GAMBLING

GAMBLING

Mike Atherton

To Isabelle

First published in Great Britain in 2006 by
Hodder & Stoughton
An Hachette Livre UK company

First published in paperback in 2007

1

A CIP catalogue record for this title is
available from the British Library

ISBN 978 0 340 89719 5

Typeset in Sabon by Hewer Text UK Ltd, Edinburgh
Printed and bound by Mackays of Chatham Ltd, Chatham, Kent

Hodder & Stoughton policy is to use papers that are natural,
renewable and recyclable products and made from wood grown in
sustainable forests. The logging and manufacturing processes are expected
to conform to the environmental regulations of the country of origin.

Hodder & Stoughton Ltd
A division of Hodder Headline
338 Euston Road
London NW1 3BH

www.hodder.co.uk

CONTENTS

Acknowledgements   vii
Preface   xi

1   The Opium of the Masses   1

2   Controlling Chance   23

3   Casino Capitalism
    Simon Cawkwell: the Financial Bettor   42

4   High Life   70

5   Low Life   91

6   All Horse Players Die Broke   116

7   Death of the Bookie
    Dave Nevison: the Horse Player   137

8   Say It Ain't So, Hansie
    Tony Bloom: the Sports Bettor   170

9   Twisted Reality   198

10   Dead Money
    Jeff Duvall: the Poker Player   220

11 The Internet Revolution
   Ray Joseph: the Internet Gambler   252

12 One Day at a Time   281

   Epilogue   303
   Postscript   307
   Glossary   315
   Bibliography   320
   Index   325

ACKNOWLEDGEMENTS

A book like this obviously relies both on written sources and interviews. The written sources – and there is a rich mine of gambling literature to prospect – are acknowledged in the bibliography. This space is dedicated to those individuals who helped me and gave freely of their time: to Richard Hickson and Fabien Devlin from Camelot; to Derek and Elaine Thompson, the lottery winners from Dorset; to Brough Scott for his contacts early in the project; to Lawrence Wadey for setting up the meeting with Alan Woods; to Alan Woods and his son Anthony for an interesting evening in Sydney; to James Osborne for his hospitality at Aspinall's; to Crockford's club for their hospitality; to Robert Sheehan for introducing me to the London club scene and for reading through various bits of the manuscript; to Stuart Wheeler, again for reading various parts of the manuscript; to the professional gamblers – Ray Joseph, Jeff Duvall, Tony Bloom, Dave Nevison and Simon Cawkwell – who gave freely of their time for interviews and allowed me an insight into the rarefied world of professional gambling; to the managers of William Hill, Portobello Road, and Paddy Power, Kilburn High Road, and to their punters for their patience and forbearance; to Edward Gillespie and Alan Lee for their hospitality at Cheltenham; to Barry Dennis and Andy Smith for their insights into the world of bookmaking; and to Andrew Black for telling me the story of Betfair; to Des Wilson for an introduction into the poker world; to John Duthie who allowed me to play in the World Masters; to the poker players in the Vic generally, who were fantastically helpful and generous with their time; to Anthony Holden for his contacts in Las Vegas; to Michael Craig for alerting me to the biggest poker game of all time, and for sending me his article on the same; to Howard Schwartz of the Gambler's Book Shop for his time (and sound advice to get a taxi back to the Strip, which means that I'm still here to tell the tale); to the addicts of the Hammersmith branch of Gamblers Anonymous for allowing me to listen to their stories; to Adrian Scarfe of GamCare; to Malcolm Lorimer at Lancashire CCC, and Graham Cowdrey at Cantor Index.

John Ford gave useful advice early on in the project and acted as a sounding board throughout. Stephen Fay read early chapters and offered encouragement. Roddy Bloomfield of Hodder came up with the idea in the first place and offered wise counsel throughout. David and Brendan de Caires read early chapters. Isabelle de Caires read the entire manuscript and made her usual feisty comments. To her, and to my children who had to put up with a year dominated by odds and sods, my grateful thanks.

Photographic acknowledgements

The author and publisher would like to thank the following for permission to reproduce photographs:

AFP/Getty Images; AP/Empics; British Library, London/Bridgeman Art Library; Camelot; Corbis; The Rt. Hon. Earlo of Derby/ Bridgeman Art Library; Mary Evans Picture Library; Gamma/ Camera Press; Gerry Images; Justin Griffiths-Williams; Houlton Archive/Getty Images; Kimbell Art Museum, Fort Worth, Texas/ Bridgeman Art Library; Littlewoods Football Pools; David Lomax/ Camera Press; PA/Empics; Popperfoto.com; Harry Price Collection, University of London/Mary Evans Picture LIbrary; Reuters/ Las Vegas Sun/Steve Marcus; Victor Chandler Ltd; Tessa Wheeler; Brad Willis/PokerStars.com.

'Where is the sin? We bet. It has all been passed down that there is a God. We bet our life on it. We calculate the odds, the return that we shall sit with the saints in Paradise. Our anxiety about our bet wakes us before dawn in a cold sweat and God sees us suffer. I cannot believe that such a God, whose fundamental requirement of us is that we gamble our mortal souls – it's true that we stake everything on the fact of his existence – I cannot believe that such a God can look unkindly on a chap wagering a few quid on the likelihood of a dumb animal crossing the line first, unless it might be considered a blaspheme to apply to a common pleasure that which is divine. Shall we play?'

Peter Carey, *Oscar and Lucinda*

'The plate of the hunter, the gambler, and the fisherman is nine times empty and one time full.'

Cretan proverb

PREFACE

Inside the gleaming walls of the Oasis Casino in Jericho, the slot machines continue to whirr, the chips are stacked neatly in piles, the green baize is brushed and the roulette wheels are oiled on a daily basis. Only the gamblers are missing.

Jericho is a quiet city in the West Bank, eighteen miles from Jerusalem. It is close to Jesus's baptismal site and the city is overlooked by the barren mountain on which he is purported to have spent forty days and forty nights resisting the temptations of the Devil. Between 1998, when the Oasis Casino was built by a joint Austrian-Palestinian conglomerate, and September 2000, when the second intifada began, gambling was the region's greatest temptation. Although gambling is outlawed in Israel, three thousand Israeli punters a day – double that number at weekends – flocked over the Palestinian borders to the casino, swelling its coffers by $54 million in 1999 and keeping 1,600 Palestinians in full employment. Brett Anderson, the New Zealand-born manager of the casino, said, 'Israelis have a passion for gambling. The State of Israel is a gamble, so perhaps that's why they go at it with such intensity.'

Since the intifada, Israeli gamblers have stayed away and the casino has stood empty. A skeletal staff of fifty keep the 285 slot machines and 124 gaming tables in working order, ready for the moment when peace and security will bring a resumption in play.

That moment came closer on 16 March 2005, when in the

glasnost that followed the death of Yasser Arafat, and under the terms of the Sharm el-Sheikh peace accord, Israel returned five towns in the West Bank to the Palestinian Authority. In the Knesset the day before the handover, an Israeli politician, Benny Elon, questioned why Jericho was the first of those territories to be returned, especially since the assassins of the Israeli tourism minister Rechavam Ze'evi were held in a prison in Jericho, and Mahmoud Abbas, the newly elected leader of the Palestinian Authority, had promised to release them once Jericho was handed over to Arab control. Was it, he asked, because of the close links between Ariel Sharon, the then Prime Minister of Israel, and Martin Schlaff, the Viennese Jew, who part-owned the Oasis Casino?

The day after the announcement that Jericho was to be returned to Arab control, Israelis jammed the telephone lines of the casino to enquire as to when it would reopen. That possibility looked increasingly remote after Hamas's victory in the 2006 Palestinian elections. Citing Islamic law, under which gambling is illegal, Hamas vowed never to open the Oasis Casino whilst it remains in government. Israelis will have to look elsewhere to feed their addiction.

Precisely one year to the day before Jericho was returned to Arab control, a 'chic and beautiful' (according to Scotland Yard) Hungarian woman walked into the Ritz casino in London accompanied by two 'elegant' Serbian men. The owners of the Ritz, the reclusive millionaire twins David and Frederick Barclay, were not thought to be in residence during the two nights that the trio played the tables. Had they been, their acute business antennae might have twitched at the outrageous good fortune that the three Eastern Europeans seemed to be enjoying. On the first evening they walked away with

£100,000 and on the next £1.2 million – £300,000 in cash and a cheque for £900,000.

On the basis that the casino should hold the whip hand and not the punter, and working on the same principle as high-street bookmakers, who love suckers and hate winners, the closed-circuit cameras were scrutinised the next day. It transpired that the three gamblers had smuggled into the casino a laser scanner linked to a microcomputer in a mobile phone. As a croupier released the ball onto the roulette wheel, the scanner noted where it had dropped and measured the declining speed of the wheel. All these factors were beamed to the microcomputer, which calculated the section of six numbers upon which the ball would finally settle, and then flashed the information onto the mobile phone before the third spin of the wheel, thus enabling the bets to be placed. The odds of winning were so reduced from 36-1 (the house percentage is guaranteed by the thirty-seventh number – zero) to 5-1.

Scotland Yard were duly informed and the trio were arrested at a nearby hotel and charged with obtaining their winnings by fraudulent means. After a nine-month investigation, they were released. They were allowed to keep their money and they were able to leave the country. Since the scanner had not interfered with the ball or the roulette wheel, no law had been violated.

On the last Saturday in October 2004, whilst the Hungarian beauty and her two acolytes were awaiting their fate, Jack Lee, a 75-year-old pensioner from Newcastle, walked into his local betting shop and placed a £2 bet on the Scoop6 – a competition run by the Tote which offers a jackpot prize to anyone who can pick the winners of the day's six televised races. The jackpot had not been won for a number of weeks and the rollovers had swelled the pot to just over £850,000. After leg five, Jack was in possession of the only ticket in the country with a chance of winning. His selection in the last race – the Ben Marshall Stakes at Newmarket – was a horse called Babodana trained by Mark Tompkins. In a rough race, Babodana crossed the finishing line first. A stewards' inquiry was duly called, Babodana was disqualified, and Jack's bet was nullified. The official form book's comment was this: '[Babodana] was unlucky not to follow up as he was somewhat harshly thrown out after passing the winning post a narrow winner. A controversial end of a decent contest and the result may well be turned over on appeal.' Not that the appeal would have helped Jack, who saw his dreams of a lifetime's win disappear with the sound of the steward's klaxon. When asked for his reaction, Jack said, simply, 'That's gambling.' The next day's papers gave him the sobriquet 'Britain's unluckiest punter'.

Jack's bad luck didn't stop there. The following week the jackpot had rolled over to £1.1 million and it was finally won by a punter called Stuart Bolland from Irlam in Greater Manchester. His outlay was 240 times more than Jack's modest £2 and was no mere shot in the dark. 'Luck is in the mix,' he said, 'but there is a lot of know-how and empirical knowledge involved.' His win entitled him to go for the bonus fund the following week, worth almost twice the original win. He announced that if his selection in the bonus race won he would like to share some of his winnings with Jack. His selection, a horse called Monkerhostin, finished third, but the local bookmaker, Fred Done, agreed to give Stuart a further £30,000, which he decided to split with Jack. A photoshoot of the cheque presentation was arranged for the following Wednesday. Jack died in his home in Newcastle on the Tuesday.

One year after Jack had died, Graham Price, a financial consultant from Swansea, was jailed for twelve years after it was discovered that, over a four-year period, he had stolen £10 million from the bank he consulted for and from eighty-four private clients. He had stolen the money to pay for his gambling addiction. Although authorities had not been able to trace all the money, it was known that he had spent £1.7 million on racing tipsters, £1 million on internet gambling, £250,000 on shares in thirteen horses and £32,000 on their training fees. Many of his victims were elderly people who had lost their homes, savings and pensions. Price was finally discovered when an auditor found an IOU pledge to the Halifax for £7 million. His counsel actually used this information in his defence. It indicated, said Peter Douglas-Jones, that Mr Price was 'clinging to the hope, the belief, the prayer, that his bets would come good.' When the police arrived to arrest him, Mr Price demonstrated the eternal hope that addicts cling to – what is known as the 'gambler's fallacy'. 'I was going to win it all back,' he said. 'You have come one week too soon.'

Gambling has infatuated human beings since the beginning of time. In Greek mythology the world was even created by a divine game of craps – Zeus winning the skies, Poseidon the seas and Hades the underworld. The desire to seek out risk seems to be a universal human phenomenon, uniting all societies – ancient and modern, western and oriental. In the 4th century BC, two Chinese gamblers bet their ears on which side a leaf would land. The loser severed his lobes and presented them to the winner on the leaf. Thousands of years later the Andaman Islanders still played a peculiar form of human roulette to convict suspected criminals.

Not just all societies but all levels of society, too: from royalty – the Queen of England is known to like a flutter on the nags and on internet companies; to academics – Isaac Newton lost a bundle in a punt on the South Sea Bubble; politicians – Richard Nixon funded his early political career with his winnings from poker; and writers like Dostoevsky, who was as addicted a gambler as any. The urge to gamble unites the aristocrats, who lost vast estates in the gaming clubs of 18th-century England, with the working man whose natural habitat is Jack Lee's betting shop. Nor has it made any difference to this urge to gamble whether the activity has been frowned upon, which historically it has, or whether, as in Israel, China, Islamic countries or certain states of America, it is illegal.

The stories of the casino in Jericho, the Ritz heist, Britain's 'unluckiest punter' and Graham Price's deception suggest that gambling incorporates many of the experiences and emotions that we would regard as essential to a life worth living – hope, expectation, excitement, intelligence, winning, generosity of spirit; and a few that we may regard as anathema – crime, greed, addiction, ruination, political chicanery and losing.

Of course, the very act of living necessitates taking chances at every turn, but that is too wide a definition of the notion of 'gambling' per se. To gamble – a verb not found in English usage until 1775, but thought to derive from the Anglo Saxon word 'gamen', meaning 'sport', 'pleasure', 'joy' or 'pastime' – implies a positive choice to seek out risk in return for reward. This apparent desire to surrender to the forces of chance regularly afflicts more than two-thirds of the adult population in Britain, if the statistics from the National Lottery are to be believed.

Indeed, all the anecdotal evidence suggests that Britain, at the start of the 21st century, is in the grip of a gambling craze fit to rank alongside any period in British history. In 2005, the gambling industry was worth just over £50 billion, more than the state's spend on transport and defence combined. High-profile cases, such as the £700,000 frittered away in five short months by Wayne Rooney, keep gambling in the headlines, as they always do. Rooney's loss, whilst staggering, was small beer in comparison with the American golfer John Daly. In May 2006, Daly announced that he had lost as much as £32 million in the last twelve years. But there is a deeper unease: for many, the government-inspired liberalisation of the industry, enshrined in the Gambling Act 2005, threatens to destabilise an area of life that has been regulated, crime-free and relatively controlled for four decades.

This book aims to put gambling in 21st-century Britain into some kind of historical context, whilst looking at the very recent technological changes that have altered the face of gambling for ever. It is these twin developments – the increased access to gambling via the internet, and the liberalisation of the industry – that will form the essence of the debate over gambling that is sure to rage as preparations for the first Las Vegas-style casino to hit these shores get under way, and as the realisation dawns that we are becoming a nation of gamblers.

1

THE OPIUM OF THE MASSES

'The Lottery, with its weekly payout of enormous prizes, was the one public event to which the proles paid serious attention. It was probable that there were some millions of proles for whom the Lottery was the principal if not the only reason for remaining alive. It was their delight, their folly, their anodyne, their intellectual stimulant.'

George Orwell, *Nineteen Eighty-Four*

On a sweltering June afternoon in 2005, about a hundred and twenty gamblers stroll though the revolving doors of the BBC and into a studio, where the bright lights of the cameras increase their discomfort. Their ages vary from early twenties through to late middle age, and they are well dressed, the men in slacks and open-necked shirts and the ladies in floral dresses. At first glance they might be taken for a book club, or a group going out for an evening at the theatre, rather than gamblers. But gamblers they all are: each possessing at least one lottery ticket, each hoping against hope that lady luck might visit them that evening. And why not? The jackpot (£15 million on this particular evening) is usually won by somebody, even if the odds of the finger of fate touching you are close on 14 million to 1.

The BBC show *Come and Have a Go* has twin attractions for the audience: the live draw, at around 8.20 p.m., and the quiz that precedes it, in which £50,000 can be won. Much of the quiz element of the show is prerecorded, hence their mid-afternoon arrival at the BBC. They sit perspiring, applauding and laughing to order, throughout the afternoon, until 7.30 p.m., when the show goes out live to an audience of around six million. It has consistently been the highest-rated entertainment show on a Saturday evening, benefiting from a surge of around three million viewers at the end of the programme when the jackpot draw is made.

Tonight's show is being hosted by possibly the oddest couple in broadcasting: Julian Clary and Emily Maitlis. At the start of the live portion of the proceedings, Clary minces onto the stage wearing a shiny mauve suit, white tie, white shoes, peroxide blond hair and near-orange make-up. He tells the audience, in a simpering voice, that 'We have goodies galore for you this evening. On my right is someone who is scorching on the outside, cool as a cucumber on the inside – a bit like a baked Alaska, really! Emily Maitlis!'

Maitlis, a Cambridge University graduate, a former business correspondent for NBC, a hard news journalist who has covered such diverse topics as the US presidential elections and the Afghan refugee crisis, and who speaks Mandarin, French, Spanish and Italian, but who is now clearly trying to break into the big bucks of light entertainment television, blushes slightly and half raises her face in a coquettish Princess Diana-like pose. She is the quizmeister.

After each question, Clary tries out a lame joke, usually with some sexual innuendo. After a question about poker, he says, 'I tried playing with a stud last night too, but we didn't get along so well!' The floor manager holds up a piece of card instructing the audience to 'Laugh!', but their only response is a half groan. Clary gallops on, undaunted.

The set is wreathed in starlike lights. The intended impression must be of a place where dreams come true, or Nirvana. (It was the advertising group M&C Saatchi that came up with the name Camelot for the conglomerate that runs the National Lottery, based, they said, on 'dreams of romance'.) At the back of the set are two pairs of machines: one to draw the lottery known as Thunderball; another for the Lotto itself, when the jackpot is up for grabs. Amidst the kitsch surroundings, the five-foot-high solid white machines look strangely stark and forbidding. The balls (prechecked by the National Weights and Measures Laboratory) have been placed inside them (in a pre-arranged order stipulated by analysts from the University of Hertfordshire) and are ready to be spun around by the rotators before, in the case of the jackpot draw, seven of them emerge to make someone's dreams come true.

All the machines are manufactured by an American company in New Jersey called Smartplay. Originally there were sixteen such machines made for Camelot, who named them, appropriately, according to Arthurian legend: Guinevere, Lancelot and so on. The originals have been replaced now and Guinevere stands on permanent exhibition at the Science Museum. There are currently six machines in operation, the more prosaically named Opal, Pearl, Garnet and Topaz, and Moonstone and Amethyst – the two on duty tonight. There are five Thunderball machines in operation and they retain the link to the kingdom of dreams and romance: Excalibur I, II, III, IV and V.

At 7.45 p.m. an auditor, dressed in a pinstriped suit and white gloves, turns on the machines. They must run for a certain length of time, and the rotators must spin for a certain length of time, before the draw can begin. Another auditor, also in white gloves, stands in the shadows with a stopwatch. At 8.05 the clocker raises a thumb and the 'Voice of the Balls' announces that it is time for the Thunderball draw. As each ball falls, it is invested with some kind of individuality and personality, as if to con the viewers that this is something more than a draw determined by pure chance. Number

25, says the Voice, is a particularly lucky number, it being the most-drawn-out ball throughout the history of Thunderball. This marketing strategy clearly works, for 60 per cent of those who choose a lottery ticket do so by agonising over their own numbers: birthdays, date of divorce and so on. The other 40 per cent simply let a computer choose a random set of numbers.

Despite the marketing, Camelot makes no secret of the fact that the draw is governed totally by randomness or chance. This is from the National Lottery Commission website: 'We have a rolling programme of research to check for elements of non-randomness in the UK Lottery. All the research we have commissioned to date states, unequivocally, that the UK National Lottery shows no evidence of non-randomness.' It is the only evidence you need to tell you that all the books advising you on how to win the lottery are a complete waste of time; that it is pointless listening to the *Sun*'s Mystic Meg who, in the early days of the lottery, exhorted the *Sun*'s readers to rub their lottery tickets on her psychically charged red dot; that it is pointless listening to the *Daily Mirror*'s Claire Voyant, who this evening has recommended the numbers 2, 16, 22, 11, 12 and 5 (none of which turn up), and that choosing your own numbers is no more likely to result in a win than letting the computer choose them for you. Unless, of course, you think you are destined to win, that fate has decreed that you, and not 14 million others, will be the one, which is, of course, a delusion common to most gamblers. The National Lottery helped promulgate this belief in its earliest advertising slogans, showing a huge finger of fate descending from the heavens with the slogan 'It could be you!'

We all know people who irrationally believe that their daily lives are controlled in some way by omens, good or bad. Gamblers seem to be especially vulnerable: they have lucky positions around the roulette table, lucky items of clothing, lucky days, or unlucky days on which they won't gamble. Anthony Holden, author of the bestselling book about poker *Big Deal*, goes out of his way to emphasise that poker is not gambling because it is a game of skill, and yet he won't go down to the tables without wearing his lucky watch. This belief in the power of fate or luck convinces gamblers that somehow they can bend the forces of mathematics or probability or pure chance to their will. That they will be lucky tonight.

Winners of the lottery have often ascribed their success to a lucky omen rather than pure chance. This is from the National Lottery website: 'Edwin Thrasher was stony-broke before he won and one day he touched the ring his father had left him when he died and said, "Dad, please send me some money." That afternoon he won £50,000 on an instant scratchcard.' Or Billy Gibbons, who picked his winning numbers after his pet chicken 'Kiev' trampled all over his calculator producing six numbers. After the numbers came up, 'Kiev' was renamed 'Lucky' and now the fowl chooses Billy's numbers every Saturday.

At 8.17 p.m. the Voice announces that it is time for the jackpot draw. The total prize fund tonight is £27.4 million and the jackpot is £15 million. Clary can barely contain himself. 'Here come the balls!' he squeals. One couple in the audience are holding hands, both clasped around a ticket. A woman is gripping what looks like a lucky pendant hanging around her neck. Some of the cameramen have a lottery ticket taped to the back of their cameras. (Apparently during one rehearsal a cameraman's numbers actually came up. If it happened now, would he simply walk away from his job and leave his camera unmanned?) Six million or so viewers are watching expectantly.

The Voice announces each ball as it emerges: 49, 44, 38, 15, 23, 27 and the bonus ball is 34. Each is greeted with rapturous applause. One of the floor managers scrunches up his ticket in disgust. Within seconds, an employee from Camelot groans back-stage, 'Oh no! There's a single winner.' Thanks to the combined efforts of Moonstone and Amethyst someone's dreams have indeed come true. I enquire why the news of a single winner is greeted with such depression – surely another lottery multimillionaire is a marketing dream. But no, Camelot's marketing department want a rollover of £20 million for the Wednesday draw, which would guarantee a pick-up in sales of at least 10 per cent. They are not happy. The 60 to 70 per cent of the adult population who habitually gamble on the lottery are not happy – some of them will succumb to what has been called 'lottery stress disorder' in the coming days. One person, who subsequently decides to spurn any publicity, is £15 million richer.

The lottery, as the descendant of the practice of casting and drawing lots, is perhaps the most ancient form of man appealing directly to chance. Those who drew lots in the Old Testament, however, to divide the lands of Canaan, or, in the New Testament, to distribute Christ's garments, were not gambling in the sense that we would understand it today. They were casting lots to divine the will of God: the casting of a lot was a direct appeal to God and the drawing of it was interpreted as His will. In that sense, the concept of pure chance could not exist at all. In a world ruled by an omnipotent and omniscient God, there was no room for chance to exist. (This practice of divining the will of God through the casting of lots lasted well into modern times: in 17th-century England men on death row were often reprieved by such methods, and the lucky ones were given a ticket labelled 'Life given by God'. Unbelievably, American soldiers were sent to Vietnam in this way – not so much to divine the will of God, as, no doubt, to ease the conscience of their commanders.)

On his travels during the expansion of the Roman Empire, Tacitus saw how the tribes of Germany drew their lots: 'To divination and the lot they pay as much attention as anyone: the method of drawing lots is uniform. A bough is cut from a nut-bearing tree and divided into slips: these are distinguished by certain runes and spread casually and randomly over white cloth . . . after prayers to the gods and with eyes turned to the heaven, take up one slip at a time till he has done this on three separate occasions, and after taking the three interprets them according to the runes that have already been stamped on them.' This was the lottery as a system of decision-making.

Despite the fact that this ancient process of divination had little to do with gambling per se, it is here, in these sacred rituals, that the earliest forms of the concept of chance are to be found. It was here that man deliberately embraced, for the first time, what we would now understand as a chance event. Later, individuals brought themselves into this process, by wagering on the outcome, thus no longer just waiting for divine pronouncement, but making the process of divination a more interactive one. It is from this combination of the sacred and the playful that all the oldest forms of gambling are derived. And it is, surely, in the gradual subjugation of the sacred to the playful that the source of the historical antipathy of the Church to all forms of gambling must be found.

The lottery as a game of chance rather than a system of decision-making began to develop in ancient Rome. At the games, emperors threw down parchments on which were written numbers that represented claims on prizes, and it became customary at the biggest parties to distribute gifts to guests by way of a lottery.

As the medieval world gave way to the modern, as orthodox religious beliefs began to be challenged, so the practice of divination gradually retreated and the idea of chance began to emerge in its own right. By the 16th century, lotteries were widespread in Europe, especially the Italian city states, where the merchants used lotteries to sell their wares. The juxtaposition of the medieval and modern is perfectly illustrated in the Parisian lottery of 1572: cash prizes of 500 francs were on offer, but on the winning tickets the phrase 'God has chosen you' was written and on the losing tickets 'God comforts you'. This lottery even received Papal approval, as the promoters were granted remission of their sins.

The earliest English lotteries resembled premium bonds (essentially an interest lottery) rather than the lottery as we recognise it today. Money spent could not be lost and the state would pay back the value of the ticket, plus interest, over a number of years. The lottery of 1711, for example, sold 150,000 tickets at £10 each. Interest was to be paid at 6 per cent and 25,000 prizes were on offer, ranging between £20 and the top prize of £12,000. In all, close to three quarters of a million pounds was given away in prize money. A greater element of chance was gradually introduced. From 1719, only a portion of the tickets were entitled to this annuity and from 1768 the value of all tickets that drew a blank was cancelled. So the lottery gradually developed into a game of pure chance in which cash prizes could be won but also a game in which the stake might be lost altogether.

Inevitably, governments began to latch on to the fact that the lottery was a way of raising revenues by circumventing unpopular increases in taxation. In England, the government has traditionally played the role of the middleman between the pro- and anti-gambling lobbies. The gambling pendulum has continually swung back and forth between liberty and constraint.

The very first English lottery, in 1569, was designed to raise revenues and was presented as a patriotic undertaking by Elizabeth I: 'A verie rich Lotterie Generall, without any blancks, containing a good number of good prizes, as well of redy money as of plate, and certain sorts of marchaundizes, having been valued and priced by the comaundement of the Queen's most excellent majestie, by men of expert and skill; and the same Lotterie is erected by her majestie's order, to the intent that such commoditie as may chance to arise thereof, after charges be borne, may be converted towards *the reparation of the havens and strength of the Realme and towards other such publique good works*. The number of lots shall be four hundredth thousand, and no more; and every lot shall be the summe of ten shillings sterling only, and no more.' (my italics)

Lotteries continued to be held in order to boost the state's coffers, to finance its growing debt provision, and to fund its endeavours: the 1612 lottery helped finance settlements in Virginia; the lotteries of 1627, 1631 and 1689 established London's water supply; Westminster Bridge was partly funded by five lotteries between 1694 and 1765, and the British Museum likewise from a lottery in 1753 that raised £300,000 (approximately £3 million in today's money). Between 1769 and 1826 lotteries raised close to £9 million for the Exchequer, thus helping to bankroll England as an emerging power. It might be said that the modern lottery funds the recreational needs of a declining one.

The lotteries proved to be enormously popular with the public. The earliest lotteries were drawn from a specially designed timber house at the great west gate of St Paul's Cathedral and huge crowds turned up to watch. Later, the lottery was drawn in front of Banqueting House in Whitehall from two six-foot-high wooden wheels. When the wheels stopped turning two orphans from the Blue Coat School dipped into a large wooden box to draw the winning tickets (later the boys had to wear tightly buttoned tunics, with stitched-up pockets, and whilst drawing they had to hold their left hands behind their backs and keep their right hands open with fingers extended to prevent any chance of fraud). The draw would last up to six weeks, with the biggest prizes

9

drawn last, so heightening the tension and encouraging the trading of tickets.

In late 17th-century London, the *London Spy* gave a good account of the kind of feverish activity that accompanied each lottery: 'The Gazette and Post Papers lay neglected and nothing was pored over in the coffee houses but the ticket catalogues . . . one stream of coachmen, footmen, prentice boys and servant wenches flowing one way with wonderful hopes of getting an estate for three pence . . . Thus were all the fools in town so busily employed in running up and down from one lottery to another . . . the common people make it a great part of their care and business hoping thereby to relieve a necessitous life, instead of which they plunge themselves into an ocean of difficulties.'

The fear of the ruinous effect on the lower orders and the destabilisation of a rigid social hierarchy were the principal reasons behind the banning of the lottery in both 1699 and 1826. In 1699 it was declared that lotteries were a 'common and public nuisance'. When they returned a decade later the minimum price of a ticket was £10 – clearly an attempt to price the poor out of the market. Yet whilst the upper classes were over-represented in the winners' enclosure – the Duke of Newcastle won eleven times in 1711 and the Dukes of Buckingham and Rutland won eight times each – it failed to prevent the common man from playing the game. People clubbed together to buy tickets. Some tickets were bought 'on margin' – that is, having only partly been paid for, with the promise of only a share of any proceeds. Speculation flourished: brokers conducted a flying trade, buying in bulk and selling at a premium. People paid more to insure themselves against a losing ticket.

It was entirely understandable that the poor were likely to grasp with both hands the concept of getting rich through pure chance. The belief that people got their rewards through hard work found favour with the aspiring classes – the artisans, the merchants, the shopkeepers and the growing number of professionals. Amongst the poor and the disadvantaged, this belief was less likely to find acceptance. A belief in chance and luck helped reconcile them to their circumstances – and gave them hope of a better tomorrow.

At a time of more rigid social stratification than today, the lottery provoked understandable fears amongst those charged with making legislation. After all, the chances of winning or losing – and therefore provoking social mobility both ways – had nothing to do with simple status or hard work. In 1819 parliament moved that: 'A spirit of gambling injurious in the highest degree to the morals of the people is encouraged and provoked.' The national lottery was no longer considered synonymous with the nation's honour, as it had been, and with Christian values; it was seen to undermine the Protestant work ethic and the meritocracy of a capitalist society. And so in 1826 the last English lottery for 168 years was drawn.

By 1994, England was the only European country, bar Albania, without a lottery. European regulations, though, stipulated that European lottery tickets could be sold in the UK and the spectre loomed large of both huge amounts of money exiting the country and the government losing out on taxable revenues. And so on 19 November 1994, 168 years after the last national lottery had been drawn, Britain underwent what *The Times* described as the country's 'greatest collective experience' since the end of the Second World War.

The reaction to the National Lottery typified the ambivalent attitude towards gambling that has always existed. The anti- view was espoused, unsurprisingly, by the *Guardian*, who railed against it on the grounds that it had 'replaced the circus as the opium of the people'.

Alasdair Palmer went one step further in the *Daily Telegraph*, taking a moral stance against the winners: 'An element of struggle is essential to a sense of purpose and sense of worth. Enormous wealth deprives people of both. No wonder so many hugely wealthy people are deeply miserable.' *The Times* was more relaxed, urging its readers to have a flutter: 'The British puritanical heritage persists in finding a cloud before every silver lining . . . But for most of the nation tonight, a man is seldom as harmlessly employed as in fantasy about a pot of gold at the end of the rainbow.'

The British public was more in step with *The Times* than the *Guardian* or Alasdair Palmer. First-day sales topped £7 million and by the end of the first week the British people had shelled out close to £50 million and most of the adult population – close on 40 million people – had purchased a ticket. By the end of its first operating year Camelot was a bigger cash cow than either Marks and Spencer or Sainsbury's.

Overnight, had we become a nation of gamblers? The government, and Camelot, were keen to dispel that suspicion. The National Lottery was marketed not as a gamble but as a harmless flutter, a bit of fun, and one that would contribute massively to five good causes: charities, the arts, sport, National Heritage and the Millennium Fund. Slogans such as 'you play, the nation wins' brought to mind the patriotic backdrop to the 1569 lottery. Whereas the rest of the gambling industry was under the auspices of the austere Home Office, the responsibility for the National Lottery fell to David Mellor's much-derided 'Ministry of Fun'. And whilst the rest of the gaming industry was regulated by the Gaming Board (now the Gambling Commission), the National Lottery had its own regulators: Oflot until 1999 and the National Lottery Commission thereafter. From the outset, the attempt was made to remove the National Lottery, in the public's perception, from gambling proper.

Of course, it was all nonsense. Playing the lottery is gambling whichever way you look at it. The Rothschild Commission in 1978 gave this definition of gambling: 'Gambling consists of an agreement between parties with respect to an unascertained outcome that, depending on the outcome, there will be a redistribution of advantage amongst parties.' In general terms, the embracing of a chance event which leads to a redistribution of monies amongst players or between players and a commercial house is as good a definition of gambling as any. The National Lottery presses all those buttons. In the sense that absolutely no skill is involved, it is one of the purest forms of gambling that there is.

Certainly, the advent of the National Lottery in 1994 increased the propensity to gamble amongst the British people. In the British Gambling Prevalence Survey of 1999, 72 per cent of people admitted to gambling in the previous year, 65 per cent of whom gambled on the National Lottery, so that within five years of the introduction of the National Lottery the number of regular gamblers had increased from 15 million to 25 million.

And there is no doubt that one of the effects of the National Lottery in this country has been the homogenisation of gambling. The lottery, as it always has, remains a regressive tax, with a higher proportion of the total spend on the lottery coming from the poorest socio-economic groups. But the purchasing of tickets cuts across every age group, every class and every ethnic group. Historically, the middle classes have instinctively frowned upon gambling, sneering down from above at the working classes, whom they considered incapable of organising their leisure time productively, and tut-tutting at their social superiors, who they felt should really have known better. Through the National Lottery, the middle classes have been brought into the gambling fraternity – even if they would neither recognise nor admit that playing the lottery is gambling.

Inevitably, the popularity of the National Lottery declined a little after its inception, although in 2005 Camelot posted a remarkable set of figures which would indicate that they have arrested that decline: in 2004–05 the British people spent 4.77 billion on the National Lottery in its various guises. In the third quarter of 2005, Camelot had an 11 per cent increase in sales – its biggest since the inception of the lottery over a decade before.

The argument against the National Lottery, most often espoused by the 'liberal elite', is that it is a monument to imbecility and irrationality. The odds are so outrageous (so much so that hardened professional gamblers would never buy a ticket) and the game so lacking in skill that only a fool would play.

And yet, because the National Lottery has few addictive properties, it would seem that it is one form of gambling where the potential upside (however remote the chances of winning) outweighs the serious losses. GamCare, the gambling addiction helpline, records next to no complaints about the National Lottery. The average spend per capita is around only £2.77, making the National Lottery the forty-eighth largest in the world in terms of per capita spend, even though it is the fifth largest overall. It exhibits few properties which the experts regard as being dangerous to potential addicts: the purchasing of tickets occurs within normal daily routines, such as shopping, rather than necessitating special trips to a gambling 'site'; with just two draws every week, the rate of play is slow and unrepetitive, with no instant gratification (apart from scratchcards); and there is little sense of urgency or excitement as the punter chooses his numbers. Those who play the National Lottery do so for one simple reason – the remote chance that they can win a life-changing amount of money – rather than for the buzz, kick or adrenalin surge that characterises 'harder' forms of gambling.

With the proviso that scratchcards, because of their instant gratification, are dangerous, and that the dangers of buying tickets via the internet need regulating (internet sales were up 600 per cent in 2004–05), and bearing in mind that Camelot has been chasing its losses slightly by introducing newer forms of games and bigger jackpots to maintain its market share (as I write, this week's Euro draw is worth £45 million, odds of winning 76 million to 1), Camelot does seem to have been a genuinely responsible operator. So far they have resisted the temptation to introduce more addictive games such as keno or rapido, which are common elsewhere in Europe. And as yet, in this country, we have witnessed none of the hysteria that accompanies some other European lottery draws.[1]

In ten Italian cities, for example, a twice-weekly draw occurs in which numbers between 1 and 90 are drawn. In Venice, for 153 consecutive draws between May 2003 and February 2005, the number 53 had refused to show itself. The effect of its nonappearance was staggering: despite the fact that 53 was no more or no less likely to be drawn than before, Italians seemed to lose their equilibrium completely, so that it seemed Orwell's vision had come to pass. In two years almost £2.4 billion were spent on the number 53 (averaging out at £277 per family). Each time it stubbornly refused to show itself, stories of bankruptcies and even deaths emerged. One insurance salesman shot his wife and son, after racking up huge losses on 53, before shooting himself. Another was arrested after beating his wife out of frustration at 53's nonappearance. A woman drowned herself off the coast of Tuscany, leaving a note that she had spent her entire savings on 53. It was the worst case of lottery mania in Italy since the number 8 had failed to

[1] On 3 February 2006 lottery mania gripped Britain as the EuroMillions Lottery, after eleven successive rollovers, reached a record total of £125 million. In my local newsagent's the 'proles' avidly discussed what they would do with their winnings, despite the fact that it was reported that they were four times as likely to be eaten by a shark as win the lottery that day – and that in the centre of London!

appear for 201 consecutive draws during the Second World War. Then, Mussolini had been suspected of rigging the draw, so keeping the lottery spend high in an effort to finance Italy's war effort. The '53 mania' became so bad that a consumer group urged the government to ban the number, to halt the country's 'collective psychosis'. On 9 February, to huge relief, it finally appeared, costing the government a payout of £400 million.

Although the National Lottery is considered a form of 'soft' gambling, is marketed as nothing more than a harmless flutter and its addictive properties are minimal, the longer-term effects of its reintroduction on the gambling industry as a whole have been far-reaching and are likely to be even more so in future.

The government's relationship with gambling has been radically altered. Prior to 1994, the government's attitude to gambling was framed by the Betting and Gaming Act of 1960. By legalising off-course cash betting for the first time in over a century, the 1960 Act recognised gambling as a legitimate leisure activity. But at its core remained the philosophy that the government should not stimulate demand for gambling. They were happy to tax gambling activities, but, almost as if gambling represented something foul and noxious, they wanted to keep it at arm's length. The reintroduction of the National Lottery in 1994 changed all that. It was easy money. Camelot did all the work and the government could sit back and watch the money – 12 per cent of revenues – roll in. In the first year alone the government received £372 million in taxed income. Now that the activity has proved to be so profitable, the government is hardly likely to throttle back in the future.

The marketing of the National Lottery as a harmless flutter and not a gamble fooled no one – certainly not the gambling industry. Not only was the government cashing in on gambling, and legit-imising an activity it had once held to be illegal, it was now seen to be sponsoring, advertising and promoting it.

As a result, the gambling industry began to lobby the government to be placed on the same advantageous footing as the National Lottery. The National Lottery enjoyed massive advantages in terms of marketing and exposure on mainstream television, whilst the rest of the industry operated within an archaic regulatory framework. The government's position was suddenly at odds with this framework. The gambling industry wanted a level playing field.

Gradually the industry underwent growing liberalisation. The pools companies were allowed to reduce their age restrictions from 18 to 16 and, like the National Lottery, they were allowed rollovers. Betting shops were allowed to stay open later in the summer to cater for evening racing. The casino industry, likewise, negotiated more advantageous terms: people could now apply for membership by post, casinos were allowed to say open longer hours, the number of jackpot gaming machines was increased, and casinos were permitted for the first time to advertise in a limited way in newspapers and magazines. Bingo followed suit: the use of debit cards to fund gambling in bingo halls was permitted, bingo halls were allowed to use up to four jackpot gaming machines, and multiple bingo (played country-wide) had the limits on prizes removed altogether. Across the board, the post-1994 gambling industry was far more liberalised and unregulated than before.

This liberalisation cannot be wholly attributed to the National Lottery, as it went hand in hand with the socioeconomic zeitgeist. But there is no doubt that the government, as a peddler of gambling, was ill-equipped to resist such pressure. The outcome, as we shall see at the conclusion of this book, was the recommendations of the 2001 Gambling Review Body, chaired by Sir Alan Budd. These recommendations, to liberalise parts of the industry and deregulate others, were largely accepted by the government in their white paper 'A Safe Bet for Success', which was duly enshrined in law in the Gambling Act of 2005. A decade on from the first National Lottery draw of the 20th century, the gambling landscape was much changed.

Given that Camelot represents the acceptable face of gambling, that its addictive properties are negligible, it seems to me that a small flutter on the National Lottery is an entirely rational choice. John Maynard Keynes, the great economist, certainly thought so. He was in favour of a lottery, provided that it was 'cheap, fair and frivolous', which, by and large, it is. And, of course, you can win a life-changing amount of money.

I had hoped – probably out of jealousy – that the lottery winners I would eventually meet would be a combination of gauche, unpleasant and, despite the millions that Lady Luck had visited upon them, deeply unhappy. It would certainly have made a good story. Indeed, there are enough examples highlighted in the popular press to show that lottery riches do not necessarily bring happiness. The outright fear that befell Dolores McNamara after her massive win of £77 million on the EuroMillions in July 2005, a fear that forced her into hiding, was enough to make one wonder whether a win was a good thing. It was reported that she was 'devastated'. Instead, the couple that I tracked down, Elaine and Derek Thompson, who won £2.7 million on 9 December 1995 (their tenth wedding anniversary), were absolutely charming and seemed the epitome of contentment.

Originally from the north-east of England, they were living in Basingstoke at the time of their win. And although Derek stayed in his job as a general manager with Motorola for a couple of years afterwards, they eventually moved down to Lyme Regis, where they now run the By the Bay restaurant. It is just 500 yards from where Meryl Streep (although I'm told she had a double for fear of high winds) wandered out onto the promontory in *The French Lieutenant's Woman*. It is the same distance, down a steep meandering lane, from the house of the author of that book, John Fowles, and it is by chance that I visited Lyme Regis on the day of Fowles's funeral. Had Fowles still been alive, he might have been a good interloper on our conversation, for the questions of luck, fate, chance or divine providence – questions that Derek and Elaine have repeatedly asked themselves since their good fortune – formed the basis of his other great literary bestseller, *The Magus*.

Derek was in London on the day of their win watching Newcastle lose to Chelsea. 'Because of that our routine had changed,' he explains. 'Normally, I would buy the ticket, but on this occasion Elaine did, although she still used the same six numbers: our birthdays, and those of our children, and our wedding anniversary and house number. We kept the same numbers week after week because Elaine was convinced that we were destined to win. Funnily enough, she'd told her boss the week before that we would not only win the Lottery, but that we'd win £2.7 million as well. It freaked him out afterwards.' Why was Elaine so certain? 'She's from a lucky family. Her grandfather won the Littlewoods Spot the Ball competition and an uncle of hers won the pools. She just felt we were destined to win.'

When Derek returned from Newcastle's defeat all the lights were on in the house, which was unusual since Elaine was an early-to-bed person. Then when he walked through the front door he found all the neighbours drinking his prize whisky. His first thought was that Elaine had arranged a surprise anniversary party. Then she told him the news. 'At first I thought she meant we'd won a tenner or something. When she said we'd won £2.7 million I didn't believe her. I checked Teletext against the numbers about thirty times and then I just burst into tears.

'We rang Camelot straight away and they told us that there was still a 1 per cent chance that we would not collect the money, because possession of the ticket was everything. If we lost it between Saturday evening and Monday morning we would get nothing. We spent the next two days absolutely paranoid about losing the damn thing. In the end, I think Elaine stuck it in her bra!

'I can't really remember much about the next few days. You definitely get disorientated and lose your equilibrium. I remember the prices at the Waldorf, where we were staying, were so ridiculous that I nipped out to the corner shop to buy our food and drink, and I remember the bank manager asking us if we wanted any spending money to celebrate, and him producing a briefcase with £20,000 in cash inside. Other than that, I don't remember much.'

They don't think that the win has changed their lives beyond recognition. They were happy before the win, they say, and they are happy now, although they admit their financial worries have eased. They haven't been especially extravagant, and the most memorable consequences of the win have been a trip on Concorde with Dale Winton, followed by a meal at Number 10 with the Prime Minister.

The choices of what they did with their money do reflect the fact, however, that Derek and Elaine have a gambling mentality. They put most of it into the stock market at a medium risk level of investment, before using it all to buy a holiday resort and then a restaurant, in neither of which they had any previous experience. They weren't prepared to let it gather interest in the bank. Their extravagances have been gambling-related – three racehorses, which they placed with the Somerset trainer Philip Hobbs, and four trips to Las Vegas.

Neither Derek nor Elaine is bashful about admitting their enjoyment of gambling, although neither thinks that playing the National Lottery counts as such (Derek calls it a subscription service, using money they are prepared to lose). They are happy to admit to starting a poker school on weekday evenings in their restaurant and encouraging the staff to gamble on how many steaks, say, have been sold in an evening, or how many covers they will do on May bank holiday. They still play the National Lottery, using the same numbers, and Elaine is convinced that they will win again. 'I had my horoscope read last week, and I was told that we would win the lottery,' she says.

Their activities in Vegas highlight their different view of gambling and of the nature of chance, luck and fate. As befits someone who believes in horoscopes, Elaine is reconciled to fate – a belief that her future is already predetermined. Therefore, in Vegas, she is happy to play pure chance games that demand no skill, like bingo, roulette and the slots. Derek doesn't believe in fate and therefore chooses to play games that demand a little skill. Mindful of his lifelong enthusiasm for horse racing, which he inherited from his shipyard-working father, he allocates himself a couple of days at the racing desks. He studies the form, using split times to give himself an advantage. In other words, Derek bets and Elaine gambles.

Their different beliefs in the nature of fate, chance and luck are also reflected in their reactions to the last question I ask them: 'Why do you think you won?' For Elaine, the answer is simple: 'We were destined to win.' For Derek things are more confusing: 'It's a question I've asked myself many times. Today, if you met every adult from Cornwall to the Scottish Borders, that's about how many people were playing on the evening we won. And only three couples, out of all those people, did win. Why us? There is no explanation, really. And yet can it just be put down to pure chance? I feel there must be more to it than that. I don't know. I can't understand it.'

Neither Derek nor Elaine is religious. Yet in this simple thought process, I sense that Derek is asking about their great lottery win what most people, at some stage, ask about life. Is everything the result of pure randomness, or is there more to it than that?

The story of the lottery is the story of gambling. It encapsulates the move away from divination, from the belief that God's design or predetermination (Elaine's view) can explain every random event, to the concept of a pure chance event (Derek's view), as we would understand it today. The move from divination to a belief that chance can exist in its own right is crucial to the development of gambling. Without that freedom of thought, gambling, as a commercial enterprise, could not really flourish at all. This secularisation of chance could only occur in a questioning world, a world where science was on the advance and religion on the retreat. And it was in this changing world that the first tentative understanding of mathematics and the laws of probability, the laws that govern random events, began to emerge.

2

CONTROLLING CHANCE

'The odds are five to six that the light at the end of the tunnel is the headlight of an oncoming train.'

Paul Dickson, *Washingtonian*

Jerome Cardano – doctor, writer, mathematician, scientist and addicted gambler – was born in Italy in 1501, just on the cusp of modernity. His father, Fazio, was a lawyer from Milan and his mother, Chiara, was of lowly stock and described as 'small, fat, pious and of quick temper'. She tried to have Cardano aborted three times, disillusioned no doubt by the fact that three children from a previous marriage had all died from the plague. His very existence, therefore, owed much to luck and chance – two imponderables that Cardano would be much preoccupied with throughout his life.

Cardano was physically backward and decidedly unattractive, born with a cleft chin, thick lower lip and a wart over one eye. He suffered from poor health throughout his life, at various times being afflicted by fluxes, ruptures, kidney trouble, heart palpitations and infected nipples. During his twenties he was sexually impotent. It was possibly his own health that encouraged him in the study of medicine. More likely, his interest in science reflected the fact that he was born just as Italy experienced the first flowerings of the Renaissance – a period when curiosity, investigation, experimentation and demonstration began to break the shackles of mysticism, the occult and religious orthodoxy. This was an age of discovery – Columbus had sailed for the Americas in 1492 – and an age of scientific advance. As a result, explorers, mathematicians and scientists were the celebrities of the day.

In 1519 Cardano went to study medicine at Pavia and two years later was transferred to Padua to avoid the Franco-Spanish war. Having been denied entry into the college of physicians in Milan, he settled in Sacco running a small medical practice. Eventually, in 1539, he was appointed to the college in Milan and, for a while, was its most highly respected physician – so much so that he was sent to Scotland to cure the Archbishop of Scotland's asthma, which he duly did.

Cardano's career, beliefs and writings betrayed both his renaissance learning and a hangover from the medieval age. He was a scholar at the forefront of both the medical advances of the time and other scientific learning. He said, for example, that 'a man is nothing but his mind; if that be out of order all is amiss, and if that be well all the rest is at ease.' He wrote a thesis on evolution, gave the first ever clinical description of typhus fever, wrote about the treatment of syphilis, and introduced the first operation to cure hernias. He was a prolific author, producing in total 131 published works: his treatise *Ars Magna* was a key mathematical tract of the 16th century and his writings on astronomy, physics, morality and death were widely disseminated throughout Europe. Shakespearean scholars have identified Cardano's *Comforte* as the book that Hamlet is reading as he enters the stage to deliver his famous 'to be, or not to be' soliloquy.

But he could not completely let go of the occult. He believed that by studying a person's facial features he could determine their future. He was also a celebrated astrologer, although when he was asked to read Edward VI's chart he predicted a long life for the monarch instead of an early death at 16. For his son Aldo he predicted fame, riches and genius, instead of gambling addiction and an early death. Beneath the waters of scientific learning a whole heap of mumbo-jumbo was fighting for air.

Cardano, then, was a man of his time: both enlightened and backward, interested in the sciences and the occult. As befits a man of his time, he was also a ferocious gambler, playing night and day at university in order to supplement his paltry earnings. His gambling addiction is laid bare in his autobiography, *De Vita Propria Liber*: 'As I was inordinately addicted to the chessboard, and the dicing table, I know that I must be deserving of the severest censure. I gambled at both for many years: at chess for about forty, and at dice for twenty-five.'

In 1525 Cardano wrote a book on gambling called *Liber de Ludo Aleae* ('A book on the Games of Chance'), which he rewrote in 1565. It is a gambling classic. It describes the games of the day; it explores the gambler's psychology; it warns of the dangers of addiction; and it lays bare his losses and the occasional scrape that Cardano gets into as a result of his addiction. It is also the first book to raise the possibility that chance can be governed by certain mathematical laws – the basis for the idea that developed into probability theory.

Cardano gambled mainly at chess, dice and occasionally at cards. Chess was the gambling game of choice for the intellectuals of the day. Dice, though, were the most widespread and ancient of gaming instruments. The earliest form of dice was the astragalus or knuckle-bone, which is the four-sided bone – solid, marrowless and therefore virtually indestructible – in the hind leg of a cloven-footed animal, usually a sheep or deer. As with the drawing of lots, the first use of dice was for a combination of the playful and the sacred. It is known that the Greeks thought the 'Venus' throw (four throws producing four different sides of the astragalus) was favourable to the Gods, and the 'dog' (when four sides the same was thrown) was unfavourable.

Dice, which replaced astragali, could be made of anything from stone to wood or bone. They were easy to make, readily affordable and widely used. The most popular game in Cardano's time was hazard, an antecedent of the modern American game craps, where two dice (or sometimes three in Italy) were rolled and the combined number had to be guessed at.

Cards have a less ancient history than dice. They were known to have existed in Europe from around the 12th century but, because the printing presses were not invented until three hundred years later, their use was far less widespread. Until then, they were hand painted or hand carved and consequently they could be afforded only by the wealthiest sections of society. The earliest cards, representing the Church, the nobility, the merchant classes and the peasantry, reflected the strict hierarchical nature of medieval society. Games like whist and primero consisted of gathering combinations of suits, so that a card had no intrinsic, individual value except in relation to other cards. Primero, a kind of early form of poker, was the most common game in Cardano's time.

Liber de Ludo Aleae dispenses much wisdom about gambling. I haven't met a gambler yet who has not been acutely aware of his weaknesses: self-knowledge, however, is rarely the same as self-help. 'During many years,' says Cardano, 'I have played not on and off but, I am ashamed to say, every day. Thereby I have lost my self-esteem, my worldly goods and my time.' He goes on to say that he was forced to gamble because of his straitened circumstances: 'It was not the love of the game, nor a taste for luxury, but the odium of my position which drove me and made me seek its refuge.' He recognises, and must be one of the first in history to do so, that addiction to gambling should be seen as a medical problem: 'Even if gambling is altogether evil, still, on account of the very many large numbers that play, it would seem to be a natural evil. For that reason, it ought to be discussed by medical doctors like one of those incurable diseases.' His gambling fuels a certain amount of self-hatred: 'There is loss of time, vain words, including on occasion curses against the gods, the neglect of one's own business, the danger that it becomes a settled habit, the time spent in planning after the game how one may recuperate and in remembering how badly one played; there are also often disputes and, worst of all, provocation to anger.' In the end, after a lifetime's experience at the tables, he counsels against getting involved: 'The greatest advantage in gambling comes from not playing at all, there are so many difficulties and so many possibilities of loss that there is nothing better than not to play at all.' *Liber de Ludo Aleae* might be nearly 400 years old but many hard-bitten gamblers and ruined addicts would recognise its reflections as timeless.

Liber de Ludo Aleae, then, is a colourful account of one of the most colourful gamblers of the day. But it remains of importance because in it the first stirrings of probability theory can be found – a theory that is absolutely crucial in the understanding of risk and in the development of gambling and more sophisticated gambling techniques. Why is it so important? In essence, gambling is about a communion with the future. The outcome of every wager is determined by what will happen to the next throw of the dice, the next draw of the card. Probability theory is the process by which gamblers might take a peek into that future, the process by which an understanding of what has happened in the past might give some kind of clue as to what might happen in the future. It is the process that helps gamblers determine the choices they make and the level of stakes they place. It is the only way that a gambler can gain an edge in an uncertain and unforgiving world.

The greatest gamblers in history, therefore, who owe their success to the knowledge that in certain situations they are playing with the percentages in their favour, however tiny, should all raise a glass to the founders of probability theory. Without them there would still be no notion that we have a choice in the decisions we make, in the risks we take, in the gambles that we make; probability theory suggests that we can quantify that choice rationally; it gives gamblers a chance to understand the odds and so, ultimately, to win.

Throughout Cardano's writing on gambling his curiosity and his rational and modern thought shines through. Whereas he struggled to move away from the occult in certain areas of his life, with gambling he was clinical and clear-headed. He dismissed any divine or mystical influence over the fall of the dice: 'Astrologers,' he says, 'make claims for themselves, yet I have never seen an astrologer who was lucky at gambling.' Later he dismisses the influence of lucky charms: 'If it is to be or not to be, how can it be changed by the amulets?'

But whilst he accepts that it is simply luck and chance, rather than some mysterious guiding hand, that causes certain numbers to come up when a die is cast, he recognises, and is the first to do so, that certain laws govern the chance of such numbers appearing and that those laws can be expressed as mathematical fractions. He recognises, for example, that he has an equal chance of throwing any number from 1 to 6 on any given throw: 'I am as able to throw 1, 3 or 5 as 2, 4 or 6. The wagers are therefore laid in accordance with this equality if the die is honest.' Whilst working through the various probabilities of certain numbers coming up when one or more dice are rolled, he suggests the following: that the probability of a number being thrown can be expressed as the number of favourable outcomes divided by the total possible outcomes. So, the chance of throwing a 7 in a game of craps in which two dice are thrown is: six possible chances (6 and 1, 5 and 2, 4 and 3, 1 and 6, 2 and 5, 3 and 4) divided by the total number of combinations (thirty-six). A punter, therefore, has a one in six chance of throwing a 7 with two dice. As simple as it might sound now, that was a revolutionary mathematical breakthrough.

Cardano, then, was the first mathematician to calculate a theoretical probability correctly. But it was to be two brilliant French mathematicians, Blaise Pascal and Pierre de Fermat, who, almost a hundred years after Cardano's death, would complete the journey. Again it was gambling that provided the impetus. A French nobleman-cum-gambler, called Chevalier de Mere, posed something called the 'problem of points' to his mathematician friends: how should the stakes of an interrupted game of chance be split between two players, one of whom was ahead in the game? Pascal and Fermat corresponded on this problem throughout 1654. Their correspondence introduced the idea of expectation into games of chance and was the foundation upon which the theory of probability rests today.

(Pascal was keen on posing other problems through the mechanism of gambling games. He famously asked, in something which became known as 'Pascal's Wager', how we should bet on the existence or otherwise of God. His answer was that the rational man/clever gambler would bet on God's existence. If God does exist, he wins the bet. If God doesn't exist, then the bet is irrelevant anyway. If, however, he bets that God does not exist, then he is risking eternal damnation should he lose. Pascal's Wager demonstrated that a belief in God is the greatest-value bet of them all.)

By the end of the 17th century, probability theory was widely understood by mathematicians of the day, if not the gamblers, and it has formed the basis of sound forecasting ever since. So, in 1708, another French mathematician, Pierre de Montmort, could write: 'I think therefore it would be useful, not only to gamesters, but to all men in general, to know *that chance has rules which can be known* . . . The conduct of men usually makes their good fortune and their bad fortune *and wise men leave as little to chance as possible.*' (My italics.)

Alan Woods is, by any estimation, one of the most successful and ferocious gamblers the world has ever seen. He has been variously a poker player, professional bridge player, professional blackjack player, horse-race gambler, sports bettor and financial spread bettor. He made his first million 'shorting' the Hong Kong stock market (i.e. betting that it would fall in value) just before the crash in 1987, and lost it all shorting the Japanese market not long afterwards. He bet £2 million on the 1986 football World Cup, which netted him twice that amount, and has won $8 million on a single horse-race bet – and lost $3 million.

He is best known, however, for heading one of the leading computer-based gambling syndicates in Hong Kong. Over the last two decades his syndicate has won more than $400m betting on the horses in Hong Kong. Whilst mathematicians of three hundred years ago used gambling games to further their understanding of probability theory, Woods has used probability theory and sophisticated forecasting techniques to perfect gambling games and line his pockets. He understands absolutely that 'chance has rules which can be known' and, as a wise man, he leaves 'as little to chance as possible'. He could be called one of the godfathers of probability-based, computer-generated gambling.

When you think of the usual paraphernalia that surrounds horse-racing punters as they study the form, you think of a racing paper such as the *Racing Post*, which gives the day's runners and betting forecasts; you think of a form book or two, such as *Raceform* or *Timeform*, which give punters information such as the speed a horse might have run, the weight it carried and a rating to compare with other horses; you think of betting slips and short, stubby pens that you can fit behind your ear; and then you think of the racetrack, all the noise and colour and excitement accompanying the bets that are wagered. You think of an emotional attachment when the bet is struck, a pounding heart as the horse runs and a sinking feeling when it fails to win its race.

Yet Woods has not been to the racetrack for nearly twenty years, his knowledge of the form is sketchy, and he shows absolutely no emotion during and after the running of a race. To him horses are not flesh and bone but simple numbers, spat out by the computer, carrying what his system has worked out to be a positive rather than a negative expectation.

Accordingly, when I meet him in his Australian office overlooking Sydney harbour (one of nine offices dotted around the word from which his syndicate gamble), I can see no clues as to the nature of his business. There is not a racing paper or a form book in sight. No pictures of favourite horses adorn the bare walls. There are just half a dozen or so computers and a giant screen that relays the evening's racing from Singapore. The computers are being attended to by two of Woods's staff – Paul, an Englishman who trained as a geologist, and who is now one of Woods's chief analysts, and Mike, a young nerdish-looking New Zealander. Books such as William Ziemba's *Efficiency of Racetrack Betting Markets*, an impenetrable-looking volume of mathematical and statistical analysis, clutter their desks.

Woods himself has short grey hair, pallid features, with a nose that turns up at its point rather like a ski jump, and there is a cigarette constantly dangling from his lips. Despite his wealth he is shabbily dressed in black tracksuit pants, black linen shirt and black slippers. Here, at least, Woods conforms to the gambling stereotype – regardless of their success, gamblers, in my experience, seem to have no interest in fashion or style and, whereas they might spend sums on a horse which you and I would gasp at, they seem reluctant to buy a new pair of shoes or a decent shirt.

Woods has just flown in from Manila, where he now lives. He has slept throughout the afternoon and is refreshed and now keen to settle down to watch the evening's proceedings from Singapore, where his team are testing out their new system. His accent still betrays his Australian roots and he speaks slowly, with long pauses – mainly because, like all professional gamblers, he is wary about what he wants to say and how much he wants to give away. 'The amounts we'll be betting this evening are a pittance,' he says, 'because we're only at the stage in Singapore where we are testing out the system.' A pittance turns out to be $25,000 a shot.

Woods's story began fifty-eight years ago in Murwillumbah, a small town on the north-east coast of New South Wales. His first experience of gambling was playing cards, usually solo, with his parents and two siblings when he was on leave from university, where he was studying maths. He graduated to poker, reasonably successfully, then to bridge, more successfully, and then to horses, with disastrous consequences. His first horse-racing bet won at big odds – 'a regrettable incident,' he says – after which an addiction set in for the next two or three years. At this stage he was betting unscientifically and therefore unsuccessfully, until he reached the point where the losses became unsustainable and he gave up. 'I didn't bet the horses again for fifteen years or so,' he says.

He worked for an insurance company in Melbourne for a while before boredom set in. In 1972, he heard that money could be made by counting cards at blackjack. Card counting had become widely known through Professor Edward O. Thorp's *Beat the Dealer*, published in 1962. Thorp's was the first book to explore the possibilities of a mathematically based card-counting system which gave gamblers an edge in blackjack. There are now many different systems of card counting but all are essentially based on Thorp's initial methods, which involved counting a ratio of high cards to low cards. For example, you might give certain cards (two through to six, say) a positive number, and others (tens and aces) a negative number. The basic idea is to add up the value of the cards which have already gone and when the count is positive you make bigger bets, on the basis that the odds of producing tens and aces have shifted slightly in your favour. It doesn't guarantee success in the short term, but over a long period of time the house advantage will move to the player. Card counting is a classic use of probability theory – using knowledge of what has happened, to forecast more accurately what might happen, and so enabling the punter to adjust the stakes accordingly.

Woods first played blackjack in Tasmania in the latter half of 1973. His first weekend counting cards helped him double his bankroll (starting amount) and he was sold on the concept. Marriage and a young family prevented him spending more time playing blackjack, but by 1979 his wife had left and Woods went to Hobart to try his hand at playing blackjack professionally. In the first four months he made about $16,000, playing every day from lunch until midnight. In late 1979, he headed off to Las Vegas, which turned out, at that time, to be a virtual card counters' convention. Shortly afterwards, Atlantic City held a two-week period in which the casinos agreed not to ban card counters, presumably to attract custom from Las Vegas, and in that fortnight Woods and his team made close on $100,000. By this time, card counters were forming teams partly because, by doing so, they were able to increase the size of their bankroll, and partly because they found that, psychologically, it was easier to ride with the ups and downs as part of a team than it was on their own.

It was in this Las Vegas period that Woods first got to know Bill Benter, an American-educated computer technician and the man mainly responsible for pioneering computer analysis and probability forecasting in horse racing. Both men have now fallen out bitterly over a money dispute and Benter runs a rival syndicate in

Hong Kong. In fact, most of the serious computer-based gambling syndicates are known to each other from the early days of card counting in Las Vegas. Most are acolytes of Benter.

Professional blackjack players had to be itinerant because as soon as casinos latched on to the fact that a player was counting, and winning, the invitation to enter the casino was swiftly withdrawn. Card counting is not illegal, it's just that casinos remain private clubs and, as such, the rules of entry are at the whim of the owners. And casino owners don't like winners. Woods's blackjack career ended in 1981 after a four-hour winning spree of over $200,000 in the MGM casino, Las Vegas.

It was time to return to both Australia and the horses. Blackjack had taught him three important lessons: the need to have an edge, the need to bet scientifically to win, and the advantage of team theory. All of which he applied to horse-race betting. Initially, his horse-race system was a simple handicap system. His team would calculate the probabilities of each horse winning the race and whenever there was an overlay a bet would be struck. The notion of overlays is central to the theory of computer-based horse race betting: put simply, an overlay is whenever the odds offered on a horse are bigger than the calculated odds. So, if the odds of a horse winning have been calculated at 5-1 and its odds at the track are 8-1, then that differential will guarantee the punter's edge/profit over the long term. It might not mean that the horse will win that particular race but, if the odds have been calculated successfully, it should win on average one in six times and lose five, and therefore an 8-1 payout guarantees long-term financial success. Betting overlays is essentially the horse-racing equivalent of card counting.

In 1983, Woods moved to Hong Kong and his team began developing a sophisticated computer model. Hong Kong had – still has – several advantages over other horse-racing destinations. The number of horses in racing there is relatively small, maybe a thousand or so, the number of races is equally manageable, and there are few races that encourage overseas horses. Therefore the data required to keep a tab on all the horses and all the races is within the scope of a relatively sophisticated computer program. Hong Kong has two tracks, Happy Valley and Sha Tin, both of which lack the variables of English tracks, which offer Polytrack, Equitrack, grass, firm going, soft going, undulating courses, straight courses, sharp tracks and galloping tracks. The variables would make England far more complicated for computer analysis and probability forecasting. Hong Kong racing is run by the non-profit making Hong Kong Jockey Club (it simply takes 19 per cent of the total turnover) and is regarded as amongst the most honest racing in the world – which is crucial for data-based gamblers. Any crookedness would skew the probability forecasts, with disastrous consequences.

The final, and most important, reason why Hong Kong became a Mecca for technology-based gamblers is the quantities of money involved. Hong Kong is the richest racing in the world, which means that teams can bet huge amounts of money without tilting the odds against them. Hong Kong racing, unlike English book-making-based racing, is run on a pari-mutuel system. The odds are based, and fluctuate, according to the amount of money bet on a horse, rather than any expert opinion of its chance of winning. So the favourite is the horse that has most money bet on it, rather than the horse with necessarily the best chance of winning. It is a system that allows the professionals to exploit the public's miscalculations, but in order to do that successfully there needs to be enough liquidity in the system for the professionals' money not to tilt the odds against them.

It took Woods's team three years to build a computer program that had a big enough database, and was sophisticated enough, to make money on a regular basis. In 1986–87 he won $100,000; in

1987–88 he won $300,000; in 1989–90 he won $1 million; the following year he won $1.5 million and then $2.5 million in 1990–91. He had a break-even year in 1992, the only one since 1986 that hasn't been profitable. At one stage in that break-even year Woods was up $2.5 million, but by the last race day he had a deficit of $400,000 – it was the most disastrous losing sequence he has known. He puts that down to a system that still needed fine-tuning. After the fine-tuning, profitability was restored: to $1.5 million in 1993–94 and then $10 million the year after that. The profits have continued to increase ever since, so that the syndicate has won over $400 million and his own personal wealth is more than $150 million.

How does the system work? Including investors, Woods's syndicate consists of around forty people. They can roughly be divided into four categories: the analysts who control the computers and the data that is fed into them; the horse-racing experts who scrutinise the videos of every race and add what is inevitably more subjective analysis of form; those who help with the accounting and the distribution of bets; and the pure financial investors. Woods provides the main proportion of the bankroll and, after salaries and expenses, creams off the lion's share of the profits. The computer models calculate roughly a 24 per cent return on turnover.

The top analysts often receive seven-figure salaries and are regarded as the jewels in the crown of the syndicate. However, Woods cautions that: 'A purely mathematical approach without accurate knowledge of the form is unlikely to work too well. You have to have the subjective analysis as well. Our guys will spend hours studying the videos, a horse's particular style of running, and the parts of the track that seem to favour certain horses.'

The analysts feed data from every past performance of every horse and every jockey into the system, and it is this data which is the foundation of the predictive betting system. Horses are judged on anything up to 130 characteristics, such as the speed they run, their ability to break well etc. All the information goes into a database which can then be cross-referenced to help predict the outcome of any race that a particular horse might be running in. The analysts run a regression on every statistic to give it a weighting of how important each one is in the running of that particular race. Then each statistic is checked for randomness.

On the race day, every horse has its probability calculated. Every factor is taken into account. 'If, on the race day, we have given a certain horse a 20-1 chance of winning and the public makes it 3-1 on the course,' says Woods, 'then we reckon that differential to be too large and so the computer assumes the public to have some knowledge that we don't have and our probability is adjusted accordingly.' Any horse that has a positive expectation, which is essentially the same as an overlay, is a bet.

Once the positive-expectation horses are identified, the bets are placed as close to the race as possible to avoid leaving clues and traces of money that rival syndicates and ordinary punters can take advantage of. Bets are put on by a combination of four teams of four people at the track and workers in the offices manning the phone lines. For a seven-race card at Happy Valley an average outlay by the syndicate might be between one and two million US dollars.

Woods says that during the late 1990s, as Hong Kong moved over to Chinese rule, there was increasing pressure put on the syndicates. 'In 1997, the day before the handover, they closed all the Telebet accounts of ours that they could identify. We still managed to bet through our other accounts, but they have continued to close them systematically under Chinese rule. The trouble is that for the last few years, as a result, the amounts bet at the track have been falling steadily and so now they seem keen to encourage computer syndicates again. Computer syndicates can account for as much as

95 per cent of the money, so it's in their interests to encourage us to play'

And Woods's rivals? 'Well, there's Benter's team, and my team, and we're the two biggest, no doubt about that. There's an Australian individual who likes to think he's the third biggest. Then there's an American team and another Australian team that sold out to an Australian bookie for $18 million – although that amount would nowhere near be enough to buy the other main syndicates.' I get the impression that the competition is intense and that secrets and strategies are closely guarded.

The big syndicates really make their money on the exotic bets, rather than simple win-only bets. Combinations like the Triple Trio, where you have to predict the first three finishers in three separate races; the Trifecta, where you have to pick the first three horses to finish in the correct order in a single race; and the Quinella, where you have to pick the first two home in either order. The Triple Trio is the biggest bet that Hong Kong offers and it afforded Woods his biggest ever single payday – a win of $8 million. Initially, the Hong Kong Jockey Club offered those exotic bets on the assumption that the results would be more random and harder to pick. It was an attempt to level the playing field for the ordinary Chinese punter. In fact, it has given the professional syndicates a greater edge, as their extra financial muscle enables them to cover a greater number of options.

During the evening in Sydney that I spend with Woods and his analysts there is no such reward. His team have only identified two races on the Singapore card that they will have an interest in. The first race on the card has two warm favourites, both with accurate expectations forecast by the computer. No other horses in the race show a positive expectation and so no bet is made. Three other races on the card concern two-year-olds or three-year-olds, horses that have had maybe only one or two career runs, and therefore horses without enough information for the computer to predict a probability accurately. That leaves just two races: race three and race five.

Paul, the English analyst, shows me the sheet that the computer has produced for the third race. I cannot make head or tail of it. It might as well have been written in Cantonese. It is a mishmash of numbers and coefficients and mathematical formulae. He points to the key column which identifies the probabilities of the horses. Three numbers – 3, 4 and 10 – are coded in blue. They are the horses with a positive expectation and they are the horses on which the syndicate will bet – to the tune of £25,000 each, win-only. Nobody knows the horses' names. I ask Paul which one he thinks will win. He shrugs his shoulders. 'No idea,' he says.

In a way, I guess their method makes a losing run easier to cope with. At no stage are they saying that this horse or that horse will win. They are simply saying that the market has priced the horse wrongly according to their calculations. Nor are they investing any emotional attachment in the horses. Horses are simply numbers, carrying positive or negative expectations. Most punters get badly affected by losing runs, to the extent that their judgement and betting patterns are affected for the worse. Poker players have a name for it – going on tilt. My guess is that Woods and his team never go on tilt. It is all too clinical.

Everyone settles down on a leather sofa to watch the race. The only similarity with a gathering of normal horse-racing punters is the crate of beer that is produced by Woods's son, Anthony. Other than that, there is absolute detachment. Even I, a horse-racing enthusiast, can't get excited on their behalf. Number 5 sneaks home by a short head from number 3, who, at 25-1, would have provided the syndicate with a nice win-bet return. There is little reaction to the race. No blaming of jockeys. No cursing of the horse. No feeling that the gambling gods have deserted them. Alan flicks his eyes over the sheet and remarks on the amount the Singapore authorities are taking out of the pool (14 per cent), and Paul returns to his computer screen.

Before race five, Paul announces that they 'don't like' the 'dollar forty' favourite who happens to be the number 2 horse. Their computer shows a positive expectation for four horses – numbers 5, 6, 7 and 8 – but the positive expectation for number 6 is too small to warrant a bet. The syndicate has three win-only bets, on numbers 5, 7 and 8. In the end, the favourite steams home by four lengths from the number 6 horse.

I remark to New Zealand Mike on the lack of passion and emotion that the proceedings generate. 'Mr Woods refuses to allow any excitement during or after a race,' he says matter-of-factly. Does he miss the action and the passion of the racetrack? 'We win,' he says, as if the matter had never occurred to him. 'Actually,' Woods pipes up, 'I allowed you to cheer last year when we won the Triple Trio on the last day of the season. Even I enjoyed that one.'

Woods's existence seems absolutely tied to the gambling. He rarely drinks, although he can be tempted to do so if he is planning a trip to one of the girlie bars in Manila, where he seems to be on first-name terms with most of the girls. 'I got married twice,' he says, 'and I thought it was foolish making the same mistake again, so I changed my lifestyle after that.'

Other than that, he lives for 'positive numbers', to use his phrase. For many, gambling is about the excitement and the buzz and the action, whether it be in a casino, on the racetrack or at a sports event. For Woods and his syndicate, it is simply about money.

For Cardano, one of the greatest gamblers of his day, gambling represented something of the stuff of life; something of a metaphor for human existence. As he says in *Liber de Ludo Aleae*: 'The knowledge of the character of our fellow citizens during play is a rack on which anger, joy, greed, honesty and dishonesty are made clear.' Of course, Cardano's enquiring mind and mathematical brilliance were the initial bricks upon which today's professional computer syndicates have built their gambling empires. Four centuries on, I wonder what he would make of it all.

3
CASINO CAPITALISM

'Anyone taken as an individual is tolerably sensible and reasonable – as a member of a crowd, he at once becomes a blockhead.'

Friedrich von Schiller

'When I was young, people called me a gambler. As the scale of my operations increased, I became known as a speculator. Now I am called a banker. But I have been doing the same thing all the time.'

Sir Ernest Cassel, private banker to Edward VII

Some have called him a financial genius, others have called him one of the most incompetent bankers in history. What is of no doubt is that John Law was a gambler, by instinct and inclination. Law was born in Scotland in 1671, just as a gambling craze was igniting further south. Law's life, and the span of history in which he lived, is a perfect illustration of the blurred lines that have always existed, and continue to exist, between gambling and financial speculation. Law's great 'achievement' was to recognise that money was simply a functional medium with no intrinsic value – and therefore that paper credit could do the job just as well as precious metals. In doing so, he set up France's first national bank, created a major business conglomerate, sparked off one of the greatest speculative bubbles in history and brought about the first pan-European stock-market crash. John Law's story, and the story of the so-called Mississippi Bubble, has been well told, although the lessons of it have never been learnt. The herd instinct of the crowd continues to impinge on the markets, moving them in seemingly irrational ways, thus increasing the potential risk (and potential for reward if you can call the crowd psychology correctly) to investors. The dotcom bubble is just the latest manifestation.

Law's father, a well-to-do money lender and goldsmith, died when Law was 12, leaving him an estate at Laurieston (just outside Edinburgh) and rental income from it. Law was a good-looking young man, described by a contemporary as having an 'oval face, high forehead, well-placed eyes, a gentle expression, aquiline nose and agreeable mouth', and he was determined to enjoy this good fortune and his inheritance. He was, said George Lockhart, a friend in Edinburgh, 'nicely expert in all manner of debaucheries'. Law left Edinburgh for London. If he hadn't already done so, he now developed a gambling habit and a sexual appetite. He befriended Thomas Neale, the Groom Porter (whose job it was to provide the court with dice and cards, and decide disputes at play), and chanced his arm at fashionable card games. Initially, he was a disastrous gambler and in 1692 he was forced to sell his estate to pay off his debts. Worse misfortune was to follow.

No one is quite sure whether it was the gambling or his sexual appetite that caused Law to kill Edward Wilson in a duel in April 1694. His supporters claimed it was over a matter of honour concerning his mistress; his detractors pointed to a bad run at dice that had left Law needing funds, which he planned to raise by forcing an argument with Wilson, who he assumed would settle rather than agree to duel. No matter, in the ensuing duel Law killed Wilson with a single stab of his sword. He was convicted of murder and sent to Newgate prison, where he was subsequently sentenced to death by hanging. Law, though, had friends in high places. The

Duke of Shrewsbury and the Earl of Warriston, whom Law met through gambling at the Groom Porter's, arranged for his escape in January 1695. He fled to the continent.

Penniless and a convicted murderer by the age of 24: things did not look good for Law. Like many gamblers, before and since, his fortunes rose and fell with speed and apparent ease. His renaissance on the continent, like his descent, was the result of gambling – although by this time he had absorbed both the lessons of his early failings and the early rumblings of probability theory that were disseminating through Europe. (Whilst Pascal and Fermat had corresponded on probability four decades earlier, it was only around the 1690s that probability theory came to England: in 1693 Edmund Halley produced statistics on the probability of mortality rates, and in the same year Samuel Pepys and Isaac Newton had a correspondence on the probabilities of dice-throwing.)

A contemporary gambler, the Duc de St-Simon, described Law as 'the kind of man who, without ever cheating, won continually at cards by the consummate art of the method of his play.' As noted in the last chapter, the majority of gamblers, then like now, exhibited more madness than method in the gaming room, and Law's understanding of probability theory placed him in a fortunate minority. He moved through the gambling rooms of Europe, amassing a fortune as he went. Law returned to Scotland briefly in 1704, when he added the estate of Sir Andrew Ramsay, valued at £1,200 p.a., to his gambling gains. By 1711, Law's financial rehabilitation was complete: he was able to open a bank account in Amsterdam for £100,000.

Law continued to gamble throughout Europe in the 1720s. One of his favourite ploys illustrates his shrewdness: he liked to wager 10,000-1, nice odds on the face of it, that no one could throw six consecutive sixes. Law knew he was on to a good thing, as the true odds are 46,655-1. Law died on 21 March 1729 in Venice. He was buried in the church of San Gemignano, which stood in the Piazza San Marco, until Napoleon ordered its demolition, after which Law's grave was moved to San Moise. There it remains.

Had this been all there was to the John Law story, he might have featured in the gossip columns of the period but he would not have attracted the attention of a dozen or so biographers. His would have been a typical tale of the time. A feckless ne'er-do-well; a passionate if ultimately shrewd gambler, who gambled himself in and out of trouble. But leaving out the years 1713–20, when Law charmed then cheated all of France, is like omitting the Creation from the ledger of God's work.

As well as gambling, Law's European adventure had taken him to the heart of the sophisticated banking and trading cities of Italy and Holland. France, which he first visited in 1705 and then returned to in 1713, was an entirely different creature, still ruled by an absolute monarch and, in terms of financing, still medieval in outlook. When Louis XIV died in 1715, France's finances were a mess: a combination of severe famines, in 1694 and 1709, and constant war left France in a state of permanent financial crisis; the previous two decades had seen the currency devalued nearly forty times and by the time the Duc d'Orléans became Regent on Louis's death, the nation was two billion livres in debt, and effectively bankrupt. Into this mess stepped Law – an old gambling chum of the Regent's – a gambler, a financier and an alchemist, who promised to restore public faith in the nation's finances by an ingenious scheme to raise money through issuing paper credit.

In this sense Law was ahead of his time. He understood that money had no intrinsic value as such, and that supply and demand was the key. In one of his early tracts Law outlined this concept: 'Water is of great use, yet of little value, because the quantity of water is much greater than the demand for it. Diamonds are of little use, yet of great value, because the demand for diamonds is much greater than the quantity of them.' Supply and demand was at the heart of Law's financial theory; it was to be the basis for his glorious rise to the highest financial position in France, and it was to be the cause of his rapid descent into disgrace.

Initially, Law set up his own private bank – issuing shares to raise capital – which accepted coins in return for paper money, a move which was given a considerable boost when the Regent effectively made Law's paper money legal tender by announcing that it could be used to pay taxes. Law's bank became France's first national bank in 1718. The next plank in Law's system was to set up a joint-stock company (a company that raised capital by issuing shares) called the Mississippi Company, which was granted trading rights in Louisiana. Trading in Louisiana, though, was merely one element in what was to become the greatest conglomerate of its day. Soon the Mississippi Company had taken over the trading routes of the Indies, of China and of Africa; it then bought the tobacco monopoly from the state, then the mint, then France's whole tax system and then, finally, in August 1719 it took over the entire French national debt. To raise money for each stage of this expansion, Law created further share issues, issuing paper currency, bonds, credit notes and company shares in return for public money.

That he was able to continually issue shares was due to a frenzy of speculation which had overtaken French investors. The share price of the Mississippi Company, which had traded at 500 livres in August 1717, spiralled upwards as the public grasped at every new share offering. By 1719 there was a fully fledged bull market in operation: shares rose to 650 in June, 3,000 by August, 5,000 by September, 6,500 by October, peaking at 10,100 in January 1720.

Shares were traded in the Rue Quincampoix and it was a sight that bemused disinterested onlookers. Daniel Defoe recalled that

'Nothing can be more diverting than to see the hurry and clutter of the stockjobbers in Quincampoix St . . . The inconvenience of the nastiest and dirtiest street in Paris does not prevent the crowds of people of all qualities . . . coming to buy and sell their stocks in the open place; where, without distinction, they go up to the ankles in dirt every step they take.' Voltaire was more questioning: 'Have you really all gone mad in Paris? I only hear talk of millions. They say that everyone who was comfortably off is now in misery and everyone who was impoverished revels in opulence. Is this reality? Is this a chimera? Has half the nation really found the philosopher's stone in the paper mills? Is Law a God, a rogue or a charlatan who is poisoning himself with the drug he is distributing to everyone?' At this stage, France thought Law a god: three days before the shares hit a high, Law was appointed Comptroller General of France.

The legends that circulated indicate the collective madness of the time and loss of judgement on behalf of investors. Tales abounded of 'millionaire' lackeys (the term 'millionaire' was coined during the Mississippi Bubble), who on receiving their newly purchased coaches temporarily forgot themselves and took up their old positions at the back of the coach. Another relates how a doctor, whilst taking the pulse of an elderly patient, suddenly cried out 'Oh God, it falls, it falls!' – the object of his worry being the price of stock, not his startled patient's heartbeat. Another tells of how a hunchback leaning against a mulberry tree in the Rue Quincampoix earned 150,000 livres from simply renting out his hump as a writing desk on which speculators could sign their contracts.

Law's scheme had one irredeemable inflationary flaw: rising share prices led to the printing of more money, which was then ploughed back into shares. Even so, he could not have foreseen the herd mentality of investors, which both blew air into the bubble, and then, when confidence collapsed, sucked air from it. They started sucking in early 1720. In May, the share price fell by 4,000 livres in one week. Panic took hold and confidence in Law's paper system collapsed. The laws of supply and demand turned against him. By October, Law's whole scheme was broken when the Regent announced that only coins, not paper money, were legal tender. Coins, though, were in short supply and the mountain of paper money was worthless: the irony was not lost on the Regent's wife, who announced that whilst no one had a sou, toilet paper was abundant. A month later the French National Bank shut its doors, not to reopen for another three generations. Law went from Voltaire's god, to rogue and then charlatan in less than a year and he fled France to the gaming rooms of Europe once more.

The madness of the crowd at the end of the second decade of the 18th century was not limited to France. Across the channel, something equally nonsensical was happening. The South Sea Company, formed in 1711, was also using a trading franchise to convert state debt into company shares. Shares in the South Sea Company were relatively stable until 1719, when the South Sea Company took on the entire national debt (£31 million) and the speculation frenzy suddenly blew across the Channel and into Exchange Alley, at the heart of London's burgeoning financial district. The Mississippi boom-and-bust had a dual effect on investor sentiment across the Channel. At first, as the enormous profits to be had from Law's alchemy became clear, investors rushed to follow suit with the South Sea. As Mississippi stock crashed, South Sea received a further boost as investor funds fled from one conglomerate to another. Then, as the realisation hit home that what could happen to Mississippi was bound to happen to South Sea, market psychology flipped from confidence to panic and South Sea stock sank.

Throughout 1720 the South Sea directors 'ramped up' the stock price (in the same way as the share price of many dotcom companies were manipulated) by planting bogus stories of trading successes (even though the company barely traded at all), by allowing investors to buy shares 'on margin' with just a down-payment of 10 or 20 per cent and by announcing huge dividends to raise false hopes. The punters were well and truly sucked in. Share offerings were over-subscribed and shares in the South Sea Company rose from 128 in January to 1000 in August.

There was exactly the same collective loss of reason in Exchange Alley as in the Rue Quincampoix. Huge crowds flooded into the Alley, so that the pickpockets enjoyed a booming couple of months in high summer. Ships remained moored on the Thames as people preferred trading in stocks and shares to trading on the high seas. Sir Isaac Newton bought and sold at the wrong times, losing £20,000 in the process (add on a couple of noughts for an approximate contemporary comparison), and admitted that he could 'calculate the motions of heavenly bodies but not the madness of people.' To a Dutch banker called Crellius, Exchange Alley in 1720 resembled 'nothing so much as if all the lunatics had escaped out of the madhouse at once.' Nor was the King immune. Pre-dating the current monarch's plunge into the dotcom market when she bought shares in a company called Getmapping.com, George I bought shares in South Sea during the third money subscription at a high of £1000. The author Jonathan Swift wrote of the all-encompassing nature of share-dealing: 'What is the religion there? They tell me it is South Sea stock; what is the policy of England? the answer is the same; what is the trade? South Sea still; and what is the business? nothing but South Sea.'

The legends of the South Sea craze concern the numerous other speculative bubbles that blew up as the South Sea stock soared. Some companies were genuine – such as the company which patented the 'Puckle machine gun' and the company 'for buying and selling South Sea stock and all other public stocks' – and eighty-seven such were floated in June 1720 alone. Others were fictitious, such as the company which was purported to have patented the 'Wheel for perpetual motion' and the company which was to 'carry on an undertaking of great advantage but no one to know what it is'. Real or not, they illustrated a market gone mad, and of the 190 bubble companies that were floated in 1720, only four survived.

When the bubble burst, it did so, like the Mississippi Bubble, spectacularly. In June 1720 the South Sea directors, who had been in cahoots with the government throughout the bubble, persuaded them to pass the Bubble Act, which made the establishment of joint-stock companies illegal without parliamentary consent and which prevented existing companies from pursuing activities beyond their charter. Not only that, but the directors also persuaded the Attorney General to prosecute three existing bubble companies for such a crime. The aim was to consolidate the South Sea's position as the only haven for public capital. To their horror, government intervention along with the collapse of Mississippi (and an unfortunate outbreak of plague) had the opposite effect. Confidence in the market drained and people started to withdraw their money from the South Sea to pay for their debts with other bubble companies. The South Sea directors were well and truly hoist by their own petard. In September 1720 the price of South Sea stock fell from 800 to less than 200. The game was up. Chancellor John Aislabie and four other directors of the South Sea company were sent to the Tower. In his defence, Aislabie blamed the public: 'The unhappy affair, my lords, began when the passion and avaricious desires of mankind were grown up to a madness and a distemper.'

Modern economists are split between those who believe in the 'efficient market theory', in which every share price merely reflects its intrinsic value, and the 'inefficient market theory', which allows for periods such as in 1720, when 'irrational exuberance' on behalf of investors, to use the phrase of Alan Greenspan, Chairman of the Federal Reserve, jolts share prices away from their inherent values. Whilst there are many periods of relative calm in the stock market, there have been enough examples of speculative bubbles after 1720 to indicate that the market is, occasionally, irrational. In England, speculative bubbles blew up in the 1790s (canals), 1820s (South American mines) and the 1840s (railways). The rest of the world has been no less susceptible to them, as America in 1929 and 1987 and Japan in the 1980s have demonstrated.

The economist Charles Kindleberger recognised this recurring theme and proposed a 'paradigm' for all speculative manias: that interest is initially excited by a new form of investment, or new technology; a resultant rise in share prices encourages new, inexperienced investors into the market; this results in euphoria and a weakening of rationality; the mania then spreads to other companies or other forms of investment; credit becomes over-extended; fraud proliferates; and a period of financial crisis and recrimination follows. Another economist, J.K. Galbraith, writing after the stock-market crash of 1987, warned of the inevitability of further episodes of irrationality: 'When a mood of excitement pervades a market or surrounds an investment prospect, when there is a claim of unique opportunity based on special foresight, all sensible people should circle the wagons; it is time for caution . . . one thing is certain: there will be another of these episodes and more beyond.'

It was a warning that went unheeded. The technological revolution of the late 1990s persuaded investors that 'this time it is different' (the most expensive phrase in the English language, according to Sir John Templeton). Internet companies with business plans that had been hastily conceived, or not conceived at all, were recipients of huge amounts of money from venture capitalists eager to exploit this latest bout of investor madness. NASDAQ doubled in the year from March 1999, peaking at 5,048 on 10 March 2000. By October 2002, it stood at 1,114 – a drop of 78 per cent. Whilst the hunchback who rented out his hump as a writing desk in the Rue Quincampoix and the company to 'carry on a great undertaking but no one to know what it is' are perhaps the most famous legends from the Mississippi and South Sea bubbles, future generations will look back in disbelief at internet companies such as Boo.com (an internet retailer that offered discounted items that cost nothing at all), Flooz.com (internet currency) and Pets.com (an online pet supply store) that burnt vast sums of money and rapidly went into administration. The only difference from the legends of 300 years before is that these companies actually existed, actually received money from venture capitalists and, briefly, were the darlings of investors.

It was hard to feel sympathy for some of the entrepreneurs. Anybody who talks of his company – as Ernst Malmsten, the founder of Boo.com, did – as a 'gateway to world cool' deserves his comeuppance. Alan Greenspan shrewdly recognised the gamble that inflated the dotcom bubble: 'There is something going on here that is fascinating to watch. It is, for want of a better term, the lottery principle. What lottery providers have known for centuries is that you can get somebody to pay for a one-in-a-million shot, more than the value of that chance. In other words, people pay more for a claim on a very big pay-off, and that's where the profits from lotteries have always come from.'

From the Mississippi and South Sea to the internet: human nature never changes. Crowds are always more likely to go to extremes, as collective will is stronger than that of the individual. The 'get-rich-quick' mentality that inspired these bubbles also reflects man's gambling nature. The flip side, of course, is that such mass hysteria affects the markets in ways which make investment in such periods little more than an exercise in judging human psychology; little more than a lottery.

Yet, in between these bubbles the markets often run smoothly and share prices reflect their true values. Capitalism, though, does not cease to function; investors still invest. How risky, how inherently unstable, is the stock market in such times? Is investing little more than placing your chips on a giant roulette table called capitalism and spinning the wheel? Opinions differ: the great American financier Bernard Baruch said that 'There is no investment which doesn't involve some risk and is not something of a gamble.' Yet the great modern investment guru, the Sage of Omaha, Warren Buffett, clearly sees himself far removed from a gambler. In 1994 he told the faithful followers of his investment company Berkshire Hathaway: 'Thirty years ago, nobody could have predicted an escalation of the war in Vietnam, wage and price controls, two oil rises, the resignation of a President, the collapse of the Soviet Union . . . well, let me tell you, those events have had little impact on investors who chose to put their money into large corporations like Coca-Cola or Gillette. Whatever the state of the economy, people will always need to shave and quench their thirst.'

The potential investor, then, is faced with a broad range of options when he looks to plunge into the market. At one extreme is the prudent, almost risk-free approach of Warren Buffett, whose long-term and selective stock-holding policy is designed to ride the vagaries of fluctuations in price and potential ambushes which might jolt the market in the short term. At the other end of the spectrum is the speculator, who is looking to make short-term trades for immediate profit.

The short-term trader/speculator takes greater risks than the investor and is involved with a transfer of value from buyer to seller, or vice versa, and when the trade is complete there will be winners and losers. That, at least, seems to conform to our initial definition of what is gambling. In essence, the speculator might be defined as someone who has an intention to trade: the investor is market-passive, the speculator market-active. The very definition of the word 'speculator' indicates how close it is to gambling: to speculate means to theorise without having enough evidence to prove the theory right or wrong. A speculator backs his opinion against the rest of the market. No doubt he has done his research and will think the probabilities in his favour. Nevertheless, he does not know. He is squinting into the future just as myopically as any gambler.

This synergy between financial speculation and gambling is inevitable, because the very formation of the English stock market, just three decades old when South Sea stock collapsed, can only be understood in the context of the gambling explosion of the late 17th century onwards, which will be the focus of the next chapter. Inherent in its formation was a system designed to appeal to gamblers. According to a recent historian of financial speculation, Edward Chancellor, 'The successful establishment of the stock market and the joint-stock company over other forms of capital organisation lay in their incorporating within themselves elements of the gaming room. In the origins of financial capitalism, rationalism was very much a subsidiary element.'

London's stock market emerged in the middle of the 1690s, following a financial revolution that created a national debt (1693), and the Bank of England (1694). The government's financing of the national debt was aimed specifically at massaging the nation's gambling instincts. Thus, various lotteries were announced in the last decade of the 17th century and first two decades of the 18th: Sir

John Blunt, the chief architect of the South Sea Bubble, was also behind the 1711 'Two Million Adventure' lottery, which rapidly raised £2 million for the government. Between 1693 and 1712, the government raised £11 million from lotteries.

The 1690s also saw an explosion of joint-stock companies and from the middle of the 1690s there was regular trade in the shares of these companies, and it is from this point that we can say the stock market, in England, was born. Specifically, it was in the coffee houses – Jonathan's (which later became the Stock Exchange) and Garraway's – of Exchange Alley, a narrow street between Lombard Street and Cornhill, where the buying and selling of these shares would take place.

The middleman who encouraged this action, the late 17th-century equivalent of today's trader, was the so-called stock-jobber. He was viewed as nothing more than a gambler, or, as described in Doctor Johnson's dictionary, 'a low wretch'. Daniel Defoe, in a 1701 pamphlet called 'The Villainy of Stock-Jobbers Detected', described the stock-jobbing as simply 'play: a box and dice may be less dangerous, the nature of them are alike, a hazard.' He accused them of putting 'the dice upon the whole town'. Defoe, though, had been stung badly in this particular casino: his speculations resulted in his being declared bankrupt in 1694, to the tune of £17,000. As stock-jobbers went about their business, this synergy of financial speculation and gambling was constant: they were as likely to be trading in lottery tickets as they were shares or life insurance. (Garraway's and Lloyd's issued daily insurance rates on the lives of famous people. The ability to bet on a life other than one's own was eventually prohibited by the Gaming Act of 1774.)

The nascent English stock market of the late 17th century and early 18th century was a sophisticated affair – sophistication that arose from the need to respond to the gambling instincts of those involved. Buying 'on margin', at a fraction of the cost of a full share price, was common, whether it be for shares or lottery tickets, so enabling many to participate who would otherwise be priced out of the market. Buying 'options' – which gave the holder the right, but not the obligation, to buy or sell a stock in the future – was a common way for shareholders to hedge a risk against the future drop or rise in the price of a share. 'Futures contracts' – which unlike options obligated the buyer or seller to take delivery of or deliver a commodity at a certain price in the future – were also common. These transactions allowed speculation without ownership of shares. These are the basis of modern-day derivatives – so called because a derivative is a financial contract that derives its value from an underlying asset (a share, say, or a commodity). Many of the tools of the modern-day trader, then, were available in this market. None of which should be surprising – the Amsterdam Exchange had been dealing in these sophisticated transactions for most of the 17th century.

The 300th anniversary of John Law's birth saw the beginning of another financial revolution, not unlike that of three centuries before, which was to have further profound effects on the stability of markets. In August 1971, President Nixon suspended the convertibility of the dollar into gold, which brought about, two years later, an end to what had been called the Bretton Woods agreement. Since the end of the Second World War, Bretton Woods (named after the town in New Hampshire where the system was thrashed out) had tied the dollar to the price of gold, and the rest of the world's currencies to the price of the dollar. Effectively, the world's currency markets had been firmly anchored. By unhinging them, Nixon ushered in an era of currency speculation. It was the necessary precursor to the arrival on the scene of a currency speculator like George Soros, whose Quantum Fund forced John

Major's government to devalue its currency by taking a £10 billion punt against the pound in 1992.

Nixon's move sparked the beginning of the free-market ideology that came to dominate Western capitalism in the last three decades of the 20th century. Economic liberalism and deregulation found favour, especially, with the right-wing governments of Ronald Reagan and Margaret Thatcher. The deregulation of the London Stock Exchange in 1986 – the so-called 'Big Bang' – encapsulated this ideology and transformed London into a major financial centre.

One of the by-products of this deregulation was the explosion of the derivatives market. (As we have seen, derivatives in the form of options or futures in shares and commodities had existed in the 17th century. Now these transactions, in other less tangible areas such as currencies and indices, came to dominate the market.) In May 1972, on the back of the unfettering of the world's currency markets, the Chicago Mercantile Exchange was given permission to open a derivatives market on currency futures. Within the next ten years, new derivatives markets were opened on share options, gold futures, bond futures, oil futures, currency options, interest rate futures and stock market index futures. The increasing complexity of the derivatives market was illustrated when in 1982 the Chicago Board of Trade offered a market for options on futures.

The development of the 'over-the-counter' (OTC) market increased the lack of transparency and the confusion surrounding derivatives. Derivatives can be traded at one of two places: a recognised futures exchange, such as the London International Financial Futures Exchange (LIFFE), where daily statements and prices are issued; or in an OTC market, where contracts, the details of which are never published and the complexity of which means that they can be rarely checked, are drawn up by traders for special customers.

By the 1980s these derivatives markets were worth trillions of dollars worldwide. The increasing importance of the derivatives sector propelled the traders of these transient deals to the top of the giant Wall Street investment banks. The high-earning, high-spending trader became the symbol of a decade that glorified greed: the 'Master of the Universe' in Tom Wolfe's *The Bonfire of the Vanities*; the 'big swinging dicks' of Michael Lewis's *Liar's Poker* (a book about Salomon Brothers) and Gordon Gekko of Oliver Stone's film *Wall Street*. 'Lunch,' said Gekko, 'is for wimps.'

Into this whirlpool of speculation stepped a young trader who was ultimately able to bring to its knees one of the most famous names in British banking history. When Nicholas Leeson joined Barings Bank at the end of this decade of excess, he was 22 years old and ambitious. Barings were much older – 209 years older, to be precise – but this once staid and stuffy blue-blooded bank was equally ambitious, and through a subsidiary in the Far East they joined the rush to expand into futures and options. Despite failing his maths A level at the first attempt, Leeson had impressed in the futures and options department of the American firm Morgan Stanley, and was subsequently poached by Barings.

He was initially sent to Jakarta and then, in 1992, to Singapore, where Barings had formed a subsidiary called Barings Futures (Singapore) Ltd. In May 1992, Barings applied for three seats on the Singapore International Monetary Exchange (SIMEX). At about the same time Leeson sat and passed his futures-trading exams and in August 1992 Leeson's navy and gold trader's jacket could be seen for the first time on the SIMEX trading floor.

The reason why Leeson was allowed to trade such extraordinary sums and how he was able to conceal his tracks, with the result that Barings were completely blind to his activities for two years or so, has been well told elsewhere[2]. One of the key elements to his fraud is that Leeson was involved simultaneously in both the settlements

[2] *The Collapse of Barings* by Stephen Fay.

department (called the back office) and the trading department. The settlements department is supposed to keep the trading department on the straight and narrow: Leeson had his finger in both pies.

What concerns us most is not the woeful failure of management at Barings (and the Bank of England) but Leeson's gambling mentality, which illustrates how dangerous derivatives can be in the wrong hands. At the nub of the story is the derivatives market in Nikkei 225 futures. To recap: a future is a financial contract that obliges the buyer to fulfil his obligations at some point in the future. He buys the contract 'on margin' – that is at a fraction of the cost of the whole – and if his position begins to move against him (i.e. if the market falls when he has a 'long' position), then those margin calls will increase. In this instance, the contract in futures was derived from the Japanese stock market index called the Nikkei 225 (the Japanese equivalent of the FTSE 100).

To make matters slightly more complicated, Leeson was trading in Nikkei 225 futures in both Singapore and Osaka. The presence of two markets ought to have given Leeson the opportunity to arbitrage – that is, the ability to trade in the same asset in two different markets in order to take advantage of the slight price discrepancies. The differences between the two markets gives traders the chance to hedge their risks. Hedging risk – being long in one market and short in another, buying a commodity at one price and selling it at another – is the bread and butter of most traders' existence. The trouble is that Leeson was a gambler not a trader, and he failed to hedge his positions. As he admitted in an interview to David Frost: 'I was not offsetting the risk. I was looking for a big return.'

In July 1992 Barings opened an error account on SIMEX – account 88888 – and it was in July, a month before Leeson actually received his SIMEX registration, that he traded his first Nikkei 225 futures. His first trade lost him £40,000. By the end of August his losses had amounted to £320,000. In September they amounted to £3 million, a figure which climbed to £4.5 million in October. At this stage Leeson also moved into trading options (where the buyer has the right but not the obligation to fulfil the contract, again buying 'on margin' at a fraction of the cost) on his futures to cover his losses, even though he was not supposed to be trading in options at all. A year later, by the end of 1993, his losses stood at £24.39 million, his trades amounted to over 7 per cent of the total trades on SIMEX. His positions were worth more than Barings' entire capital, and by December 2004 his losses stood at £200 million.

In the summer of 1994, Leeson had changed the password on his computer to 'Superman', so cocksure was he that his losses could stay hidden in account 88888. As the economist J.K. Galbraith has said: 'financial genius is before the fall.' On 17 January 1995 a giant earthquake hit the Japanese city of Kobe (echoing the unfortunate outbreak of plague that precipitated the bursting of the South Sea Bubble). Unknown to Leeson's bosses, Leeson had not been arbitraging between Singapore and Osaka: instead Leeson had built up huge 'long' positions in both markets. He needed the market to rise. The market's response to the Kobe earthquake was to go into freefall. On 23 January it fell 1,175 points in a single day. For every 100 points the Nikkei dropped, Leeson lost £20 million. On 23 February he lost £144 million. It was too much, even for a gambler like Leeson, and he fled to Kuala Lumpur. All told, Leeson gambled away £869 million.

It was enough to bring down Barings, and end Leeson's career as a trader. The gambling bug stayed with him, though – in January 2006 it was reported that one of Leeson's main sources of income was playing online poker on a website called CelebPoker.com. After winning a pot of £25,000, he was quoted as saying, 'The returns are phenomenal, but I am well aware that I can lose too, so

I won't be repeating the mistakes I made in the past.' It is a different story, I guess, when you are gambling with your own money.

It would be comforting if Leeson's story was a one-off: the high roller who played big in a casino that was characterised, in general, by prudence and good stewardship. But Leeson's story is not exceptional. In the right hands derivatives play an important function in the capitalist process as a whole, enabling firms to offset their exposure in other areas. In the wrong hands – in the hands of a gambler rather than a trader – derivatives can be explosively dangerous. As the *Financial Times* columnist James Morgan explained: 'A derivative is like a razor. You can use it to shave yourself . . . or you can use it to commit suicide.'

Leeson is not the only derivatives trader to have 'committed suicide'. Most of the major financial disasters in the 1990s came from derivatives traders holding unhedged positions. In the same year as Leeson's fraud came to light, a Daiwa trader called Iguchi was discovered to have placed 30,000 unauthorised trades in New York over a period of eleven years – it cost his firm $1.1 billion. A year later, Yasuo Hamanaka received a seven-year jail sentence for incurring losses of $2.6 billion for the Japanese bank Sumitomo after he bought enough copper futures to exceed the entire copper consumption of the United States. Allied Irish Bank was nearly brought down after it discovered a $691 million hole in its accounts, in a scandal that had many of the hallmarks of the Barings collapse. In 2005 derivatives traders for China Aviation Oil were found to have huge unhedged positions in oil, a gamble which cost the company $550 million.

As I write, in a disturbing echo of the Hamanaka copper fiasco, a respected metals trader for the Chinese government, Liu Qibing, has mysteriously disappeared. He was known to have taken a massive 'short' position on copper futures – a gamble that went disastrously wrong when copper hit a high of $4,200 a tonne in

November 2005.[3] Throughout the autumn of 2005 the Chinese government sold copper and put out spurious information about the size of its copper reserves in order to depress the price and protect its position. Its failure to do so led some analysts to deduce that the Chinese government had now hung Qibing out to dry and was blaming its massive loss on the activities of a rogue trader.

Derivatives seem to have brought unnecessary instability to the markets as a whole, as a result of the increasing complexity of the contracts, the proliferation of the over-the-counter market that makes the whole process increasingly opaque, and the fact that the markets seem overwhelmingly reliant on these products. Some, like George Soros, have warned against their proliferation: 'There are so many of them [derivatives], and some of them are so esoteric, that the risk involved may not be properly understood even by the most sophisticated investor, and I'm supposed to be one. Some of these instruments appear to be specifically designed to enable institutional investors to take gambles which they would otherwise not be permitted to take.'

The gambling instinct of speculators has been central to the development of the capitalist process. They give the system vitality and liquidity. Without risk there can be no reward and the system would ossify. The system itself has responded magnificently to their needs: transactions such as options and futures were established early on, and then developed, to enable speculators to play the market.

[3] Copper reached the dizzy heights of $7,385 a tonne in early 2006. The Secretary General of the International Wrought Copper Council, Simon Payton, blamed hedge fund speculators for taking copper's price away from its inherent value based on supply and demand. 'This,' he said, 'is a feeding frenzy driven by hedge fund speculation. This would not be happening if the price was left purely to industrial supply and demand.'

The world of modern high finance, though, does seem to be overly reliant on such transactions, which in turn rely on correctly predicting the future changes in the market and, on occasions, rely on correctly predicting the psychology of the crowd. It is highly speculative.[4]

Bearing in mind the frequent financial crises that have dislocated the markets in the last two decades, the activities of rogue traders like Nick Leeson, of rogue companies like Enron and the collapse of hedge funds like Long-Term Capital Management (which had taken a $1.4 trillion position in the market on a capital base of less than $1 billion), it is worth recalling the words of the great economist John Maynard Keynes who, eight decades ago, warned of the dangers: 'Speculators,' he said, 'may do no harm as bubbles on a steady stream of enterprise. But the position is serious when enterprise becomes the bubble on a whirlpool of speculation. When the capital development of a country becomes a by-product of the activities of a casino, the job is likely to be ill-done.'

And if you think investing in 'blue chip' companies is any less of a gamble, just remember where the name 'blue chip' comes from: it is the colour of the most expensive chip in the casinos of Monte Carlo.

---

[4] The financial markets suffered their latest bout of investor madness in May 2006. Soaring commodity prices meant that gold, copper and oil saw a sixfold increase in the previous four years. Stephen Roach, the chief economist at Morgan Stanley, said that the commodities markets had become the latest bubble: 'It too will burst; the only question is when.' Sure enough, it burst in mid May, with silver declining by 20 per cent in one week and copper by 14 per cent, with similar falls in aluminium, nickel, tin and zinc. These sharp falls induced the Bank of England to warn investors that they had become dangerously complacent about the underlying risks in a market that many thought was damagingly speculative.

SIMON CAWKWELL
(aka 'Evil Knievil')

The Financial Bettor

The study in Simon Cawkwell's South Kensington lair is a shrine to gambling. Photographs of his favourite horses adorn the walls, as does a list of bookmakers he can and can't bet with. ('Most of them have stopped me now,' he says.) On the wall behind a desk – cluttered with the *Racing Post*, the *Financial Times* and an array of spreadsheets – are four large computer screens upon which the share prices of the London and New York Stock Exchanges are flickering away.

Cawkwell has gambled for most of his life, despite the fact that there were no family influences. His father is an emeritus fellow at Oxford University and about as 'financially risk averse as it is possible to be'. His father's second name is Law, which makes Cawkwell wonder about any family connection with the financier John Law. Disappointingly, though, Cawkwell cannot find any evidence of such a link: having John Law as an ancestor would fit in perfectly with Cawkwell's image of himself as a financial maverick.

Cawkwell is convinced that most people emerge from adolescence as either gamblers or not. His theory is that most gamblers experienced a heavy degree of parental authority. At least he is convinced of that in his own case, and dates his success at gambling from the moment he stood up and argued successfully, for the first time, against his own father.

It was at Rugby school that Cawkwell's lifelong interest in gambling started. 'A boy called Peter Cundell had his study opposite mine at school. His father, Ken, had a runner in the 1963 Oaks called Pourparler ridden by Scobie Beasley. Peter told me to have a small bet on it, which I did (four shillings each way), and it came third at 14-1. I was hooked and I've been hooked on the horses ever since. It struck me as being all about a combination of weighing up evidence, chance, assessment and opinion, and then backing your judgement accordingly. In that sense, picking stocks is quite similar.'

Cawkwell's gambling on the horses has been a roller-coaster ride of enormous wins and huge losses. 'I've won more than £100,000 on a bet more than once. My biggest bet was £35,000 on a horse of mine at Royal Ascot which won at 11-2. That was very pleasing. I had an excellent 2000, a very good 2002, I won over £250,000 last year but I'm down at least that this year.

'Very early on, on Betfair[5], I had a eureka moment. At Cheltenham in March 2002, I saw someone post a bet of £100,000 on a horse called Like-A-Butterfly. I thought, "There's no chance of that being taken up." But it disappeared before my very eyes. Suddenly I thought that Betfair was a very good, what you would call in the city, "volume and price indicator". That means that Betfair gives you a clue where the smart money is going. A couple of months later on Betfair, at an evening meeting at Newmarket, I saw that someone was trying to have £4,000 on a horse at 8-1. This was all very strange, because that horse was freely available at 11-1 with the bookmakers. I had my Eureka! moment. If this chap wanted 8-1 on Betfair when 11-1 was freely available elsewhere, it meant that he couldn't get on elsewhere, which meant that he was very well informed. He knew something. I simply followed the money. I had

---

[5] See chapter seven for an explanation of how Betfair works.

£2,000 each way at 11-1 and netted £27,000. It was the start of a good run on Betfair. I made more than £500,000 off the bookies in 2002 and every account of mine was closed.'

Cawkwell shows me the list of who he can and can't bet with. 'Ladbrokes will still give me a couple of hundred quid – after a board meeting – as will Stan James, whilst Blue Square will only let me bet ante-post. The rest won't let me bet.' 'But after this year they might want your custom back,' I venture. 'It's too late for the bookies: I've lost it all to Betfair.' Why has this year been so bad? 'I had a moronic bet on the election. I took a position at £4,000 a seat and there was a swing of twenty-five seats away from me. Cost me £100,000. I lost a lot on Lindsay Davenport at Wimbledon, too.' And the horses? 'It's just a matter of not landing a couple of big blows. I'm lying low at the moment. Unless you have a compelling reason to have a bet, I'd suggest that means there's a compelling reason not to bet.' Cawkwell is candid enough to accept that he is, ultimately, a losing punter when it comes to horse racing. 'I'm definitely a loser overall. I've probably lost a six-figure sum.'

Cawkwell's financial security comes from his long-term success at stock picking. 'I've always been a very good stock-picker. On average I've taken about £100,000 out of the market on an annual basis ever since I qualified as an articled clerk with Cooper's.' It is important to stress that, aside from Cawkwell's penchant for gambling, he has an acute analytical mind that is able to see through balance sheets and weigh up the strength or otherwise of a company and, therefore, he can coolly assess the probabilities of those shares rising or falling regardless of public sentiment. 'It's not about what they want to tell you in the balance sheets, it's about what they don't!' he shouts. The best example of Cawkwell's forensic financial skills was his role in unravelling the accounting frauds of Robert Maxwell. It was how he came by his nickname of 'Evil Knievil'. After dissecting Maxwell's financial irregularities he sent around a note under that assumed name to the City institutions outlining the discrepancies. It has stuck with him ever since. He made £250,000 selling Maxwell stock in 1991. Despite the fact that he has made and lost much more than that on many days since, his analysis of Maxwell's fraud remains the achievement he is most proud of.

When firms started offering spread betting on individual shares in the mid 1990s (crucially, with any gains free of tax), it was time for Cawkwell to bring his expertise of the markets and his enthusiasm for gambling together. It is as an aggressive short-seller – identifying overvalued stocks and shorting them aggressively – that he has made his name and his fortune.

What is 'short-selling'? Short-selling is the happy situation whereby an investor can see the value of his investments go up in a 'bear' or declining market. If you are sure that a share will decline in price you can short-sell. That is, you borrow a certain number of shares, and sell at a certain price and the money is accredited to your account. At an agreed date in the future, you 'close the short'. That is, you agree to buy back those shares at market price and the difference is your profit or loss.

It helped, of course, that 'Cawkwell's moment' coincided with one of the most irrational markets that the City has ever seen. The dotcom boom was under way. Whilst Cawkwell is a 'bear' and, therefore, a seller by nature, he recognised that he had to ride this particular beast and he made more than £1 million between January 1999 and March 2000 going 'long' on technology stocks. The difficulty was then deciding when the bubble would burst. 'It's not as though a letter goes around, you know, telling everybody that it's time to sell! And when you think that a bear market is about to begin, there are many ambushes along the way – stocks that you think should fall but that the irrational market pushes up. It can be a very dangerous time.'

Sometime in 2001, he recognised that investors were starting to lose their courage and faith, and he short-sold aggressively just before the bubble burst. 'I made about £1 million in 2001, and then about £3 million the following year (as well as around £330,000 on the horses). It really was a very agreeable year.'

It might be supposed that, since Cawkwell is such a good financial analyst, his form of short-selling is not gambling at all. Yet I would argue that it is. Short-term predictions are notoriously difficult and open to all kind of unforeseen circumstances, so the market often reacts irrationally and shares trade way outside the boundaries of their intrinsic value. In that case, it doesn't matter how expert you are. Shorting, as opposed to going long, also means that the potential for losses is limitless (there being no ceiling to what a share might appreciate to, whereas a share cannot go lower than zero) and there is always the possibility that a short-seller won't be able to close his position if there aren't any sellers out there. This is known as a 'bear squeeze'. Shortly after Cawkwell's very agreeable year in 2002, he and his brother-in-law lost close to £3 million on short-selling a company called Regus. 'This is not a game for wimps,' he says.

How then does Cawkwell cope mentally with these massive fluctuations of fortune? Firstly, he has salted away enough money from short-selling in the last five years (around £5 million) to make him financially comfortable ('I'd have to be extremely dim to lose it all now,' he says); secondly, he says, it is all about self-belief. 'With gambling you must have self-belief that you are going to win. A lot of people live in a kind of miasma where they are happy to be dominated and humiliated by bookmakers. To keep this state of affairs going, they have to keep losing. Even if they knew how to win, they wouldn't be able to handle it.' Thirdly, he doesn't regard money as important and therefore can take the blows with equanimity.

It seems strange that a man who has spent his whole life around money, and whose every waking hour seems to be focused on making it, should have so little regard for it. 'I've never attached much importance to money. Just because a guy is worth £100 million doesn't mean much to me. I'm more interested in a way a chap thinks and conducts himself. I suppose I could buy a Rolls-Royce if I wanted to, but I don't. I drive an old Mercedes that cost me £500, my wife drives an old Fiat Punto and, look around you, this is not the grandest apartment in Kensington. I don't regard myself as imprudent – as I'm always taking a position on the balance of probabilities – and I've never been bankrupt, although I've come close once or twice. No, money is nice but not that important to me. It's just a means of keeping score.'

As I'm about to leave, the phone rings. 'That will be my brother-in-law,' he says. 'A few years ago he gave me £4,000 and I've turned it into £2 million. He'll want to know how we've done today. He answers the phone brusquely and says to his brother-in-law, simply: 'We've had a good day.' With that he puts the phone down and wishes me farewell.

4

HIGH LIFE

'A thousand meadows and cornfields are staked at every
throw and as many villages are lost as in the earthquake that
overwhelmed Herculaneum and Pompeii.'

Horace Walpole

The high point of gaming in England can roughly be dated from the
Restoration of Charles II in 1660 through to the Gaming Act of
1845. Before this period, gaming was challenged by Cromwellian
Puritanism, and afterwards by Victorian morality. In between,
although gambling continued to be popular with all classes, it was
the excessive and often ruinous gambling of the aristocracy that
induced most comment from contemporary observers.

Inevitably, the aristocracy took its lead from the court. Given the
Puritanical nature of the Protectorate, it is perhaps not surprising
that there was a reaction when the monarchy resumed. Nor, given
the upheaval which saw a divinely ordained king beheaded and the
natural order of things turned upside down, is it surprising that the
ruling classes lost their sense of perspective. The popularity of
gaming at the court should also be seen in a wider European
context: in its exile, the Stuart monarchy would have no doubt
picked up the habits of its European cousins, and the French court
of the *ancien régime* was particularly prone in this regard. Gambling, and knowledge of the card games of the day, was de rigueur
if entry into the French court was to be granted.

Samuel Pepys and John Evelyn observed the goings-on at the court of Charles II with a combination of interest, even awe, and obvious disapproval. Evelyn watched the King 'throwing the dice himself in the privy chamber, where was a table set on purpose.' On another occasion he observed 'the wicked folly and monstrous excess of passion amongst some losers', and denounced the fact that such a 'wretched custom as play to that excess should be countenanced in a Court which ought to be an example of virtue to the rest of the kingdom.' Pepys was shocked to discover that the Queen and the Duchess of York played cards on a Sunday. Just before the death of Charles II, Evelyn famously described the scene he witnessed at Whitehall: 'I can never forget the inexpressible luxury and profanity, gaming and all dissoluteness . . . which I was witness of, the King sitting and toying with his concubines . . . whilst about twenty of the great courtiers and other dissolute persons were at basset round a large table, a bank of at least £2000 in gold before them.'

Gaming was still strictly illegal unless permitted by the royal office of the Groom Porter, which dated from the reign of Henry VIII. His job was to see that the King's lodgings were well furnished, to provide dice and cards and to decide disputes at play. Traditionally, gambling was permitted at the court between Christmas and Epiphany. When the King wished to gamble, the Groom Porter would announce that His Majesty 'is out' and when His Majesty was 'at home' gambling was not permitted. The office of the Groom Porter was re-established after the Cromwellian Protectorate, when he was allowed to keep a grace-and-favour apartment at Whitehall. In Queen Anne's reign the Groom Porter's role was extended to licensing gaming establishments outside the court – a key development for the commercialisation of gambling which was at hand. The office lasted until 1772, when George III – 'unaccustomed to play at hazard' – ordered a handsome gratuity for the Groom Porter and discontinued the office.

Proof of the popularity of gambling in the late 17th century is the publication of the first English book dedicated to gambling – Charles Cotton's *The Compleat Gamester*. It begins with the memorable phrase that 'gambling is an enchanting witchery' and it goes on to provide a compelling testament to the spirit of the time, describing the gambling games of the day: sports, from billiards, to chess, to cock-fighting; card games, some of which, like cribbage and whist, will be familiar, others, like l'ombre and lanterloo, are not; and dice games like hazard, which, he says, is justly called since it 'speedily makes a man or undoes him.' Cotton indicates that huge losses were already common: 'Consider how many persons have been ruined by play. I would nominate a great many, some who have had great estates lost to them, other having good employments have been forced to desert them and hide themselves from their creditors in some foreign plantation.' Cotton devotes twice as much space to cards as to dice, which suggests that cards had become the predominant gaming instrument by this time.

As we move into the 18th century, so a demarcation gradually develops between aristocratic gambling at the royal court and other private palaces and estates, and the development of other centres of gambling – private clubs, such as White's, and spa towns, such as Bath – where the aristocracy could continue to gamble in surroundings that, while still private, were more commercial, and gave the entrepreneurs an opportunity to take their cut.

Francesco Bianco set up White's Chocolate House on the east side of London's St James's Street in 1693. Shortly afterwards the place morphed into a private club, presumably so that the undesirables could be kept out. That gambling quickly became central to the club's raison d'être can be seen by looking at the list of the first club rules. Rule 9 stated that 'Every member who is in the room after 7 o'clock, and plays, is to pay half a crown.' The club's coat of arms, designed by Horace Walpole, shows two jacks of clubs holding a card table upon which there are three aces and two dice, above which a hand is shown shaking a dice box. Below, the motto of the club: *Cogit amor nummi* – 'love of money compels'.

In the first half of the 18th century, the 'deepest' play (defined by the philosopher Jeremy Bentham as gambling that was so big and so unpredictable as to be entirely irrational) took place at White's. In 1744 Horace Walpole tells us of Lord Coke, who was 'always drunk, has lost immense sums at play and seldom goes home to his wife before eight in the morning.' A year later we hear that 'there had been extreme deep play and that Harry Furnese went drunk from White's at six o'clock having won the dear memorable sum of 1000 guineas.' Occasionally, gambling was so deep that members paid the ultimate price. In 1754, the betting book notes that Lord Montford wagered Sir John Bland 100 guineas that Beau Nash would outlive Colley Cibber. Unfortunately, neither of the intrepid gamblers outlived Nash or Cibber. Underneath the evidence of the wager is written 'Both Lord M and Sir Jn Bland put an end to their own lives before the wager was decided.' Lord Montford was a regular in the betting book at White's, with over sixty wagers to his name. He can have won but few, for, having run out of money, he shot himself on New Year's Day 1755. In September of that year, Bland followed suit, having lost enormous sums (£32,000 at one sitting, according to Walpole) at hazard.

The betting book at White's, which dates from 1743 (the first betting book was lost in an earlier fire), suggests that gambling at the club encapsulated both the private and the commercial. For, whilst gambling games against a bank were common, the notion of the private wager between individuals continued to thrive. The first wager written down in the book is between Lords Lincoln and Winchelsea, who wagered 150 guineas that the Duchess Dowager of Marlborough would not outlive the Duchess Dowager of Cleve-land. Many of the wagers seemed to concern the issue of the timing of death. Others were of a sporting nature (in 1757 Lord Eglinton bet Mr Vernon that he could find a man who could kill twenty snipes in twenty-three shots before May), others of a sexual nature (in 1748 Mr Boone bet Mr Rigby that his penis was within an inch as long as Mr Halsy's). Some sensibilities remained: the outcome of that particular wager is not recorded. The predilection for betting on anything and everything led to an apocryphal wager or two passing down into the club's legend. Walpole recounts how a man collapsed on the pavement outside White's, only for the members to haul him in and immediately start betting on whether he was alive or not. When it was suggested that the man be bled to find out if he was alive, there was an uproar, as it was felt the bleeding would affect the status of the bet. No such wager, however, exists in the betting book.

(One of my favourite wagers in the entire book is between Tony Milbanke and Richard Sutton in 1939, when Milbanke wagered Sutton a fiver and a set of golf clubs that Sutton could not get from the far side of Tower Bridge to the front steps at White's in under 2000 strokes. Sutton dressed in a lounge suit and Milbanke a fur coat. Sutton teed his ball up on a bus ticket, took out his putter and smashed the ball forty yards down Tooley Street. The *Daily Mail*, which reported the match, noted that Sutton 'kept to the gutter', 'averaged 40 yards a stroke' and never once used any other club. The long 14th down Northumberland Avenue and the water hole at Trafalgar Square were negotiated without much difficulty, although the dog-leg from Pall Mall to St James's Street caused a 'bit of bother'. And so to White's, where Sutton arrived in 102 strokes. He still had to get the ball from the gutter on to the pavement, which he did in forty more. The wager was Sutton's, presumably paid up on the 19th hole in White's.)

The club's betting book of the 18th century simply reflected the customs of the time. The wager became the accepted method of settling a dispute with the now universal measure of value – money. The weekly paper the *Connoisseur* tells us in 1754 that 'there is nothing, however trivial or ridiculous, that is not capable of producing a bet.' And when naturally occurring events – births, deaths etc – were not sufficient to whet the appetite of a gambling-hungry public, eccentric and artificial wagers were dreamt up. In 1735, Count de Buckebergh laid a large wager on riding to Edinburgh whilst sitting backwards on the horse – a feat duly accomplished in just under four days. In 1750 Lord March bet a thousand guineas that a four-wheeled carriage could be drawn at a minimum of nineteen miles in an hour. The event took place over a mile in Newmarket and Lord March won his thousand guineas with seven minutes to spare. In 1770 two earls struck a bet that one could ride from London to Edinburgh and back in less time than it took the other to draw a million dots. In 1778 a young Irish gentleman called Buck Whaley had £20,000 pending on whether he could walk to Constantinople and back within the year. He won his wager. My favourite concerns a northern baron who laid a considerable wager that he would go to Lapland and bring back two native females and two reindeer within an allotted time. He did so, and the Laplanders lived with the baron for about a year until they asked to go home. He paid for their return but didn't accompany them. It seems that this particular form of gambling – the eccentric wager – was peculiar to England. When, in 1754, the Ambassador to Paris, Lord Stair, laid a wager that Louis XIV would survive beyond September, Voltaire later noted in *Siècle de Louis XIV* that Stair had betted 'according to the custom of his nation'.

It was not just in the private clubs and the gambling 'hells' of London that gambling flourished. Bath was already a fashionable spa town by the turn of the 18th century, but it became predominantly so over the next fifty years, largely because it became a resort dedicated to pleasure – and the chief of all pleasures was gambling. Richard 'Beau' Nash, the son of a lowly glass-maker, arrived in Bath sometime during the first decade of the 18th century, and whilst a gambling room already existed, it was Nash who transformed Bath into the Las Vegas of its day. He appointed himself 'Regulator of Diversions and Moderator of Disputes at Play' – a kind of Groom Porter for Bath (but without royal consent), and whilst he created a resort to which all the fashionable aristocrats of the day would look to spend their summer months, he also enriched himself in the process. Holding the bank at faro or basset was a sure and quick route to riches, and Nash was happy to rake in at the expense of those foolish enough to play. He won vast estates off the Lords Howard and Bedford, which he converted into an annuity of £1,200 for life. Indeed, the unfortunate Bedford was so addicted to gambling that Nash offered him 100-1 that Bedford could not get through a gambling session without losing £10,000. After a particularly bad session at Newmarket in 1731, Bedford had to pay up. Nash settled for £5,000 up front and 400 guineas per annum thereafter. In Bath and 'Beau' Nash, we see the early results of the commercialisation of gambling: aristocrats losing and shrewd entrepreneurs winning.

Fashion can be an ephemeral thing and in London the deepest gambling moved from White's to another club called Almack's in about 1760. According to the diarist Horace Walpole, 'the gaming at Almack's, which has taken the place of White's, is worthy of the decline of our Empire, or Commonwealth, if you please. The young men of the age lose five, ten, fifteen thousands pounds in an evening there. Lord Stavordale, not one and twenty, lost eleven thousand there last Tuesday but recovered it by one great hand at hazard: he swore a great oath – "Now, if I had been playing really deep, I might have won millions." His cousin, Charles Fox, shines equally there and in the House of Commons.'

The Whig politician, and third son of Lord Holland, Charles James Fox was considered the most brilliant man of his day – at anything other than gambling. He was a founder member of Almack's, although that didn't induce any loyalty on his part. When William Brooks opened his club in 1778, Fox was quick to transfer his custom. 'Brooks,' he said, 'opens his new house and invites all or as many as please to come from the club in Pall Mall. Almack desires us to stay but there can be no reason for preferring a bad old house to a good new one.' Deep gambling moved to Brooks's, where it stayed for the next three decades. Although the club was also political in nature – frequented by the Whiggish acolytes of Fox – gaming was essential to its success. Faro, the new fashionable game, conferred an enormous advantage to whoever held the bank, which for a while Fox and his chums did. Fox, though, was a punter at heart and needed the rush that throwing himself at the feet of chance provided. His temperament demanded that he play at faro and hazard, rather than rake in a cut whilst others lost. By the time he was 25 years old, Fox was £140,000 in debt and had to be baled out by his father. Later his friends clubbed together when Fox was again broke to raise £70,000 to pay further debts and to raise him an annuity for life.

On 6 February 1772 it was reported that Fox performed poorly in the debate in the Commons. It was no surprise: from the evening of the 4th until five in the afternoon of the 5th he had played hazard continually at Almack's, losing £11,000 in the process; after speaking in the Commons debate, he went to dinner and then on to White's, where he drank until seven in the morning; then on to Almack's, again, where he won £6,000 at hazard, and then to Newmarket for the afternoon's racing, where he lost £10,000. On the 13th of the same month, Fox lost £10,000 more. Fox's talents, especially in the first half of his life, were drowned in a whirlpool of gambling. A contemporary recalls that 'he was unquestionably a man of first-rate talents, but so deficient in judgement as never to have succeeded in any object during his whole life. He loved only three things: women, play and politics. Yet at no period did he ever form a creditable connection with a woman, he lost his whole fortune at the gaming table, and with the exception of about eleven months he remained always in opposition.' Fox would not be the first young talent, down the years, to be squandered at the feet of addiction, but it does show how deeply ingrained gambling was amongst the fast set, as Fox was clearly no fool.

The young ladies of the day were not immune to gambling's peculiar charms. Georgiana, the Duchess of Devonshire (1757–1806), was a noted socialite, part of Fox's coterie and equally addicted to gambling. But, since clubs like White's and Brooks's were out of bounds for women, she hosted gambling parties at home. These were both private and commercial: private in the sense that exclusivity was a given and commercial because she transformed her London residence, Devonshire House, into a veritable casino. Professional croupiers were hired for the evening and a commercial faro bank was in operation. The *Morning Post* reported in September 1776 that the 'gaming amongst the females at Chatsworth [her country house] has been carried to such a pitch that the phlegmatic Duke has been provoked to express of it and has spoken to the Duchess in the severest terms against conduct which had driven many from the house who could not afford to partake of amusements carried on at the expense of £500 or £1,000 a night.' Whatever the Duke said had little effect: in 1789 Georgiana went bankrupt and secretly asked the Duke's personal banker to advance her £5,000 to pay her debts. He did. She promptly kept a little for herself, sent some to the lottery office and put the rest on ante-post bets in the Oaks, Oatland Stakes and Derby. 'The risk is so little,' she said, 'and the gain might be so much.'

*   *   *

The ball has landed on 26 black in this Monte Carlo casino and it looks as though only a smallish percentage of the punters will be happy. The losers are unlikely to walk away. Roulette is a game of pure chance and a calculating gambler would be unlikely to play the odds, which routinely favour the house, especially in Las Vegas, where there are two zeros.

Cheating and gambling have always gone hand in hand. Before cards were machine made, card marking was rife. In this instance, the gentleman in the foreground is hoping to make fools of his female companions by hiding the ace of clubs in his cummerbund.

Primero, the game in question in this painting, was all the rage in 16th century Europe. It took up much of Jerome Cardano's time and he gives a full description of it in his 'Book on the Games of Chance'.

Jerome Cardano (1501–76) was a gambler extraordinaire. He was also a doctor, astrologer, author and mathematician, and his early foray into the probabilities of dice throwing gave him lasting fame. Probability theory is the basis upon which all serious gamblers ply their trade.

Genius or charlatan? John Law (1671–1729) reached the height of his powers as comptroller-general of France but, as the late J.K. Galbraith said, 'financial genius is before the fall', and shortly after this painting was made, Law was forced to flee France. A fine line has always existed between speculation and gambling.

The lottery draw was as widely anticipated in 18th century London as it is today. Here, orphans from the Blue Coat School prepare to pull numbers out of the giant wooden wheels at the Guildhall in 1763. A lottery is one of the purest forms of gambling, and the introduction of the modern lottery in 1994 paved the way for a transformation of the gambling industry.

Aristocratic ladies, as well as gentlemen of the highest rank, were attracted to games of chance, especially faro. Lady Archer reputedly made a lot of money by setting up a faro bank, and the Prince Regent, seated next to her in this Gillray cartoon of 1792, was said to have taken a share of the profits.

Count D'Orsay calls a 'main' while playing hazard at Crockford's in 1843, just two years before the club was to shut down. Captain Gronow described the 'gentlemanly bearing and calm and unmoved demeanour' of the aristocratic gamblers of Crockford's club. *How* you won or lost was invariably as important, or even more so, than *whether* you won or lost.

Greedy Old Nickford eats oysters, leaving the poor devils from minor hells (lower-class gaming houses) to starve. This satire on William Crockford shows that he was as unpopular as he was rich.

Above left: A pigeon fancier releases his pigeons in Northallerton, Yorkshire, in 1953. Pigeon racing, over long and short distances, was popular in the north of England and there would always be a few quid resting on the outcome.

Below: Whippet racing was popular in East London. A dock worker tries to give his dog a flying start, no doubt hoping to reap the rewards later. Dog racing, born out of whippet racing and coursing, became the classic working-class sport – 'animated roulette' according to Winston Churchill.

Crockford's spirit lived on in John Aspinall. The Clermont slavishly followed the style of a Georgian gaming house and Aspinall's punters were just as susceptible to following the disastrous gambling tendencies as the aristocracy of the late 18th and early 19th century. Here money changes hands over a game of backgammon, with Charlie Benson, former racing correspondent on the *Daily Express*, making a move. His opponent is Stephen Raphael, a leading player of his day.

I can't imagine that Joan Collins 'did the pools'. For the working man it was a regular weekend treat, its dominance reduced only with the re-introduction of the lottery. The actress hands out cheques worth £60,000 to two lucky winners.

Derek and Elaine Thompson look contented at their Dorset home, and why not? Wouldn't you be with a couple of million salted away after picking six lucky numbers?

Whilst Fox and other young aristocrats threw their money away, the shrewd entrepreneur, following the example of Nash fifty years earlier and the more recent examples of Almack and Brooks's, could prey with great reward upon aristocratic folly and addiction. The nonpareil of the gambling entrepreneurs of this period was born in 1775, three years before Brooks's opened. William Crockford was born the son of a humble fishmonger, just on the wrong side of the city walls at Temple Gate, which separated Fleet Street from the Strand. Crockford's home was in smelling distance of the putrid Fleet ditch, and watching distance of Newgate prison, which became the centre for public executions when Crockford was nine years old, and continued to show public disembowelments until 1814. The contrast with where Crockford exhaled his last breath could not be greater. Number 11 Carlton House Terrace was considered to be the second grandest house on The Mall, after Buckingham Palace, and Crockford's neighbours included the Marquis of Cholmondley at number 12 and the Earl of Lincoln at number 14. Crockford had sent his children to Harrow and Oxford and Cambridge and he left three-quarters of a million pounds in his will. The difference between the world where he was born and the world where he died was entirely down to gambling and the profits made from the feckless aristocrats of the day.

Crockford showed a penchant for gambling from an early age and he frequented the many gambling hells around the Strand and Covent Garden. He was apparently a shrewd card player – good at whist, piquet and cribbage – and he had a good head for figures, due, no doubt, to the many early mornings spent bartering for fish at Billingsgate market. He was known to gamble frequently in St James's: at the Tun Tavern in Jermyn Street and the Grapes in King Street. It was in one of those taverns that the young Crockford challenged a butcher to a marathon game of cribbage over 10,001 holes, for £1 a hole. Crockford emerged £1,700 to the good, an amount that he used to purchase a quarter share in a tavern in King Street, where he was known to put up a bank of £500 a night. Right from the start, the shrewd Crockford realised that real profits were to be made in owning the house, rather than gambling against it.

By 1820, Crockford was wealthy enough to purchase the first of his houses on the west side of St James's Street at number 50. He was soon able to buy the house next door and it was said that his profit from the first year of his St James's establishment cleared £200,000. Two more neighbouring houses were bought, and in 1827 Crockford decided to merge them into the grandest gaming establishment that London had ever seen. No doubt the old cronies of White's, directly opposite, stared disapprovingly through the famous bay window during the building works throughout 1827. Disapproval became more widespread when the neighbouring Guards' Club fell down on account of the scale of Crockford's endeavour – an expensive accident to add to the mounting costs of erecting his dream.

A year later, Crockford's grand design came to fruition and Crockford's – or 'Fishmonger Hall', as it was snootily known – opened in January 1828. It was a stunning success: Ben and Philip Wyatt, the architects, had built the most glorious club in London; Crockford employed the Gordon Ramsay of his day – Louis Eustache Ude – to cook peerless meals that highlighted the drab fare at White's and Brooks's; members from those elite clubs were welcomed by Crockford – provided that they paid the 30 guineas joining fee; and a committee of gentlemen, including the Earls of Chesterfield, Sefton and Lichfield, ensured that the club would have the right sort of social connections. If the fashionable set sneered at Crockford's Fishmonger Hall behind his back, they were soon eager to join the most exclusive gaming club in London.

Crockford's ascendancy lasted a dozen years, during which time it became the place for the young bucks of the day who fancied their chances when playing 'deep'. Hazard, not faro, was now the 'in' game, and the passion. Each night Crockford put up £5,000 and provided three pairs of new ivory dice (at a cost of £2,000 per annum), so that it became known as a fair gaming house. Credit was rarely advanced, although Crockford would often take payment in kind for debts (Lord Seagrave was forced to give Crockford his house in Bruton Street as payment). It became the place to be seen largely on account of the fact that the greatest aristocrat of the day – the Duke of Wellington – was a member, even though he rarely gambled. Exclusivity was a given, although The *English Spy* tells us that 'the members of Brooks's, White's, Boodle's, the Cocoa Tree, Alfred and Travellers' clubs only are admissible; but this restriction is not always enforced, particularly when there is a chance of a good bite.' For Crockford it was always simply about making money, not social advancement.

Who were Crockford's victims? William Molyneux, the second Earl of Sefton, had estimated losses of £250,000 at Crockford's. When he died in 1838 he owed Crockford £40,000, which his heirs paid up immediately. George Stanhope, the 6th Earl of Chesterfield, was also ruined. The best contemporary description of the gaming room, and one that provides a clear flavour of the passion for play, is provided in the memoirs of a contemporary observer of Regency society, Captain Gronow: 'In the play room might be heard the clear ringing voice of that agreeable reprobate Tom Duncombe, as he cheerfully called "seven", and the powerful hand of the vigorous Lord Sefton in throwing for a ten. There might be noted the scientific dribbling of a four by "King" Allen, the tremendous backing of nines and fives by Ball Hughes and Auriol, the enormous stakes played for by Lords Lichfield and Chesterfield, George Payne, Sir St Vincent Cotton, d'Orsay and George Anson and, above all, the gentlemanly bearing and calm and unmoved demeanour, under losses or gains, of all men of that generation.'

Watching on in anticipation was the sly Crockford, described contrastingly by Gronow: 'His cheeks appeared whitened and flabby through constant night work. His hands were entirely without knuckles, soft as raw veal, and as white as paper . . . On settling day, old Crocky sat himself down at the seat of custom and generally had some thousands of Bank of England notes pinned to the table by the dainty flexible fingers we have noted, having the heavy ledgers secured by the thumb, the fifties, twenties and tens under his three longer prongs and a sheaf of fivers under the guardianship of his little finger.' By the time Crockford stepped down from his club, it is said that he netted some £1.2 million and that he retired, according to Gronow, 'much as an Indian chief retires from a hunting country when there is not enough game left for his tribe.'

Crockford retired in 1840 and died four years later. The club didn't last long without him, shutting down in 1845. His passing, and the club's, brought an end to the period of aristocratic excess. There was a new monarch, Victoria, on the throne and a new Gaming Act in 1845, which empowered the police to close down many of London's gaming establishments. A new mood prevailed.

What explains the degree to which, for a century or more, the aristocracy seemed hellbent on dissipating their fortunes? The explosion of gambling in the 17th century can be explained by the developments highlighted in the last two chapters – the rise of numerical awareness through the development of probability theory and the development of a mercantile society whose standardised measure of value was money. Both were clearly key developments if gambling was to flourish. But as well as the increase in gambling, it was the extent of the losses in this period that was particularly noteworthy: they were on a scale little seen before or since.

Historians have suggested that the excessive gambling of this period should be seen in the wider context of a society that was rapidly changing, and an aristocracy whose role and importance within that society was being challenged. The craze for eccentric wagers, for example, using the now universal arbiter and measure of value – money – can be seen as a replacement for the old chivalric codes of honour: the wager replacing the duel as a way of settling disputes.

The traditional ruling classes had little choice but to go along with this new mercantile world. It didn't mean that they had to like it, and in their dissipation of vast fortunes at the gaming tables can be seen their disdain for it. Whereas traditional authority and position in society came by dint of birth right, title or royal patronage, now it could be bought or sold like any other commodity. What was society coming to when the son of a fishmonger owned the second grandest house on The Mall? In response, it has been argued, the aristocracy showed their indifference to money by gambling it away as if it didn't matter at all. Hence the importance of Captain Gronow's description of Crockford's gaming room, where the nobles showed 'gentlemanly bearing and calm and unmoved demeanour' regardless of whether they were winning or losing a fortune.

The historian Gerda Reith has argued that the battleground in this rapidly changing world – new money against aristocratic privilege – was the gaming room where games of chance were played out. Gambling debts were not recoverable at law and therefore paying out huge losses depended upon old-fashioned, aristocratic virtues of dignity and honour. Gambling and losing huge amounts was one way of showing that old-fashioned values were still important. The aristocracy who were fleeced by Crockford were not playing to win at all – and even, possibly, wanted to lose – so that they could show their true selves and the values of their class in the face of enormous losses.

(In that sense, it could be argued that their gambling was entirely rational. Such an explanation rests easily with the interpretation given to the Balinese cockfight by the anthropologist Clifford Geertz. Geertz argued that the Balinese wagered many times their average daily wage on cockfights precisely because it was in such circumstances that manliness, honour, esteem and dignity could most be shown. For the Balinese at a cockfight, 'deep' play was more meaningful than 'shallow' play – where only money could be won and lost.)

The types of card games that were played in this period could be seen as reflecting the battle between old money and new. As noted in the last chapter, the card games of Cardano's day – whist, trumps etc – were largely those where the suit of the card was important. Now, as the 19th century dawned, numbers were placed in the corners so that every card had its own value. Games such as vingt-et-un (blackjack) and chemin de fer (baccarat) became fashionable, games that depended on counting the numerical value of each individual card. Just as the individual challenged the old feudal order, so every card was given some individual value, and the picture cards, the cards of the nobility, were even downgraded so that they all carried the same value.

There are unmistakable echoes of the William Crockford story in that of the most recent entrepreneur to fleece the English aristocracy. John Aspinall was born in Delhi in 1926, like Crockford, into relatively humble beginnings, the son of a lieutenant in the Lincolnshire regiment. Like Crockford he desired financial security from an early age, although, unlike the fishmonger, this was accompanied by a pressing need to feel part of the social set he was to mix with for most of his life. At Oxford, therefore, he took to strolling down the High Street in a pink suit and gold waistcoat, carrying an ebony cane, and he went by the name of Jonas V. Aspinall.

He quickly realised that gambling was his metier, taking his place in a regular poker school at Oxford and missing his finals to attend Royal Ascot. 'From the first time I settled down to play,' he said of his early gambling experiences at Oxford, 'I felt at home as I had never before.' Gambling, and later wild animals, were to be the passion for the rest of his life. He later remarked that people who didn't gamble at all were 'emotional cripples'.

Like Crockford, Aspinall soon realised that it was easier to make money offering odds than taking them. He went into bookmaking, with another addicted gambler from Oxford called Ian Maxwell-Scott, both on-course and as a credit bookmaker off-course under the name of Jonathan and Carlyle.

He began to host private gambling parties, even though they were still strictly illegal under the terms of the 1845 Gaming Act. Fine wine, good food and decorous surroundings were essential if the big-staking players were to be attracted and so, with Maxwell-Scott, he began to organise poker parties at the Ritz. Soon he began to offer chemin de fer parties in various Mayfair homes. Because of the illegality, they moved from house to house – a kind of upper-class version of Nathan Detroit's famous floating craps game in the musical *Guys and Dolls*.

Chemin de fer was a licence to print money, just as hazard was in the early 19th century. The 'cagnotte' (or pot) was the house rake and was fixed for every game at around 20 per cent of the total pot. Although expenses for hosting a game would be high, with free food and drink on offer (once an Old Master painting was hired for the evening), Aspinall knew he was on to a good thing. His first three parties netted him £20,000 and the first year brought him an estimated profit of £350,000.

Late 1950s London was an auspicious time to be holding private gambling parties, despite their illegality. Gaming houses and public casinos were still both illegal, under the 1845 Act, and it was a time of rising property prices and rents in London, so that the aristocracy, who still owned most of the real estate in London, had cash to spare. Aspinall's private gambling parties were screened for exclusivity, much as Crockford's club had been in 1828. Lord Derby, the Duke of Devonshire, the Earl of Cadogan, the Lords Suffolk, Bedford, Effingham and Carnarvon and, most infamously, the 7th Earl of Lucan were all regular players.

It was only in January 1958 when Aspinall rented a house in Hyde Park Street, which fell under the supervision of the Paddington Police Station, that things went wrong. The police arrived in the middle of a game of chemin de fer and Aspinall was charged with 'keeping a common gambling house'. (It is said, apocryphally no doubt, that Lady Osborne countered the police charge with the words 'Young man, there was nothing common in this house until you entered it.') No matter, Aspinall and the Lords Mond and Blakenham were carted off to the nick.

The charges were eventually dismissed (on the basis that one gambling party did not constitute keeping a regular gaming house), which opened the way for a flood of private gambling parties – and competition for Aspinall – until the Betting and Gaming Act of 1960 made casinos legal. As a result, Aspinall decided, like Crockford 134 years before him, to open his own club – the Clermont Club – in 1962. The style of the Clermont was based very much on the Regency style that Crockford created: it was a beautifully restored Georgian townhouse and served exquisite food. The membership list included five dukes, eight viscounts and seventeen earls.

Aspinall continued to offer chemin de fer and aristocrats continued to be fleeced. The 'cagnotte', made illegal by the new Act, was replaced by a table charge for every game. It was still lucrative. One of the biggest losers was Andrew Cavendish, the 11th Duke of Devonshire. A descendant of Georgiana, Devonshire described his time at the Clermont as 'a not uninteresting part of my retarded adolescence'. For a while he was clearly addicted: 'For me,' he said, 'the real attraction of gambling was the terrible excitement of losing. This gave every evening an extraordinary atmosphere of risk. I found it utterly addictive and before long I was unable to resist.' Devonshire, though, had an inbuilt defence mechanism that prevented him from falling over the precipice: 'In fact, I could afford to lose, and though I lost a lot and my losses were often embarrassing, they were never actually disastrous. I remember waking up one morning after another night of heavy losses at the Clermont. I felt like death and said to myself: what you are doing is totally ridiculous and a total waste of a life. There and then, as I lay in bed, I decided I would stop. I have never entered a casino again.'

Luckily for Aspinall, not everyone had Devonshire's self-awareness or strength of mind. The Clermont was sold for £500,000 in 1972 and Aspinall's, which he opened in 1978, sold for £90 million, just before the stock-market crash in 1987.

The ghosts of William Crockford, John Aspinall and the periods of aristocratic excess haunt London still, although the days of the aristocracy dominating 'deep' play have long since passed. At the north end of St James's Street, on the eastern side, Tory grandees still gather in White's for long, liquid lunches. The betting book is still in existence, although modern-day bets tend to be paltry – a tenner here, a fiver there – with honour, rather than the thrill of wagering deep, of paramount importance. The old men of White's, no doubt, still watch sneeringly from the famous bay window as young bloods of no discernible breeding flock into the casino opposite – once called Crockford's, now called Fifty St James's.

The magnificence of Crockford's vision is still to be marvelled at, though: the great Corinthian columns stretch up from the balconies where Wellington and others once looked down upon London society in the second decade of the 19th century. The interior has recently had a facelift and is dripping with gold leaf. The central feature remains the huge, sweeping staircase which forced one noble lord of Wellington's day to take three pauses for breath on the way up. Only the gamblers have changed: Fifty is a members' club, but when I rang to enquire I was told that, provided I could stump up £750 and show a passport or driver's licence, I didn't even need to be proposed. The stakes at the gaming tables cater for the smaller punter, too. Crockford would be dismissive of the £5 low limit for the blackjack tables.

There is no mention of Crockford himself in Fifty. That remains the prerogative of Stanley International, the group that owns the casino in Curzon Street which still carries the old fishmonger's name. In the hallway, there is a portrait of Crockford in a top hat, three-quarter-length coat and riding breeches, looking every inch the English gentleman he was not. There is also the Crockford family tree, replete with the family arms and motto. Crockford might have chuckled at this brazen attempt to erase his humble beginnings. He would certainly have seen the irony in the motto: *Non nobis solum* – 'not for ourselves alone'.

Fifty yards further up Curzon Street – so close to Crockford's that you would wonder at the sense of it all – Aspinall's offers further competition for the discerning gambler. The atmosphere, as at Crockford's, seeks to recreate the opulence of the Georgian salon of the early 19th century. That Aspinall held a special place in his heart for that period is clear from the bust of Charles James Fox which adorns the staircase. Under it, a quote from Aspinall in honour of Fox: 'He lost everything he possessed at the tables – except his friends.' Just above Fox is the bust of another losing aristocrat, Lord Lucan. The bonds of gamblers – or should that be the bonds of exploiter to exploited? – remain stronger than respect for the law: 'What would you do if he walked into the room?' is the question posed under Lucan's bust. 'I would embrace him,' is Aspinall's reply.

Aspinall's half-brother, James Osborne, is the current chief executive of Aspinall's and he gave me an insight into the high rollers who replaced the Aspinall set of the 1960s, once Lucan's disappearance had heralded the end of its fling with chemin de fer. Oil money flowed through in the 1970s, then the Chinese came, and then the Russians. Osborne says that the Chinese and the Arabs are back now, although their presence is most conspicuous during half-term when foreign parents are over to see their offspring. Osborne says that the serious gamblers don't seek out London in order to go gaming specifically, but Aspinall's and its like benefit when they are here on other business.

Time and money are always the prerequisites of the high roller, the latter being the more important. Osborne recalls that Hugh Fraser 'virtually lost Harrods in here'. He was such a sick gambler, apparently, that he had to play more than one roulette table at once, rarely waiting for the ball to land before he was off placing his chips elsewhere. Osborne remembers Kerry Packer, the late Australian billionaire, walking in after having had a near brush with death on his private jet. 'I'm feeling lucky tonight,' said Packer, and he duly walked away with £2 million. Packer reportedly dropped £11 milion at Crockford's during a three-week losing streak in September 1999. Those losses dwarfed the previous biggest loss (£8 million), also at Crockford's, by the Greek millionaire Frank Sarakakis.

Another creative entrepreneur, Philip Green, reportedly won around £3 million at blackjack in another swanky London club, Les Ambassadeurs, at the end of 2004. Chelsea footballers Jimmy Floyd Hasselbaink and Eidur Gudjohnsen reportedly lost £1.4 million between them during a short spell of casino addiction at the start of José Mourinho's spell as manager. 'We started gambling,' said Hasselbaink, 'because we were having trouble with our girlfriends. We didn't want to go home, so we went to the casino.' Even footballers' wives might have been less expensive than their casino trips. Time and money. Time and money.

Within six years of Crockford's passing, the doors of Crockford's casino were open once again, although it had now become a cheap eating house called the Wellington. Captain Gronow complained of the changed circumstances and the new clientele: 'How the mighty are fallen! Irish buccaneers, simple captains, welchers from Newmarket and suspicious-looking foreigners may be seen swaggering, after dinner, through marble halls and up that gorgeous staircase where once the chivalry of England loved to congregate.' I'm not entirely sure that Gronow would approve of those who 'swagger' through Fifty St James's now, or even Crockford's or Aspinall's. We need not be so sniffy, except to say that the chips which adorn their tables today are purchased by new money, not old.

5
LOW LIFE

'The greatest support for organised gambling once came from the bored and ill-educated aristocracy; it comes today from the bored and ill-educated proletariat.'

The Economist, 1947

Paddy Power betting shop, Kilburn High Road

'Rooster Booster runnin' in this race?' Moses, a Jamaican with a raw accent and a down-turned felt soup bowl for a hat, thrusts his neck forward to get a better view and then stares disbelievingly at the screen in front of him. He turns to his two West Indian companions – Thomas, whose black skin and grey-flecked hair give him the look of a photographic negative, and 'Walksy' ('everyone jus' call me Walksy') – and adds, wide-eyed, 'Can you believe it! Rooster Booster in this race! Dicky Johnson's the second best jock' as well! I've got a feelin' about this. I'm gonna to back it!'

Moses withdraws a sheaf of unused betting slips from his hip pocket and scribbles down a £20 win bet on the former champion hurdler at 5-1. Walksy and Thomas make their bets, too, although they are not prepared to follow Moses to the Promised Land and they back another horse. Then, all three stand about six feet from the main screen and stare at it intently, maybe hoping their wishes can be telepathically transmitted to the several hundred pounds of horse and human flesh that are carrying their cash.

Moses was the most animated of the three before the race and, it turns out, during it. Calm at first; then increasingly agitated. 'He's goin' well. He's goin' well! Keep him on the inside, Dicky. Jump now, boy!' Moses stands on his tiptoes as Rooster Booster jumps a hurdle and then he creeps towards the screen, hunched over as if he too were sitting on the back of a horse. He begins to point at the bearer of his hopes. 'He's still on the bit! He's not shaken him up yet, y'know! He's winnin' it! Yes, sir!' Just as Rooster Booster's jockey, Richard Johnson, stands up in the saddle and punches the air twice in celebration, so Moses turns to his mates and does exactly the same thing. 'I had a feelin', you know! 5-1, 5-1! What a price! Fifth in the champion hurdle this year and now runnin' against this lot! I have a good judgement!'

Thomas and Walksy seem genuinely pleased, even though they won't be following Moses to the counter to collect. Except that Walksy does go up to the counter. On his way back he whispers to me: 'That's why I bet with Paddy Power, y'know. They had a special on that race. Any horse that finishes second to Rooster Booster, and it's your money back. With the others that's my money up in smoke!' And he strolls back to Moses and Thomas with the swagger of a man who has just hit the old enemy for one almighty lash.

William Hill betting shop, Portobello Road

'Go, Saucy, go, Saucy!' Alfred, a tall Trinidadian wearing a bomber jacket and flashy watch, holds out both his clenched hands horizontally in front of his face. He draws them back and forth, in almost a pumping action, at first gently and then frenetically, as if the horse's reins were entwined around his fingers; as if he himself were sitting on the horse. 'Where are you? Where are you? Get cover! Get cover! You bet, yeah! Eat him up! Eat him up! Go, Saucy! Go, Sauceeeeeee!' He turns to take the acclaim and revel in the collective delight of the dozen or so West Indians who are gathered around the big screen. There is much back-slapping and I-told-you-so-ing. A win for one, it seems, is a win for them all.

For the moment, the luck is with Alfred; he is the man and he has the stage. The punters ask him for his pick for the next race, the 6.15 at Newmarket. The veneer of knowledge is suddenly washed away as he chooses a horse called Evasion, basing his choice simply on the fact that he likes the number three.

Later, Alfred is crouched in a similar position in front of the big screen, hands clenched again, squeezing home a horse called Levantine. 'That's it, Levantine! You have him beat. Pull your whip now! Pull your whip now! Look at the jock'! He won't give it a single tap. Hit him! Whitworth, you're a shit-stick!' A winning bet is the vindication of a punter's judgement; when a horse loses, it's the jockey's fault.

Both betting shops, Paddy Power on the Kilburn High Road and William Hill on the Portobello Road, are in inner-city, working-class areas. By all visual signs, Kilburn is run-down, still too far north to have undergone the kind of gentrification that has affected the likes of Notting Hill and Queen's Park. From the tube station, a plethora of high-rise tenements are immediately visible, as are 'No Litter – £200 fine' signs. The place is awash with litter. The Paddy Power shop is towards the northern end of the Kilburn High Road. To get there, as I walked from Kilburn tube station, I passed five bookmakers, three pawnbrokers and a Mecca bingo hall – a sure sign that gambling has infiltrated deep into this working-class community.

At the northern end of Portobello Road, just past the junction with Westbourne Park Road, there is a William Hill betting office next to the ubiquitous Starbucks. Here, too, there is a similarly down-at-heel feeling – even though this area is much changed from the kind of slum it was four decades ago when Shelter began its housing charity for the homeless. The Portobello Market is home to a remarkable variety of traders – there are three halal butchers within fifty yards of the bookies – and on any given day, all of life is there to see.

I reckoned a high-street bookmaker in an inner-city area the best place to go to see working-class gambling in action. The clients of such places are generally those for whom gambling on credit via a telephone account or via the internet is not possible. Indeed, the regulars at Paddy Power had conformed to type. Mostly, they were manual workers. Moses worked on the railways; Walksy was a part-time waiter in a casino; Thomas didn't currently seem to be doing much at all, and behind the West Indian trio had stood a couple of Irish boys, Mickey and Freddy, both painter-decorators. In William Hill, the clientele was much the same: West Indian casual workers.

In Hill's, surrounded by West Indians, I found it impossible to escape my former life. The realisation that a former international cricketer was in their midst heightened the excitement for a short while. Suddenly, one punter started to shuffle forward and then back as if he was batting – first coming down the pitch, then feigning and rocking back to cut the ball past backward point. As he mimed hitting the ball, he squeezed his thumb and second finger together and clicked his forefinger against them, making a whiplash sound. He did this half a dozen times, before the realisation that it was having little effect sent him back to his stool.

For most of these working-class punters, time spent in betting shops is part of their daily routine. They gamble openly, unashamedly and legally, in shops that are allowed to advertise and entice people to walk through their doors.

* * *

Anybody who has read Alan Sillitoe's classic working-class novel *Saturday Night and Sunday Morning*, or seen the film of the same name, will know that the working man was not always at such liberty to bet. The hero of the novel is Arthur Seaton. His is the bleak world of industrial inner-city Nottingham and his hobbies are mainly boozing, womanising and betting. Audiences thrilled to the gritty realism of the setting and the outspoken vitality of its hero. The young actor who played Seaton had no need to research the role: Albert Finney was a working-class boy from Salford and the son of an illegal street bookmaker. When Seaton (or a young Finney, for that matter) wanted to have a bet, he had to do so surreptitiously. He had to conduct business with a bookie's runner at work, or at the pub, or in the back yard of a house, writing out his betting slips under a false name to protect his identity.

This was because the film was released in 1960, the year before licensed bookmakers re-opened after just over a century of censure. The timing of the film's release in the context of the history of gambling is fascinating, coming as it did on the cusp of the legitimisation of off-course cash (as opposed to credit) betting. Between the 1853 Betting Houses Act and May 1961, off-course cash betting (the only form of betting available to the working man) was illegal. The story of gambling legislation from the mid 19th century, when Victorian attitudes started to bite, until the liberalisation of the second half of the 20th century, is one of gross class discrimination.

Until the Victorian age, legislation designed to restrict gambling was passed out of practical rather than moral considerations. Gambling, per se, was not frowned upon, only its effects. In 1388 the first statute against unlawful games was passed, but only as an attempt to prevent interference with the practice of archery. In 1541 certain games were again outlawed for 'the maintaining of artillery'. A nation that was continually at war could scarcely afford to have its subjects neglecting practical pursuits in favour of idle gambling.

The first statute to be passed specifically against gambling, as opposed to the playing of games generally, was the Gaming Act of 1664. It is not surprising that the explosion of gambling at the end of the 17th century should have resulted in a wave of legislation, but again the objections were not so much against gambling itself, as against the excessive gaming of the upper classes. So, the Gaming Act of 1710 enabled anybody who lost more than £10 to sue the winner 'for the further preventing of all excessive and deceitful gaming'. The Gaming Act of 1738 specifically outlawed the games of faro, basset, hazard and ace of hearts (except where the Groom Porter had given his consent), with a severe penalty of £50 for those who broke the law. The following year various other games of dice were banned because, said the statute, of 'the ruin and impoverishment of many of his majesty's subjects'.

The idea that gambling was morally wrong began to formulate with the death of William IV and the advent to the throne, in June 1837, of an austere young woman called Victoria. That same year William Thackeray noted that 'play is a deposed goddess, her worshippers bankrupt and her table in rags.' The age of Regency excess was at an end. Two new threads of thought gradually emerged: that gambling was inherently bad for the soul and injurious to the state, and, whilst the rich could take care of themselves, it was the poor who had to be protected from its evils.

In the Gaming Act of 1845 the Victorian state washed its hands of gambling by making gambling debts irredeemable at law. The unintended result was to encourage cash rather than credit betting. This led to an explosion of betting houses, where bookmakers posted betting lists in premises to which men flocked to back their judgement with ready cash. The number of betting houses in London was estimated at around 100 to 150 by 1847. More legislation followed and in 1853 these betting houses were given the same status as common gaming houses for the purposes of the law, and they were outlawed. The consequence of this was that betting houses gradually disappeared and gambling moved onto the street. Where working-class gambling went, the law followed. In the Metropolitan Street Act of 1867 penalties were imposed on any group of three or more citizens assembled together for the purposes of betting. This was amended in 1873 whereby such persons were deemed to be vagabonds and vagrants and prosecuted as such. Finally street betting was outlawed altogether in one of the most discriminatory bills ever passed: the Street Betting Act of 1906.

Moralists frowned at the 'unholy trinity' of drinking, sex and gambling, which affronted the principles upon which the Victorian state should be based: thrift, hard work and self-denial. There were practical reasons for this, namely that gambling, in their eyes, threatened productivity at work and therefore Britain's economic hegemony. The late 19th century was a time of declining economic output for Britain, and economic, and therefore social, uncertainty. The 1902 Select Committee on gambling took evidence from a major employer who said that betting 'not only deteriorates a man morally but undermines his industry and makes him sooner or later listless and careless in his work.' The committee was warned that 'if the betting craze goes unchecked the sober youth of Germany will take the reins of the commercial world.'

There were also theoretical objections: that gambling appealed to chance and not, therefore, to man's rational being, and as it entailed the illegitimate transfer of money from one person to another it had the potential to undermine the very nature of the capitalist state. The outlets for these views came in the form of the Church, the National Anti-Gambling League (NAGL) and, surprisingly, given the inclination to gamble among its natural constituency, the leadership of the Labour Party.

The 1923 Select Committee which debated whether to impose a tax on betting (and therefore legitimise it) took evidence from the National Free Church Council. The Council argued that, since it destroyed any sense of value, any obligation to steady industry and any sense of thrift, betting was economically unsound. A tax on betting, it argued, would mean that the State sanctioned an activity that was dangerous to the economic interests of the nation.

The NAGL was formed out of a coalition of Nonconformist Protestant churches in 1890. Although its intention was to root out gambling, it found that there was little enthusiasm in political circles to attack a gentleman's leisure activities. Instead, they concentrated their attack on working-class gambling. By the 1940s the organisation was a dead letter, but its influence at the turn of the century was considerable: the 1902 Select Committee took advice from the secretary of the NAGL, John Hawke, advice which helped form the recommendation that street gambling be banned.

J. Ramsay MacDonald, later leader of the Labour Party, was a leading light of the NAGL. In 1905 he wrote an article entitled 'Gambling and Citizenship', in a collection of essays called *Betting and Gambling: A National Evil*, in which he laid out his objections to the working man having a flutter: 'To hope that a Labour Party can be built up in a population quivering from an indulgence in games of hazard is pure folly. Such a population cannot be organised for sustained political effort . . . cannot respond to appeals to its rational imagination. Its hazards absorb so much of its leisure; they lead it away from thoughts of social right-eousness; they destroy in it the sense of social service; they create in it a state of mind which believes in fate, luck, the irrational, the erratic; they dazzle its eyes with flashy hopes . . . Every Labour leader I know recognises the gambling spirit as a menace to any form of Labour Party.' Ramsay MacDonald wasn't the only

Labour Party grandee to pour cold water on the idea of a 'harmless flutter': when Premium Bonds were introduced by Harold Macmillan in the 1956 budget, the shadow chancellor, Harold Wilson, derided them as nothing more than a 'squalid raffle'.

Gambling was under attack. More specifically, working-class gambling was under attack. Admiral Rous, who was a key influence on Lord Palmerston's Select Committee of 1844, summed up the paternal attitude of the ruling classes: 'What should I care what a rich man does with his own,' he said, 'the poor should be protected . . . but I would let a rich man ruin himself if he so pleases.' Nine years later, Alexander Cockburn, the Attorney General, articulated perfectly the class-based nature of the 1853 Betting Houses Act. He spoke of the problems of the legislation which were 'to be found in the disinclination which was felt against interfering with the description of betting which had so long existed at Tattersall's and elsewhere in connection with the great national sport of horse racing . . . the object of this bill was to suppress these [betting] houses without interfering with that legitimate species of betting.' He could not have been more explicit: Tattersall's and other private members' clubs like the Beaufort and Victoria clubs (price of membership about 16 guineas per annum, credit betting encouraged, bookmakers discouraged) were to be left alone, whilst cash betting in ordinary betting houses was to be outlawed. Cockburn had no doubt that 'the mischief arising from these betting shops was perfectly notorious. Servants, apprentices and working men, induced by the temptation of receiving a large sum for a small one, took their few shillings to these places and the first effect of their losing was to tempt them to go on spending.' The second effect, he added, was the frequent occurrence of 'robbing their masters and employers'.

The 1901–02 Select Committee on gambling, which eventually recommended the Street Betting Act of 1906, made its concerns very clear in its opening remarks: 'The practice of betting has increased considerably of late years, especially amongst the working classes, whilst, on the other hand, the habit of making large bets, which used at one time to be the fashion amongst owners and breeders of horses, has greatly diminished.' Whilst the Committee did not think gambling 'a crime in itself', it deplored 'the spread of a practice which, when carried to excess, is opposed to the true interests of sport and injurious to the general community.'

The Street Betting Act of 1906 did have its political dissenters. Men such as Lord Durham highlighted the discriminatory nature of the bill. He felt that it would transform 'what is only a human instinct into a crime', and that it would 'seriously interfere with the amusement of the working classes and intensify the monotony of their lives'. Lord Faversham complained that 'it would enact one law for the rich and one law for the poor'. Horatio Bottomley, the Liberal MP, no doubt spoke for the great unheard majority when he criticised 'the prevailing wave of puritanical and namby-pamby, goody-goody legislation'. It made no difference. The 1906 Act outlawed betting on streets and other public places. Anybody who loitered for the purpose of making or taking a bet could be fined £10 for a first offence, £20 for a second and £50, or six months in prison, for a third offence. For the next fifty-five years, a man could only bet legally if he went to the racetrack itself, or if he was wealthy enough to bet on credit.

In the seven decades that followed Victoria's accession to the throne, attitudes to working-class gambling varied between the paternal and the moralistic; between a belief that the poor had little or no judgement in choosing their leisure options sensibly, and a belief that gambling was an out-and-out sin.

Despite the prevailing attitudes, the desire amongst the working classes to gamble was too powerful, and the legislation designed to prevent them from doing so was simply ignored. It should come as no surprise that the working classes continued to gamble in the face of this moral and legal backlash. The poor have always gambled, because it offers one of the few possibilities for a better life and social mobility. Gambling also fits neatly with working-class attitudes to life: small and irregular incomes militate against middle-class, bourgeois attitudes to insurance and saving. The working classes have always had a short-term, fatalistic view of life. Why save for an uncertain tomorrow when you could have some fun and maybe win a few bob today?

Between the 1853 Betting Houses Act and 1960 Betting and Gaming Act, cash gambling on commercial sports such as horse racing was illegal but still widely practised through the conduit of street book-makers. In Manchester in 1932 alone there were 1,034 arrests made of street bookies, which illustrates how far gambling had become woven into the fabric of working-class existence. Bookies' runners were employed around the workplace and the pub, punters used false names on their betting slips to protect their identity, and bookies were allowed by locals to do business out of their back yards. It was all illegal, but an accepted part of working-class culture.

There was also a swathe of less organised gambling, on coins and dice and cards, and on less commercial sports such as, especially in northern England, crown green bowls and pigeon racing. Street-corner gambling schools, in which coin games such as pitch and toss, heads and tails and nudges were popular, were widespread until the 1950s. My father can remember a police raid on one such school in the inner-city Manchester of his youth. These schools were illegal and would all have a lookout – a 'crow' – to warn of a police raid. Usually, the crow would be someone who had lost his money. He would be paid a little from the communal pot until he was able to rejoin the game, to be replaced by the next impover-ished gamester.

Betting on bowls, pigeon racing and on cards and coins in the streets was illegal but widely practised. The two greatest outlets for working-class gambling during the inter-war years and beyond, as incomes and leisure time increased, were dog racing and the pools, and they were entirely legal.

Greyhound racing became the classic urban, working-class sport. It developed out of the animal instinct to chase a hare and the human instinct to gamble. The countrified and gentrified sport of coursing had been established as long ago as 1776, although it was the Earl of Sefton who established its most famous meet, the Waterloo Cup, sixty years later. During the early years of the 20th century, racing with dogs, but without live bait, had become a popular pastime within the inner cities. Men kept dogs in their back yards, feeding them on high-protein diets of raw eggs and pigs' trotters, and then racing them at weekends with the aim of making a few quid to supplement their incomes. It was a popular sport amongst the mining community. The colliers of the Bradford pit, my grandfather's pit in inner-city Manchester, were especially keen. Races would take place at weekends, when the whippets would race towards a man flapping a rag (hence the term 'flapping' applied to small, unlicensed tracks), and the betting would be intense. It was hard to be confident that the result wasn't fixed, though. Dogs could easily be fed a pork pie or two to ensure the required result.

And so, from a fusion of the gentrified sport of coursing, the working man's enthusiasm for racing whippets, and the need for greater regulation and organisation to prevent fraud, the sport of greyhound racing was born. The first meeting was at Belle Vue in 1926. More than 1,700 folk turned up to gamble on dogs owned by such aristocratic patrons as Lord Stanley, Lady Cholmondeley and the Duchess of Sutherland. Two years later, attendances nation-wide had reached 5.5 million. By 1945 the sport was at the height of its popularity, with over 50 million people 'going to the dogs'. It was the perfect vehicle for working-class gambling: unlike horse racing, it was an urbanised sport; the ten or so thirty-second races kept pulses rattling; and the tight bends of the oval tracks ensured that greyhound racing was an unpredictable spectacle. 'Animated roulette,' Winston Churchill called it.

Along with greyhound racing, the growth of the football pools in the inter-war years was central to the rise of mass, commercialised betting. Lancashire was the heartland of the pools, largely because of the strength of the sporting and gambling press, which set the ball rolling by offering weekly coupons for their readers to guess the results of matches. John Moores, a Liverpool entrepreneur, was quick to identify its potential. He set up Littlewoods in 1922 with two partners, £150 capital and a small office in Liverpool. By the end of the first year he had haemorrhaged £600 and one partner, but two years later boasted receipts of £2,000. The large prizes offered by his pool-based system gave him a huge advantage over the fixed-odds bookmaker, and the business soon took off. By the mid 1930s over 10 million people enjoyed a weekly go on the pools.

Although the pools were played by a cross section of the population – Nigel Lawson, the Chancellor of the Exchequer under Margaret Thatcher, was a regular player – its growth and success can only be explained through an understanding of the working-class culture of the time. Above all, there was the potential to win big by not spending too much. It was also seen as a home-based, communal activity which encouraged the family to gather round and discuss the choices based upon a knowledge of the football scene. In this respect it was not just a harmless flutter, but socially beneficial as well.

Thus the working-class desire to gamble was strong enough to stand against both the prevailing sentiment of the time and legislation that was clearly discriminatory. The police were unhappy about enforcing laws which were unpopular and which put them in direct conflict with citizens who were otherwise law-abiding. Ironically, the Street Betting Act of 1906 was the high point of anti-gambling legislation not because it succeeded but because it was such a dismal failure. It proved to be unenforceable. The pressure to legalise was eventually too great, and the 1960 Betting and Gaming Act reversed a century of discrimination when off-course cash betting was legalised. The following May, licensed betting shops opened for the first time. Within one year, 13,340 licences had been granted.

In terms of home comforts, the Paddy Power punters on Kilburn High Road have a better deal than William Hill's clients on Portobello Road. The Kilburn shop has only been open eighteen months. It is brightly lit, well decorated and filled with comfy chairs. An air-conditioning system removes the smoke, and the staff dole out coffee, tea and biscuits liberally to their clients. It's almost a pleasure to lose your money in these surroundings.

Such a betting shop would have been inconceivable in May 1961. For, whilst the government of the day salved its conscience by allowing the working man to bet, it did not want to encourage him, or others, to gamble. So betting shops had to be strictly functional: no carpets, no drinks to be served, no television to watch the races and windows that had to be blacked out and void of advertising. It was only through another Act of Parliament, a quarter of a century later, that punters were allowed to bet in more comfortable surroundings – chairs, lavatories, soft drinks and refreshments, live and recorded sport on television became acceptable. The William Hill shop on Portobello Road doesn't look as though it has changed much since Douglas Hurd's welcome legislation in 1986, and is currently awaiting a makeover.

Everything in the two shops is designed to encourage the punter to bet. Pages of form are pasted along the walls. There is one big television screen, surrounded by a dozen other screens showing everything from football odds to snooker and general election odds and sporting action from all over the world. (Paddy Power is particularly keen on colourful bets and advertising and PR that will help them challenge the dominance of Ladbrokes, William Hill and Coral. One of Paddy Power's early advertising campaigns showed a young couple sitting on a park bench, and the caption offered 2-1 about the boy getting his hand up the girl's sweater and 5-1 up her skirt. Another typical Paddy Power stunt was setting up a betting stall in St Peter's Square and offering odds about the next Pope before John Paul II had breathed his last.) In the shop on Kilburn Road, there is a St George's Day special on football – a no-lose bet should any English player be sent off in a game on which you have gambled – as well as a 'treble the odds on lucky 15s' special, a 'guaranteed early price race' special and 'the Punchestown Paddy Power difference – money-back specials every day'.

Both shops also have a number of Fixed Odds Betting Terminals (FOBTs) in the middle of the room, on which the punter can play a variety of virtual pure-chance games such as roulette, bingo or even spoof.

The enticement to bet has been on the increase ever since May 1987, when SIS (Satellite Information Services) first beamed live satellite coverage of non-televised race meetings into a handful of betting shops. Two years later, the service was available nation-wide. Now it is complemented by a virtual racing service – that is, computer-generated horse and dog racing – so that there is on-screen action throughout the whole day, from around 11 o'clock in the morning until 9.30 at night. Virtual racing – 'Sprint Valley' and 'Steepledowns' for horses, 'Millersfield' and 'Brushwood' for dogs

– opens bookmakers up to the charge of cynical exploitation. One morning in the Paddy Power shop, I counted fourteen races from Steepledowns, and fourteen from Brushwood, all neatly scheduled around the live dog or horse racing of the day. The advent of virtual racing, as a 'filler' between live racing, means that there is an opportunity to bet every three minutes or so throughout the day. This was the schedule one morning for one half-hour between 12 noon and 12.30 p.m.:

> 12.02 Walthamstow – dogs
> 12.04 Millersfield – virtual dogs
> 12.09 Wimbledon – dogs
> 12.11 Millersfield
> 12.16 Walthamstow
> 12.18 Steepledowns – virtual horses
> 12.25 Fairview – horse racing from South Africa
> 12.29 Walthamstow

During a lunchtime break from racing, it is time for the lotto – a game called 49s, which carries the slogan 'Are your balls hot or cold today?' And so the opportunity to gamble presents itself, hour after hour, day after day.

There is even an attempt to make the virtual racing as real as possible: artificial sounds of horses and dogs can be heard during the race; a computer-generated image of a knee-length-booted, short-skirted, big-breasted young girl lowers the flag for the hare, and there are advertising hoardings on all the racetracks – advertising gambling sites, of course, like the Irish lotto, or a website called www.Win-On-Numbers.com. Even some of the names of the virtual dogs and horses are enticements to gamble: one morning, a horse called 'Winnalotto' ran in the first 'race' from Steepledowns.

Virtual racing elicits a variety of responses from punters. Bernie, a goggle-eyed punter who frequents the Paddy Power shop in the mornings, was clear in his views. 'It's an insult to punters everywhere. It's just another way to fleece us – if there's a spare minute on the screen they've got to find something to fill the gap. They've got racing from America, Germany and South Africa – anything to tempt us. If the evenin' racing finishes at 8.30, they'll put on an hour of American racing just to fill up the hour till closing time. All it does is creates bad blood between the staff, 'cos it keeps them here till all hours.'

Bernie did not play the game, but knew people who did. 'I know a guy from Brondesbury, a smart guy, who can work out the most complicated things, and he puts hundreds of pounds on virtual racing. He has a theory that there's always a 9-1 winner during the day. If he comes in and there's not been a 9-1 winner that day, he'll back the 9-1 shots blind. They go for it, these suckers!' Bernie shook his head and chuckled at the sheer lunacy of it all.

In Notting Hill, the West Indian punters generally seemed to be more in favour. Deon, a painter: 'Yeah, we have a go.'

'Why? It's just pure chance.'

'So are the horses.'

'But there's no form to go on.'

'Well, odds-on shots get turned over all the time in real racing. It's still a lottery.'

'How do you choose your "horse"?'

'Just a lucky number or a name we like.'

Deon's mate, a jet-black, gap-toothed West Indian, joins in the conversation.

'The horses have form,' he says, and everyone nods.

'The races have stadiums,' he says, and everyone nods.

'They even have jockeys who are ferried to the races in helicopters.'

As I'm taking my notes, there's a silence. I look up and the whole crowd explode with laughter, pointing at me. For a moment, I'm the sucker. Deep down they all know the whole virtual-racing thing is nonsense, but they are happy to play along.

One William Hill punter bet on every single opportunity throughout the hour that I watched him. His bets were small, in the £1 to £2 range, but he stayed throughout the morning that I was there. He didn't communicate with anyone; he didn't seem to study the form for the live dog racing that he was betting on; he muttered obscenities under his breath throughout each race ('Fuck off, six!'); and at the end of each race he would screw up his losing bet and flick it down at his feet. I asked him why he bet, since it seemed so joyless. All he could reply was that, 'They're all crooks anyway, so it doesn't make any difference.' When he walked out of the shop just after lunchtime, there was a small pile of screwed-up betting slips, as a monument to his defeat. Sonny, a Nigerian punter, shook his head as the loser left.

'What about you, Sonny, do you win?'

'If I won, I'd be in the Caribbean right now.'

Apart from class, losing is the one thing that unites betting-shop punters. Bernie professed last year to be his first winning one for twenty or more years of solid punting, 'and that was only because I got lucky on golf.' Walksy's first bet, which is typical of many hardened punters, was a winning 33-1 shot in 1965 with a book-maker called Baines, but he has long since lost that magic touch. Professional punters say that winning on horses is hard, that it takes self-discipline and knowledge – precisely the qualities that betting shops discourage. With a race every three minutes, there is no time to study the form, and as for self-discipline: if you're not in the shop to bet, what are you there for?

Both shop managers are sure that the majority of their customers are losers. John, in William Hill, simply raised his eyes and looked at me as if I was mad when I asked him the question. After a prolonged silence he realised that I was waiting for an answer. 'That's the game, isn't it?' he said. Graham, in Paddy Power, estimates that he takes around a 10 to 12 per cent profit on a weekly turnover of around £40,000. He says that only 3 per cent of his turnover is accounted for by virtual racing accounts, and between 3 and 5 per cent by his four FOBTs, which as far as I could see were mainly played by Eastern European men, and Asian women. In Notting Hill the picture is skewed by one big punter who accounts for much (about a quarter) of the shop's business. The shop was in its seventeenth week of business that year, and had already turned over £3.5 million. Because the big player was having a bad time, profits were good at around 17 per cent. There the machines accounted for a slightly higher percentage – 8 per cent of turnover.

Fixed Odds Betting Terminals have changed the face of high-street bookmaking. They have enabled the bookie to bypass laws that for years prevented them from hosting casino-style games. Because the wheel in virtual roulette is spun by a machine, it does not count, technically, as a casino game. The government has yet to challenge this legal interpretation, instead doing a deal with book-makers, which limits them to four FOBTs per shop, with online help pages for customers. The customers need all the help they can get: the roulette game pays out at 97.3 per cent, allowing the punter the thrill of the occasional win, but ensuring that the house is always the ultimate winner.

Ignoring the big Notting Hill punter, the profile of both shops is similar. In the mornings, when the shops are at their quietest, a high proportion of the punters are pensioners. They put on small, multiple bets (doubles, trebles, lucky 15s), hoping for the unlikely big payout from a small layout, and at the same time the routine of putting on their morning bets gives some structure to their day. The afternoons are the busiest and loudest times, when the punters tend to bet slightly bigger amounts – typically £10 to £20, but both shops have their punters who bet in hundreds – on single horse-racing bets. The evenings quieten off again, a time, says John, for the 'real diehards'.

It might be imagined that the sole purpose of frequenting and punting in a betting shop is to win money, but if it is, there are only a tiny percentage who achieve their aim. Comments such as 'I'll tell you what, I'm going to give you my last quid', as one punter went up to the betting counter, or 'We're all in the deep end, drowning in here!' suggested that most had a defeatist attitude, that they knew they were losers and that they would keep on losing.

What, then, explains their continued presence? In the past, sociologists have argued that punting was a positive feature of working-class existence, because the form study that went with making a choice on the horses was mental stimulation in a life otherwise devoid of it – that betting was a kind of working-class intellectual pursuit, if you like. It was said that many a northern working-class housewife in the inter-war years became literate reading the *One O'Clock* – the afternoon paper that gave the day's racing form. Making a positive selection on the horses was at least a choice of sorts in a life otherwise lacking choice and responsibility.

It that was the case, then it is no longer. In the betting shops I visited, I saw absolutely no evidence of any serious form study. The races come so quickly, one after the other, that the timetable allows no study of any kind. Making bets becomes simply a matter of routine. In fairness, the horse-racing punters in the afternoons did seem to have some residual knowledge, in a way that those who punted on the dogs didn't. A horse race might take, from parade to finish, a good ten minutes – long enough for punters to develop some kind of relationship with certain horses, jockeys and race-tracks. Even so, most bets were made on instinct, gut feeling, lucky numbers, interesting names, or a tip that had been passed around. Intellectual pursuit it was not.

Does addiction explain the presence of the betting shop's regular punters? Those same studies also suggested that working-class punting, although regular, tended to be considered and controlled; that there was no evidence of gambling-induced poverty and no link between gambling and poverty, except that it was poverty which encouraged people to gamble in the first place in the hope of changing their circumstances. Mostly, they found that working-class gambling was controlled by economic restrictions – poverty – and, as a result, addiction and ruination was a small problem.

I did encounter addiction. Mickey and Freddy, the two Irish painter-decorators who stood silently as Moses called Rooster Booster home, were both self-confessed addicts. Alcoholics, too. Freddy is a little overweight now, although 'people still tell me I look a bit like Darren Gough', and has a smiling, open face. Mickey was a jockey in Ireland, and the way his nose is squashed and bent suggests he might have done a bit of fighting in his time as well. Freddy used to take home between £400 and £450 a week, of which he might have punted away £250, 'depending on whether I came to the betting shop before I went home.' Mickey, sipping on a bottle of water, says he has given up drinking, although he still bets.

One afternoon, I was talking to Mickey when a friend of mine, who owns a horse called Chef Tartare, rang. It happened to be running that afternoon at Perth and he thought it worth an investment. I quickly checked out its form; I learnt that it had been turned over a few times at short odds, but that it was also trained by Paul Nicholls, the excellent West Country trainer who, by the closing stages of the season, was vying with Martin Pipe for the trainers' championship. There were only a couple of days to go and clearly any Pipe or Nicholls horses would be trying, especially if they had done a 400-mile round trip to the track. At odds of 9-2 it seemed worth the risk of accepting a tip from a mate – which is usually the quickest and surest way to the poorhouse.

I wondered whether I ought to tell Mickey and Freddy. There is nothing worse than a losing tip – except perhaps a winning tip that you have kept to yourself. Moreover, there was a moral issue at stake here: Freddy was a reformed addict; Mickey was doing his best to stay 'clean'. Probably, neither could afford to fritter money away on a hopeless tip. I decided to tell them – but added hastily, for the sake of my own conscience, that if they were going to bet they must 'tread lightly'. Freddy politely declined. Mickey joined me in a small win bet. We watched the race together. Being naturally pessimistic, I didn't like the way the Chef was jumping. Mickey liked the position the jockey had taken on the rails. 'He's goin' the shortest way round,' he said, gripping my arm tightly. Neither of us could summon up the kind of *joie de vivre* that the West Indians exhibited when their money was down – too much Southern Irish and Mancunian reserve for that. Mickey did let out one 'Go on, the Chef!' as it jumped the last fifteen lengths clear. The triumph brought a firm handshake and a bundle of notes.

Freddy has given up betting now, largely thanks to his own efforts in going to Gamblers Anonymous. 'Gamblers Anonymous,' he says, 'is very similar to Alcoholics Anonymous. It's the same twelve steps. There's lots of crossover.' Freddy also highlighted the similarities he encountered between alcoholics and gamblers: the desire, to drink or to gamble; the buzz and excitement during the process; and then the let-down afterwards. Freddy was a serial loser. 'It began to make me depressed, so I stopped.'

William Hill must also be aware that addiction is a potential problem because in every branch there is a leaflet advertising GamCare – the gambling addiction helpline. The blurb on the leaflet states: 'Gambling is an exciting pursuit which, when taking place in the social environment of a licensed betting office, is harmless fun.

For the great majority of people who use betting offices, gambling is an enjoyable leisure pursuit. For a very small number, there can be problems and gambling can cease to be fun. Gambling can be a problem for people who: continue to bet until their money has gone; borrow money to continue betting; because of gambling neglect the welfare of themselves and their family. As part of William Hill's social responsibility policy, our staff are trained to offer help and advice on request. This includes a self-exclusion agreement where, if you wish, you can arrange to have your custom refused by our staff for a period of no less than six months.' It's rather like having a 'No Firearms' poster in the middle of a war zone. John, the manager of the Portobello Road shop, says, unsurprisingly, that he has never had a punter plead for his custom to be refused.

GamCare is especially worried about the corrosive effects of the FOBTs. More than one in five first-time callers to GamCare in 2004 cited FOBTs as their problem. Overall some 28 per cent of GamCare's clients cited FOBTs as their main problem – making them the second biggest cause, according to GamCare, of gambling addiction after punting on horses.

Adrian Scarfe, the clinical director of GamCare, told me this: 'FOBTs are a huge problem at the moment. They have a double-whammy effect: their addictive nature, fuelled by the fact that people using them are already predisposed to gamble. We have lots of anecdotal evidence that suggests people who were losing small amounts in betting shops, or at least keeping their gambling under control, are now struggling to do so. It is changing the nature of betting shops and of gambling: for the first time casino-type games are now available on the high street and we think that is very bad news. One of my counsellors sees six clients on a Wednesday – all are there because of FOBTs.'

Not surprisingly, since the FOBTs are worth £520 million to the bookmakers' industry, they, the bookmakers, challenge Scarfe's concerns. In 2004 the Association of British Bookmakers produced a report which indicated no link between FOBTs and addiction, which is a bit like the smoking industry producing a report on the properties of nicotine. Ironically, the Association of British Bookmakers explained the increase in calls to GamCare as the result of the bookmakers themselves promoting GamCare's helpline in their shops. Addictive or not, FOBTs are hugely profitable for the industry. In 2005, the average net profit per terminal per week for the William Hill group was £400 and they expect to have 7,500 in operation soon. The government says that FOBTs are still 'on probation'.[6]

Despite the fact that Freddy has given up betting, he is still a regular in the Paddy Power shop on Kilburn High Road. This, I think, gives the best clue as to why so many punters continue to spend a large proportion of their day in betting shops even though they lose regularly. Freddy goes in because his mates go in, and because 'They look after us in here. There's a nice atmosphere, the staff are great and they even give us coffee, tea and biscuits.' Watching the West Indians enjoying themselves in Notting Hill, it is hard not to come to the same conclusion. One afternoon, a Rastafarian walked in. He paused at the door, and with great ceremony he bowed to all corners of the room and then approached, high-fiving the assembled throng. This is a regular crew. All are known or become known to each other (even though their socialising seems to stop at the exit from the betting shop door), and the atmosphere is similar to that which you might find in any local pub. In both shops, I encountered clients who simply used the shop as a resting place. In Paddy

[6] In his 2006 Budget, the Chancellor of the Exchequer, Gordon Brown, hit FOBTs with an annual levy of £1,965 on top of VAT.

Power, one Indian gentleman slept off his hangover all morning; in William Hill, a West Indian slept one evening right in front of the screen, the cacophony around him failing to have any impact at all.

Ultimately, this seems to be the best explanation for the inherent, and at first puzzling, contradiction of the betting-shop punter: the principal aim of gambling must be to win money, and yet, in time, they all become losers and, more than that, they know that they will continue to lose. Ultimately, for Freddy (before he stopped), Mickey, Moses, Thomas, Walksy and the rest, losing money is a price worth paying for the buzz that an occasional win brings, and for the feeling of community that the habitués have created for themselves.

6

ALL HORSE PLAYERS
DIE BROKE

> 'Son, no matter how far you travel, or how smart you get,
> always remember this: some day, somewhere, a guy is
> going to come to you and show you a nice brand-new
> deck of cards, and this guy is going to offer to bet you that
> the jack of spades will jump out of this deck and squirt cider
> in your ear. But, son, do not bet him, for as sure as you do,
> you are going to get an ear full of cider.'
>
> Damon Runyon, *The Idyll of Miss Sarah Brown*

It is two hours before the start of racing and the Guinness tents are
thronged with punters. A band strikes up an appropriate Irish tune
and the queues are five deep at the bar. Paddy Power, the Irish
bookmaker, is brazenly offering 2-1 on 200,000 pints of Guinness
or more being drunk during the Festival and this is one bet that the
punters have some control over and are determined to win. Everywhere, groups of men and women – young and old, well-dressed
and shabby, hands thrust deep into coat pockets to protect them
from the biting chill – are chatting animatedly with the unmistakable air of anticipation. At the heart of gambling is a communion
with the future: a way of buying hope, however transitory. Over
the next four days, hope will, more often than not, turn to
disappointment and many a now-bulging wallet will be emptied.
But the first day of the Cheltenham National Hunt Festival is not a
time for pessimism, or even realism. It is a time for optimism.

In modern Britain the symbiotic relationship between sport and gambling is best seen in horse racing, a sport which would cease to exist were it not for the public's love of a bet on a horse. And in horse racing that relationship reaches its most glorious expression at this annual shindig in the Cotswolds. First run in 1904, at a time when racing had completed the journey from an aristocratic pastime to a mass leisure pursuit, the Cheltenham Festival has developed into a championship affair for the best National Hunt horses in the world. It is also incredibly popular with humankind, so much so that this year, 2005, the organisers have extended the Festival to a fourth day for the first time.

The Festival is held every March, just on the cusp of spring, so that the weather can veer dramatically from the glorious to the diabolical. Regardless of the weather, the natural amphitheatre of the undulating racetrack – enclosed on the one side by the enormous grandstand and on the other by the great green clump of Cleeve Hill – is home to a throng of fifty thousand or more punters united in a desire to have a bet, win some money and forget, for a short while, about the miserable constraints of respectability and the daily grind.

It is a meeting for the true believers, a proper racing and gambling crowd, unlike the social occasions-cum-fashion stakes that characterise some race meetings during the flat season, or the once-a-year dabblers who blindly stab at finding the Grand National winner. Cheltenham's racegoers have a right to let their hair down: most of them have braved the bitter months of winter in rain, sleet or snow at desolate country tracks like Fontwell, Ludlow, Taunton or Tipperary.

As a punter, it is hard to win at Cheltenham. Most of the races are championship affairs, races full of the highest class of horse-flesh. This often means that very good horses go off at seriously tempting prices, which has lured many a dreamer to an early financial grave. Because of this potential (for reward and ruin),

Cheltenham attracts the high rollers of racing, just as Las Vegas is a magnet for the high rollers of the poker table. It is a place of fearless bettors and equally fearless bookmakers, a place where the frisson of danger is never far away.

This year the gravest financial danger is to nine anonymous punters who are the subject of an article in the *Racing Post*. The nub of the story concerns the fitness of an Irish horse called Kicking King, the new 7-2 favourite for the Gold Cup, feature race of the meeting. Kicking King is trained by Tom Taaffe, the son of Pat Taaffe, who rode the legendary Arkle to three successive Gold Cup victories, and it is in the bar named in that horse's honour that my friends and I are chuckling over the now traditional pint of Guinness. Two weeks before the Festival, Taffe announced that the horse had trained badly and was subsequently found to have mucus in his lungs. Taffe pulled him out of the Gold Cup reckoning. Accordingly, his odds on Betfair, the online betting exchange medium[7], had drifted out from 7-1 to 999-1, reflecting the fact that his chances of landing the crown had all but disappeared.

Gamblers are always on the lookout for a risk-free bet. For these nine punters, Kicking King's withdrawal represented such an opportunity. They decided to 'lay' Kicking King to win the Gold Cup at 999-1 (that is, they were playing the role of the bookmaker, offering odds of 999-1, which other people could accept). Some people did accept and these nine punters eventually found themselves laying £54 (i.e. an average of £6 per head) at 999-1. Their stupidity can only be marvelled at: they were willing to risk £53,946 for a potential gain of £54 (although they believed their risk to be nil, since Kicking King had been withdrawn from the race).

If only they had read Damon Runyon, a man who knew a bit about betting and about life, which he rated 6-5 against. This was

[7] For an explanation of the workings of Betfair see the next chapter.

the classic case of the Jack of Spades waiting to leap out of a deck of cards with a syringe full of cider. A week after he had withdrawn Kicking King, Taaffe announced, to widespread Irish rejoicing, that his horse had made a near-miraculous recovery and was back on the Gold Cup trail.

It was now Tuesday. The moment of truth for Kicking King, and nine very nervous punters, would come at 3.15 p.m. on Friday, the day after St Patrick's Day.

Gambling has always been the *raison d'être* of racing. A minority might argue that they go racing to pay homage to the thoroughbred at its most refined, that rare mixture of stamina, speed, class and courage which defines the great horses; some might even say that they go to marvel at the bravery of the jockeys as they go hurtling towards a six-foot fence. A minority might say all that. The majority come to bet. In any case, it's a whole lot more fun to have a financial interest. As *The Times*'s sportswriter Simon Barnes noted, 'Racing without betting is like dancing without sex.'

Indeed, sport purely for leisure didn't exist as a concept until the mid 19th century. Until then, sport was either simply a brutal extension of an agrarian society, as seen in bloody and violent pursuits such as cockfighting, bull- and bear-baiting, and dog-fighting (all of which were, in any case, good activities to wager on), or, in the case of sports such as prizefighting, cricket and racing, a convenient tool for gambling. Sports like racing and cricket would not have spread so quickly and developed into commercial enterprises, had it not been for gambling; nor would gambling have become a mass leisure activity, had it not been for sport. The one nourished the other.

Organised racing can be traced back to the 16th century in England. But early races were mostly private affairs in the form of match bets between aristocratic owners. The Earl of Bristol's beating of the Duke of Devonshire in 1698, when his horse Lobock beat Devonshire's Looby over eight miles for the sum of 325 guineas, was a typical example. Both owners rode their horses, this being before the advent of the professional jockey.

The motivations for aristocratic involvement in horse racing stretched further than the love of a bet. It was a sociable pastime, it helped sustain the deference shown to them by their social inferiors, and owning and racing horses allowed them to conspicuously display their wealth and status. Much of that is true of the racing 'nobility' today. Nevertheless, making horses pay their way has never been easy. J.P. McManus, for example, ran 223 horses in the 2006 jumps season (up to February). His training costs were estimated by one racing correspondent to be in the region of £2.5 million, and yet the average prize monies won by his horses was £4,000. A hundred years before, it was the same story: it cost 360 guineas to keep a horse in training, and the average prize money was £149. A winning bet, therefore, could help narrow the difference. No wonder *The Times* reported in 1827 that the 'noble Lords' at the St Leger 'were constrained to stand on tables and chairs in their eagerness to have a bet'.

It was the passion for betting that forced the sport to change and to broaden its popularity. Races between two horses, often run over long distances, were not particularly interesting races to bet on. Gradually, such match bets were replaced by sweepstakes, races with larger fields and younger horses, run over shorter sprint distances – much more enticing betting propositions. Until 1750 match bets were the predominant form of competition. By 1843, however, there were only eighty-six match bets run, compared to 897 sweepstakes. The five classics that are still the premier races of the flat-racing season today were an important part in this evolutionary process. The St Leger was first run in 1776, the Oaks in

1779, the Derby in 1780, the 2000 Guineas in 1809 and the 1000 Guineas in 1814. These were races which punters could really get their teeth into, backing horses ante-post at huge prices and then hedging their bets as the race drew near. Developments such as two-year-old races, with their increased uncertainty of outcome, and handicap races, where the weight allocation gives every horse a theoretically equal chance of winning, were the culmination of this desire to find interesting betting propositions.

As racing grew in popularity in the 18th and 19th centuries, the race day became an important occasion in the local calendar, often coinciding with local holidays. It became more than just a horse-racing spectacle. Whereas racing now looks to increase its support base by tacking on family-based entertainments – a concert, perhaps, or a jazz band – a day at the races two hundred years ago required an over-18 certificate. Alcohol and prostitution were rife, as were all kinds of ancillary entertainments, often based around gambling. Gambling games such as E&O (a primitive form of roulette, where you simply bet odd or even) were popular. At Ascot in 1792, there were ten marquees dedicated to E&O. Each tent cost 100 guineas a day to rent, which shows the level of betting that accompanied a big race meeting. Sometimes the entertainment was of a more gruesome kind: in 1739 Dick Turpin was hanged on the Knavesmire, a piece of common ground that had become the venue for York races six years earlier. A day at the races was an occasion, even in Victorian England, where conventions could be tossed aside and risk embraced.

Today, gambling remains no less important to horse racing. With over six million people going to the races last year, horse racing is Britain's second most popular spectator sport behind football. But how many racegoers have ever sat on a horse, raced a horse or owned a horse? There is no horse-racing equivalent of backyard cricket or football. Although ownership has spread in recent years thanks to the introduction of syndicates, participation in the sport remains out of the financial reach of the majority. And there aren't many grown men who can do nine stone in the saddle, as most flat jockeys must do. Racing is a spectator sport, and the thoroughbred is a betting mechanism.

Horse racing's share of the betting market is declining as internet poker, sports betting and Fixed Odds Betting Terminals become more popular. Yet it remains at just under 50 per cent of the total betting market (although five years ago it was nearly 70 per cent). And without the levy charged on off-course betting (10 per cent on profits of over £75,000), then racing would simply be unable to continue. In 2004–05 racing benefited to the tune of £98 million from bookmakers (or, more accurately, from losing punters), £74.3 million of which came from off-course betting. And of the £100 million offered in prize-money, £62.5 million came from the levy. Lord Rosebery, former Prime Minister, Derby-winning owner and member of the Jockey Club, famously said of the racing public that they 'don't count'. It would be a fool who repeated that claim today.

Two hundred thousand people will attend Cheltenham over the next four days and, as an illustration of the central place that betting has in horse racing, they will be given plenty of opportunity to part with their money. As you meander down the main concourse there are numerous Tote betting booths to the left and right, interspersed with hole-in-the-walls for the cash-strapped punter. Up the stairs and out of reach of most, there is even a Tote booth at the entrance to the Royal Box, should the Queen fancy a flutter (apparently she does). In front of the main grandstand is the betting ring – where the biggest punters and bookmakers do annual battle. This year the usual suspects are there, from the youngest, the 26-

year-old Ben Johnson, who trades under the banner 'security and civility', to the most fearless, a bookie called Freddie Williams, who will think nothing of laying a six-figure bet on a single horse. All are happy to be at Cheltenham, where the competitive nature of the racing tends to play to their favour. If the punters go home skint, which at Cheltenham they frequently do, there's only one place the money has gone – straight into the bookies' satchels. Win or lose, though, the bookies love Cheltenham: as the slogan of Rickert Ltd says: 'A bad day at the races is still better than a good day at the office.'

If you don't fancy the rough and tumble of the betting ring, then you can still bet against the old enemy in the more refined surroundings of the Centaur Room. The Centaur Room is a recent addition to Cheltenham and during race day it resembles a mini stock exchange, with the bookmakers setting up their stalls in the middle of a circular ring where some punters prefer to sit through-out the day, ignoring the smell, the sounds and the fury of the live action outside. It is a poor substitute for the real thing but, in addition to protection from the elements, it does offer 'betting in running', where punters can back their judgement as the race unfolds and bookmakers will change their odds accordingly. Betting in running, though, can be a dangerous game, as the Champion Hurdle, the feature race of the first day, showed.

Coming over the last fence, with the hill and the winning post in front of them, the Champion Hurdle seemed to be a two-horse race: last year's champion and this year's favourite, Hardy Eustace, was in front, but looming ominously was another Irish raider, Harchibald, with the fearless Irish Jockey Paul Carberry on board. With 400 yards to go, Conor O'Dwyer was, in racing parlance, 'hard at work' on Hardy Eustace: in truth, he was whipping the shit out of his horse. In his slipstream, Carberry sat motionless, as quiet as a church mouse. In the Centaur Room odds were being shouted and bets struck with alarming frequency. The odds of Harchibald winning the hurdler's crown were around 4-1 *on* – that is, to win one pound you had to risk four – a measure of Harchibald's perceived advantage. Hardy Eustace lived up to his name and battled gamely up the hill, but when Carberry pushed the button on Harchibald he got no response, and in the Centaur Room thousands of pounds went up in smoke. Carberry felt the lash of the punters' tongues on the way back to the enclosure, but it was the horse's heart, not the jockey's tactics, that was to blame for a thousand discarded betting slips.

Shortly afterwards, events took a happier turn for the Carberry clan as Paul's sister, Nina, brought the first day's action to a close with a winner in the 'getting out stakes', the final race of the day. She provided a nice story for the racing hacks, though at 20-1 she provided little solace for the punters. But at the end of a day's racing few hang around to discuss the one that got away. For most, it is a quick getaway to a pub, guest house or hotel, whose prices have increased three- or four-fold during Cheltenham week. There, it's down to serious form study and analysis of the next day's racing, for horse players are eternally hopeful, optimistic creatures.

Although I was staying by the racetrack, I arranged to have dinner in a pub in Stow-on-the-Wold with some friends that I punt with every Saturday on an exotic bet run by the Tote called the Scoop6. One miraculous Saturday, which lives long in the memory, we had actually won the damn thing, netting over £80,000, including the bonus race the following week. My friends were part of a bigger group who have been going to Cheltenham and staying in the same hotel for twenty-six years. The festival inspires that kind of loyalty.

Over dinner in our pub, the generally sombre mood of a losing start was punctured by the excited tones of Irish Mike, who had picked four winners on the opening day, and who was now in the process of dispensing his considerable wisdom on the next day's big race, the Queen Mother Champion Chase. Moscow Flyer would be carrying Irish hopes, although not Irish Mike's money. 'I want it to win so badly, I think I'm not going to back it,' he said. Occasionally, just occasionally, emotion overrides financial interest.

Towards the end of the evening, the atmosphere became maudlin, as triumphs of previous years were remembered. Like the time the group won the jackpot, winning £21,000 for an £8 stake, proof of which was hanging in the form of a replica cheque in the pub's dining room. It was a horse called Spectroscope that carried the confederates' hopes in the final race that day and it was called home by him who had picked it with the never-to-be-forgotten phrase 'Mine eyes have seen the glory!' Since then, the eyes have been dulled rather, but it was the kind of one-off experience that can lead to a lifetime's addiction.

I had joined the group for the evening but was staying elsewhere, and just to show how racing and betting dominate Cheltenham life during the Festival, my taxi driver, 'Ging', saw fit to dispense 'an absolute cert' for the next day as he drove me back. 'Persian Waters tomorrow,' he said, 'it's come from my friend, the jockey Tom Dreaper. He was going to ride it, until his boss got one in the race and forced him to ride that. He says Persian Waters can't lose.' How many times have you heard that at a racecourse? At Cheltenham, especially, whispers from friends of friends of a trainer become tips, and those tips become certainties, and before you know it, all your hours of careful form study and reasoned, logical analysis have been supplanted in an instant by wild and unsubstantiated rumour. Sometimes it adds colour to the scene – and there was no more colourful racecourse tipster in the 20th century than Ras Prince Monolulu, whose colourful headdress and garb were matched by his frequent cries of 'I gotta horse! I gotta horse!'

– but most of the time acting on a tip is the surest and quickest way to the poorhouse.

There was no Ras Prince Monolulu at Cheltenham on day two, but there was one chap who collared me early on: he grabbed me firmly by the arm, looked around furtively to make sure no one was in earshot and then whispered through the side of his mouth, 'Back McCoy today!' Now, Tony McCoy is the champion jockey, probably the best jockey of all time, and the winner of over a thousand races in the last five years alone. His mounts warrant careful consideration at all times, but this joker was imparting the information in a manner which suggested he had just heard that oil had been found in Liverpool or gold in the Mersey.

There was a noticeably less exuberant feel to the second morning. It was not just that the reality of how hard it is to win at Cheltenham had hit home, but news had seeped through that one of the contenders for the big race of the meeting, the Gold Cup, had died that morning. Farmer Jack was trained by West Country trainer Philip Hobbs and it was on Hobbs's gallops that Farmer Jack had collapsed and died. Not that it stopped the betting market on the Gold Cup being adjusted accordingly. In gambling, sentiment is short-lived.[8]

As the faithful gathered again, flitting from paddock to parade ring, from bar to betting stall, it was hard not to appreciate that the democratisation of racing, through gambling, was complete. There was an army of tweed; there were the pallid, suited and booted city types hoping to have a few days at the bookies' and their employers' expense; and then there was the jeans and T-shirt brigade. The

[8] The ultimate proof of this occurred in the run-up to the 2006 Cheltenham Festival, when Best Mate collapsed and died of a heart attack halfway through his comeback race. Scarcely had news seeped out about his demise than punters were laying him on Betfair at attractive odds for the Gold Cup in an attempt to sucker in anybody unaware of Best Mate's sad demise.

racecourse itself genuflects to the rigid social stratifications of the past – no jeans and T-shirts in the owners' and trainers' enclosure, thank you very much – but in the betting ring they all rub shoulders. Perhaps the cross section of racegoers was best summed up by the connections of the first winner of the previous day, a horse called Arcalis: the trainer, Howard Johnson, is a country man, a former cattle farmer who is deaf in one ear after being kicked by a recalcitrant cow; the owner is Graham Wylie, a newcomer to horse racing who has made many millions in the computer business and who now has invested some £4 million of that in bloodstock, and the jockey is a typical little Irish ball of fire called Graham Lee. In microcosm, their association sums up racing.

It wasn't always so, of course. Not for nothing is racing called 'the sport of kings'. Charles II, James II and Queen Anne all patronised the sport, built houses at Newmarket and gave their names to races that are still run today. The nickname of Charles II – 'Old Rowley' – was commemorated at Newmarket by naming the mile-long racetrack after him. Through match betting, 17th-century racing was, as we have seen, a preserve of the upper classes. As late as 1674 a tailor was punished for racing his horse, 'it being contrary to the law for a labourer to make a race, it being a sport for gentlemen.'

But gambling on sport has always proved stronger than the barriers of class. The great chronicler of prizefighting Pierce Egan noted a democratic feel to the fight between Tom Spring and John Langan at Worcester in 1824: 'Not less than 50,000 people were assembled together on this milling occasion. It was a union of all ranks, from the brilliant of the highest class in the circle of Corinthians, down to the Dusty Bob gradation in society, and even a shade or two below that. Lots of the Upper House, the Lower House and the Flash House.'

Gradually racing, too, underwent this democratisation and by the end of the 19th century it was hugely popular and deeply rooted in the fabric of the whole society. The Jockey Club, the arbiter of the sport, remained a bastion of upper-class privilege, but the advent of the railways, a nascent sporting press and an increase in real wages and leisure time meant that, by the end of the 19th century, racing, and gambling upon it, was a mass leisure pursuit. The results of the St Leger had to be sent by carrier pigeon to the manufacturing towns of the North, such was the eagerness to know the result. Even the middle classes put their concerns to one side to embrace the economic advantages that a race day or racing week brought.

This cross-class support for racing is the main reason why it withstood the late 19th-century anti-gambling backlash. Cock-fighting had been banned by the middle of the 19th century, prizefighting declined markedly from about the same period, and cricket purged itself of bookmakers and gambling from around 1830. Even the ancillary gambling that characterised a day at the races was affected. But racing itself and on-course cash gambling remained untouched, even as betting houses and then street betting were outlawed. After 1847, parliament adjourned for the running of the Derby and by the turn of the century the Jockey Club could boast seven former members of the cabinet and two former prime ministers amongst its ranks – no wonder racing was well looked after.

The democratisation of racing is best summed up by the changing face of the owners of the great horses. Early on, the list of Derby winners came straight from Debrett's. Yet in 1830 the Derby winner Priam was owned by plain Mr W. Chifney and two years later Mr R. Risdale was the envy of many a blue-blooded owner who had yet to taste Derby success. One of the greatest horses ever, Eclipse, was owned by an Irish ruffian called

Dennis O'Kelly in the 18th century. O'Kelly had spent time in prison as a debtor, worked as a sedan chair carrier and a billiard marker. Through a shrewd combination of punting and bookmaking, he came to acquire great wealth, and Eclipse for some 1,750 guineas – a steal, since the horse earned a reputed £25,000 at stud. Despite his great wealth and his success as an owner, he was never allowed to join the Jockey Club or the elite credit betting clubs in London. When one of his lordships, on seeing O'Kelly's ostentatious display of wealth, asked as to the whereabouts of O'Kelly's estates, the Irishman replied, 'My estates! If that's what you mean I've a map o' them about here,' and he unfurled a gleaming sheaf of notes.

The nature of owners was changing, as was the nature of betting. Until the mid 19th century much betting was characterised by the type of aristocratic 'deep play' that we witnessed in chapter four. Men like Harry Hastings, the 4th and last Marquis of Hastings, who was the biggest bettor of his day. When Hermit won the Derby in 1867 it cost Hastings over £100,000. The loss hit Hastings hard – he had to sell his Scottish estate to pay his debts and he died a broken man at 26. On his deathbed his last words were purported to have been, 'Hermit fairly broke my heart. But I didn't show it, did I?'

Hastings's death coincided with a change in the pattern of betting as smaller, more prudent sums but from a much wider source fed the bookies' satchels. The shift was noticed by the observers of the time. One such, Thormanby, sniffily complained: 'Nowadays betting in large sums, confined to a few professional layers and backers, has disappeared in favour of thousands of petty wagers by men and women who hardly know a racehorse from a hack.'

*　　*　　*

After a quiet first day at Cheltenham, it was time for the current generation of great owners to enter the fray, and there is no bigger owner than the pint-sized Irishman John P. McManus. McManus is a living link to Dennis O'Kelly and Harry Hastings, being both a self-made man and an almighty bettor. Born in County Limerick, McManus has been punting regularly since childhood. He set up as a bookie at 20, later diversifying into currency trading, where his keen mathematical brain stood him in as good stead as it did within the betting ring.

Like Hastings, McManus is fearless. Unlike Hastings, he is remarkably shrewd. His punting has been elevated to mythical proportions by the Cheltenham faithful, who have given him the nickname 'the Sundance Kid' for his frequent and successful raids on the ring. They have never forgotten his £250,000 coup on Mister Donovan in 1982, or a win of similar proportions on Forgive 'n' Forget at the following year's Festival.

His only real action during the first day of this meeting had been a £20,000 bet on his horse Spot the Difference at 7-2 with Freddie Williams. It won. It was now rumoured that McManus had a six-figure amount – again with Freddie Williams – riding on the outcome of Moscow Flyer's attempt to win the Queen Mother Champion Chase. To a crescendo of cheers, but no doubt little emotion from McManus, Moscow Flyer proved himself to be the champion that Irish Mike so dearly wanted him to be. (His victory prompted the inevitable headlines in the *Racing Post* that Williams had been 'massacred' by Moscow and that he was on the retreat. Unlike Napoleon, though, Williams stayed the course, finishing just £15,000 down on the meeting overall. At the end he said, 'It was a super place this week and if I go skint at Cheltenham, you'll never hear me complain. I'm looking forward to next year already.' Bookmakers get a bad rap, much of it deserved, but types like Williams who stand the biggest bets and pay up without a whimper will always carry the punters' respect, even on the day when he leaves with his satchel bursting at the seams.)[9]

David Johnson, another self-made man and another big owner and shrewd punter – more McManus than Hastings – was also ready to show the colour of his money on day two. In the Royal & Sun Alliance Chase it was rumoured that Johnson had had a hundred grand on his horse Comply or Die. I found myself watching the race alone (that is, detached from friends), on the lawn in front of the Arkle bar. Just in front of me was the trainer Nicky Henderson, who was running a horse called Trabolgan in the same race. Henderson had been having a bad time of it, his horses out of form for much of the run-up to the Festival. Now, he was watching Trabolgan and he looked anything but relaxed: on his tiptoes, scanning the runners with his binoculars in one hand and a fag in the other. But there was something in his taut body language – a kind of nervous but expectant tension – that made me take notice. As Trabolgan jumped the last ahead of Comply or Die, Henderson went what can only be described as doolally. He ran one way, then the other, arms and legs barely connected to his body, then he checked to make sure that, yes, his horse had got up the hill and passed the wining post first, at which point he jumped up and down repeatedly, punching the air with a clenched fist, waving his trilby around maniacally, until he quietly stubbed out

---

[9] Whether Freddie Williams will be favourably inclined to Cheltenham after the 2006 Festival remains to be seen. His rivalry with J.P. McManus continued and after Reveillez romped in at 6-1 and Kadoun at 50-1, McManus had lifted £925,000 from Williams's satchel. To make matters worse, Williams and his daughter were victims of a carjacking on the way home after day three. He was relieved of a further £70,000. The Cheltenham faithful's appetite for a bet went undiminished in 2006, with over £50 million wagered on course over the four days. £150 million more was wagered off-course, in bookies up and down the land.

his fag, looked around to make sure that nobody had seen him, and walked off to the winner's enclosure, mobile phone glued to his ear. Nobody, except me, had noticed Henderson.

The third day of the Festival coincided with St Patrick's Day. Father Breen, an Irish cleric and racing fanatic, gave a sermon for the travelling Irish at a nearby church. Breen was far more in tune with the gambling inclinations of his congregation than the institution he represented. 'We pray for winners,' he said, 'for they are hard to get. And we pray for Irish winners – wherever they come from.' After the Flyer's victory the day before, no doubt his audience were taking communion with the mother of all hangovers, paracetamol and the form book in close attendance.

Breen knew his audience well, as the Irish have long held a special place in their hearts for jump racing and Cheltenham in particular. The first chase supposedly took place in County Cork in 1752, between the steeples of the churches in Buttevant and Doneraile, five miles apart, hence the term 'steeple-chasing'. This enthusiasm continues unabated and every year the Irish swarm to Cheltenham. Their love affair with jump racing and Cheltenham must be explained by the rural nature of the Republic of Ireland, where many of the best jumpers are reared and where the great owners, like J.P. McManus and Trevor Hemmings (who won the 2005 Grand National with Hedgehunter), keep their studs.

Why the Irish should punt with such ferocity is harder to explain. Maybe a theory could be put forward linking Ireland's painful past and the gambling mentality of its countrymen – an unstable country imbuing its citizens with a penchant for risk taking? Maybe it is better explained by simple patriotism and a desire every March to put one over the old enemy. Because the Irish, mostly, punt with their hearts and not their heads.

Regardless of the reasons why, the Irish were having a wonderful and profitable time of it this year. Their success was best typified, perhaps, by the man dressed as a leprechaun who had overindulged during the early part of St Patrick's Day and had thrown up on the main stairway, resulting in even bigger queues for the bars than usual. Now he was veering around the parade ring being passed like a parcel from punter to punter. When Oulart (trained by the Irishman Dessie Hughes, ridden by Paul Carberry) won the final race of this, the third day, it was the seventh Irish-trained winner of the week so far. More than that, they had scooped the Champion Hurdle with Hardy Eustace, the Champion Chase with Moscow Flyer and all thoughts were turning to Kicking King in the Gold Cup, which was due to bring the meeting to a close on the fourth day.

The Gold Cup is the zenith of the meeting, when the best chasers in Britain challenge each other over a punishing three and a quarter miles. It is the ultimate test of a horse: the stiff fences test a horse's jumping prowess and the final gruelling hill its stamina and what is called in professional sport its 'ticker' or heart. The greatest names in the history of jump racing have been inextricably linked with Cheltenham and its Gold Cup, amongst them Golden Miller, Desert Orchid, Dawn Run, Best Mate and the incomparable Arkle. The Grand National may be the nation's favourite race. The Gold Cup is, unquestionably, the race of champions.

The 2005 Gold Cup seemed to be jinxed – almost as if the racing gods were rebuking the festival organisers for their avarice in extending the traditional three-day meeting into a fourth day. Three days' bacchanalia have always stretched a man's stamina and wallet to the limit; four seemed to be asking for trouble. And, as far as the Gold Cup was concerned, it was trouble that the organisers got. The public's favourite horse and ante-post favourite, Best Mate, burst a blood vessel in the build-up to the meeting and was pulled out. Farmer Jack's demise reduced the entry by one on the second day. Kingscliff, another intended runner, was withdrawn. Kicking King, therefore, was the new 7-2 favourite and by far the classiest horse in the race.

As we waited on Kicking King's moment of truth, what were the nine anonymous punters feeling? Were they sweating up nervously, as the horses that were about to put their courage on the line were surely doing? What had they done since they had struck their lunatic bet? Had they reduced some of their liability by backing Kicking King at 7-2? Were they at Cheltenham to watch? Or had they merely done an ostrich impression for the duration of the day, hoping that when they emerged, blinking into the sunlight, the world would not seem such a cruel place and that they would be, communally, £54 richer instead of the best part of £54,000 poorer?

Nor would it have brightened their collective mood to read about another punter that day who stood to make £863,947 off Ladbrokes, which would have been the biggest payout in their history. This unnamed genius or lucky dipper – for it is amazing how many big wins are won by the casual and uninformed punter – had somehow managed to have a £10 ante-post (that is, a bet placed well in advance of the racing, so that the prices offered are more generous) accumulator on Arcalis (20-1), Hardy Eustace (10-1) and Trabolgan (10-1), all of whom won, which meant that he had £25,410 rolling onto the final leg of his accumulator – a horse called Sir Rembrandt in the Gold Cup. If either Sir Rembrandt (now fifth favourite at 15-2) or Kicking King won the Gold Cup, there would be joy for one or pain for nine of almost equal proportions. And on such raw emotions does the pleasure/addiction of horseplayers rest.

The off was greeted by a thunderous roar – a great, throaty primitive roar from fifty thousand punters for whom the end of four days' punishment was at hand. The roar was matched by the growing excitement brought to bear by a grand old grey horse, the 11-year-old Grey Abbey, who led the field through the first dozen fences or so. The public for some reason always take to a gallant grey – Desert Orchid, the most famous of them all, was known as 'Dessie' to grannies who wouldn't know the front of a betting slip from the back – and Grey Abbey, ears pricked and jumping boldly, was no exception.

Kicking King took quite a keen hold early on, expending too much energy, which must have worried his jockey, Barry Geraghty, as his mount was not certain to stay the trip. Kicking King had won once before over three miles, but that was at Kempton – a sharp, flat track – very different from Cheltenham's undulations and its punishing uphill finish. Geraghty, though, settled his mount soon enough.

Of the other fancied horses, Celestial Gold, trained by the champion trainer Martin Pipe, clouted the first fence and never really recovered; Strong Flow travelled well until the downhill sweep to the third last caught him flat-footed, and Sir Rembrandt, who had joined Grey Abbey at about halfway, also failed to go the pace on the downhill stretch.

With two fences to go, it was between Kicking King and Take the Stand – an unfancied 25-1 shot trained by the little-known trainer Peter Bowen. Briefly, as they turned for home, Take the Stand looked as though he might spring a surprise, only for his challenge to fade up the hill. Kicking King's class told through and, with 200 yards to go, his coronation was a formality.

And so it came to pass, on a glorious spring afternoon, the day after St Patrick's Day, that Kicking King powered clear of the finest horses in the British Isles and came home to general Irish whoopin' and hollerin'. Sir Rembrandt finished a tired but creditable third.

The Irish claimed a memorable treble – the Champion Hurdle, the Champion Chase and now the Gold Cup – which would be a long enough tale to fill the 360 evenings until the moment came to pack their bags for another trip over the Irish Sea. The big accumulator wasn't won. Somewhere in the ether of the betting exchanges £53,946 had just changed hands and nine punters had cider squirted in their ears.

7

DEATH OF THE BOOKIE

'It was better betting with a decent feller. Now it's better betting with a mobile phone or a computer.'

Carl Chinn, bookmaker turned historian

On 4 June 2000, the *Sunday Times* business section ran a small story on the imminent launch of an online betting exchange designed, it said, to exterminate the bookmaker from the gambling market. Three days later, that betting exchange, Betfair, was launched in Covent Garden to a gathering of celebrities and gamblers. Betfair immediately declared open war on the traditional bookmakers: they staged a mock funeral cortège – bookmaker, coffin and all – throughout the City's square mile, and leaflets were distributed proclaiming that the bookie, 'who emptied punters' pockets, took the shirts off their backs, never made a decent price' would wither and die 'with the birth of open-market betting'. Although it was an audacious launch, full of the kind of shrewd PR and marketing chutzpah that has since become Betfair's trademark, there was little doubt as to the seriousness of both their intent and their challenge to the established order.

An online betting exchange such as Betfair is the ultimate challenge to the bookmaker because it takes the need for the middleman (the bookmaker) out of the equation. It is simply a mechanism by which people can bet with each other in cyberspace. It allows punters, as long as they are Betfair clients, to act as both layer (bookmaker) and/or backer (punter). Not only that, but it also allows them to set their own notional odds and, as long as there is someone in cyberspace prepared to lay or back to the odds that they want, then the bet is struck. If a gambler has a computer screen to hand, a reasonable knowledge of how to use it and a mind that can quickly understand the changing odds, then, technically, there is no need ever to bet with a bookmaker again. At least that is what Andrew Black, a former professional gambler and derivatives pricing modeller, was hoping when he set about raising a million pounds from the City to get his brainchild up and running.

Bookmakers, though, have overcome many challenges over the years. Ever since the first of their ilk appeared with their pencils and notebooks on Newmarket Heath just over a couple of hundred years ago, they have constantly proved their survival instincts. They have overcome everything from the closing-down of betting houses in 1853, to the outlawing of street betting in 1906, the imposition of betting tax, the threat of the Tote and the opprobrium of a distrustful public. By very publicly setting bookmakers in his sights, Black was taking on a formidable and resourceful opponent. In every sense of the word, he was taking a gamble.

It is a dismal July day – the Sussex Downs are enveloped in a low-hung blanket of mist and mizzle – and the first day of the summer festival at Goodwood promises to be anything other than glorious. Horses have raced over this part of Sussex for more than two hundred years. It is one of England's most historic tracks and the summer festival, known as Glorious Goodwood, is one of the country's premier flat meetings. It is not difficult to see why racing developed here – the course is a natural amphitheatre, first rising and then falling in the distance until a sharp right-handed turn brings a six-furlong straight run-in to the winning post in front of the grandstand.

The atmosphere, despite the weather, will be that of a giant summer garden party. The marquees have been erected behind the grandstand next to the paddock, as have the jazz stands, where the boatered and blazered brigade will soon sip their Pimm's, nod knowingly at the horseflesh as it parades before them and dip into their pockets to back their judgement with a few readies. The racing today promises to be of decent quality: there are two Group Three races and a Group Two race on the card (group races attract the best horses and the best prize money) and so the quality of horse ought to be matched by the size of the action in the betting ring. Interestingly, and maybe this offers the first clue of the day as to how the battle between Betfair and the bookmaker is going, two of those races – the historic Lennox Stakes and Molecomb Stakes – are now sponsored by Betfair. The Lennox Stakes has been re-named the Betfair Cup, whilst the Molecomb stakes simply has the Betfair prefix tagged on.

Now, one and a half hours before racing, the course is empty of that endless mix of colour, clamour, uncertainty, joy and despair that characterises a day at the races. The only people inside the racetrack are workers: the stewards who man the gates, the caterers who are preparing for the day ahead, the journalists who are busy attending to their contacts, the stable lads and lasses who are putting the finishing touches to their horses' coats, and the book-makers who are beginning to set up their 'joints'.

Think of the traditional stereotype of a bookmaker and you think of an ostentatious, flashy type, loudmouthed and uncultured, perhaps with a bowler hat on his head and a pinstriped waistcoat wrapped around his bulging midriff, the odds being shouted through the plumed smoke of a big fat cigar. Early on-course bookies had to portray an image of ready wealth to inspire punters that a big bet could be struck and accounted for should the need arise, and so such stereotypes no doubt existed. Literature feeds this image. In Walter Greenwood's working-class novel *Love on the Dole* the reader is first introduced to the bookie, Sam Grundy, in these terms: 'A small fat man, broad set, with beady eyes, an apoplectic complexion, came out of the house, crossed the tiny backyard and stood on the upturned box, thumbs in waistcoat armholes. Preposterous-sized diamonds ornamented his thick fingers and cable-like gold guard, further enhanced by a collection of gold pendants, spade guineas and Masonic emblems, hung heavily across his prominent stomach. He chewed a match stalk; his billycock [bowler hat] rested on the back of his head; he wore spats. Self-confidence and gross prosperity oozed from him.'

Literature not only portrays the bookmaker as a flashy arriviste, but also as someone you had to be at your sharpest to do business with. Damon Runyon's classic short story 'The Snatching of Bookie Bob' tells of a bookie who has been kidnapped by Harry the Horse, Spanish John and Little Isadore, who then put a ransom on his head of $25,000. The four of them spend two days kicking around an apartment waiting for the bookie to find someone to stump up the cash; two days which they spend betting on the horses at Belmont and various other American tracks; two days during which the bookie agrees to set a book for them and accept their markers; and two days in which Harry the Horse, Spanish John and Little Isadore end up losing $50,000 to the bookie, who emerges from his nightmare unscathed and $25,000 to the good.

The bookmakers at Goodwood generally give off no such air of prosperity or in-your-face confidence. Perhaps the weather is to blame. Most are soberly dressed in dark gaberdine raincoats and felt hats. On days such as these, creature comforts – in particular, the ability to stay warm and dry – win out over any image-conscious concerns. Only the representatives of Sealey and Son ('You know it makes sense' is their imploring sign) challenge the drab scene and pay deference to high summer: they are dressed in yellow and black striped blazers and boaters.

Sixty or so bookmakers are milling about the Tattersall's area. Racing tradition dictates that bookmakers must set up their stalls in the Tattersall's enclosure, so named after Richard Tattersall who set up a meeting place at Hyde Park Corner in 1773 where racing men could congregate and do business. Sixteen years later, he added a subscription room where his patrons could settle their financial transactions in greater comfort, and it remained the pre-eminent centre for ante-post betting and post-race settling until late into the 19th century. The 'Tatts' is usually situated next to the Members'. This tradition, whereby the Members' enclosure is kept free of the socially unacceptable whilst at the same time keeping them close enough to do business with, emphasises the historically negative portrayal of bookmakers.

As well as the Tattersall's enclosure, bookies can also bet from the Silver Ring. The Silver Ring is further away from the Members' enclosure and it is this physical distance, as much as anything, that dictates that the betting action here will be of smaller proportions than in Tatts. Simon Kingshott, for example, who takes bets from the Silver Ring at Goodwood, has a minimum wager rule of £1 and will pay out a maximum amount of £500. Such limitations would not be accepted in Tatts, where a minimum bet is likely to be £5 or £10 and where punters would not expect any ceiling to be placed on maximum payouts.

In Tatts they line up, three deep, facing the grandstand. The best positions are at the front, nearest the rails bookmakers, the grandstand and the punters. The rails bookmakers, so named because they take up their positions along the rails that separate the Members' enclosure from Tatts, are the independent credit bookmakers and on-course representatives of the major bookmakers, such as William Hill, Ladbrokes and Coral. As well as betting with their credit clients, they will also take cash bets, provided that the sums are big enough. It is only recently that rails bookmakers have been allowed to advertise prices in the same way as the Tatts bookmakers, a change that has taken some custom away from Tatts. The rails bookmakers are invariably dressed sharply in dark suits and represent the corporate face of bookmaking. This is where the biggest action in the ring will take place and so proximity to this action is all-important, as is proximity to the punters themselves.

The farther a bookmaker is distanced from the rails, or from the punters, then the more generous odds he must offer to attract customers. This is called 'forced turnover' and is less desirable than 'unforced turnover'. Forcing his turnover by offering more generous odds is risky, as the bookmaker is squeezing his margins and reducing his chances of taking home a profit – but without the custom he has no chance of making a profit. For a bookmaker, turnover is king. A bookmaker's position in the ring, then, is crucial to his chances of making a decent living.

Traditionally, these positions, or pitches, were passed down from generation to generation in a system that was set up by the National Association of Bookmakers half a century ago. It was a system designed to prevent the kind of violent conflict that characterised on-course bookmaking immediately prior to, and after, the Second World War, when the most favoured pitches were fought for in often bloody battles. Subsequently, a bookmaker had to join the NAB, after which he would make a deposit, fill in an application and join a waiting list for a pitch at a racecourse. He would be allocated a pitch, usually in the back row ('in Siberia'), only when a vacancy arose. For potential newcomers it was a restrictive, non-competitive scenario; a 'dead man's shoes' structure in which the best pitches were kept by those bookmakers whose families had been in the game for generations.

This has now changed. Pitches are now bought and sold like any other commodity. The top pitches are at the Grade One racetracks. Courses such as Goodwood, Ascot, Cheltenham, Epsom, York, Newmarket and Kempton, say, are the ones which have the best races and therefore the biggest crowds, and to have a top-ten pitch at any of these guarantees a bookmaker plenty of action, if not necessarily profit. An hour and a half before racing, the bookmakers decide upon their pitch for the day. Number one pitch has first choice, number two second and so on. A representative from the National Joint Pitch Council manages the betting ring for the day, helping to allocate pitches and to sort out disputes between punters and bookmakers.

The bookmaker who is as much responsible as anybody for this more meritocratic, less oligarchical system is betting at Goodwood today and, of the assembled group, nobody more closely resembles the historical stereotype of a bookmaker than the 64-year-old East Ender Barry Dennis. Large and swarthy, he is Desperate Dan without the desperate. He is, by his own admission, loudmouthed, garrulous and no respecter of tradition or reputation. He dominates the ring, verbally and physically, and his appearances on *Channel 4 Racing*, and in the *Sun* newspaper, give him the highest profile of any bookmaker. This high profile irritates the other bookmakers, who think that his brash self-promotion is part of the reason that punters gravitate towards him. They are right. Dennis's success story, though, is that of the self-made man.

Dennis's father died in the Second World War, and his path first to gambling then bookmaking began when his mother remarried a gambler. As a schoolboy, Dennis would stop off at Romford Market to pick up the newspaper that carried the evening's racing results for his stepfather. 'I remember it now,' he says, 'the cries of "*Star, News, Standard! Star, News, Standard!*" It was the *Evening News* that carried the results and that was the paper I had to buy.'

After a while, Dennis would put the odd bet on for his step-father. 'At that stage, pre 1960, off-course bookmakers were illegal, so I had to wait at the corner of the marketplace, or in pubs, for the runners and I'd put the bets on with them.

'I started betting myself at 11. In 1954 I ran a book for the first time at my local grammar school. It was on the Derby. They all backed Never Say Die with Lester on board. It won at 33-1! It was a month before I could go back to school. But I made sure I paid off all my debts. It didn't put me off, though. Later that year I ran another book on the Grand National. By this time, my best pal had told me of a bookmaker in Romford market with whom I could lay bets off. So whenever I had a liability on my book at school I used to go to him – he had an illegal business in the back room of his house with a tickertape machine and blowers – and he'd let us lay off our liabilities with him. Gradually, I started to work for him in the evenings on the dog phones, taking dog bets. All the punters got to know me and knew that they could collect their bets from me at the various pubs in the area.

'I left school in 1958 with two O levels – in maths, which won't surprise you, and English literature, which will.' And suddenly in the middle of the bookmaker's ring at Goodwood, where we are chatting, Dennis startles all around by reciting some Shakespearian verses in a sonorous baritone. 'I went to work in the City as an office boy but I continued to work weekends with the bookie in Romford. In May 1961 off-course betting was legalised and I went straight out of the City and into bookmaking. At 20 I was managing a bookmaking operation in Romford market. In those days all you had to do was find a shop on a high street or near a pub, apply for a licence, put up a counter and a couple of blowers on the wall and that was it. We had a limit on payouts: 25-1 for a double, 33-1 for a treble and 50-1 an accumulator. In 1966 the bookie I worked for sold his 24 shops and I applied to be a bookie at Romford Dogs. I knew the business and I thought it was about time I had a go on my own.

'In 1970 I applied to the NAB to be a bookie at Brighton races. All I had to do was give them some assurances of my liquidity: at that time I'd opened a hair salon for the missus and we had £1,000 liquidity in the house. That was it. It was easy to get started but hard to get on in the game because of the pitch situation being "dead men's shoes". Anyway, the catalyst to it all changing was the advent of the all-weather at Lingfield in 1989. I had pitch number thirty-six out of the forty pitches there. Often the weather was appalling in January and February and one January afternoon it was sleeting and snowing and hardly anybody turned up. By the last race I was the only one left and I'd managed to get all the way up to pitch number one. I thought I'd made it! The next time racing was at Lingfield it was a bright sunny day and I was shunted all the way back to pitch thirty-six again. It just didn't seem right.

'So in 1991, along with five other bookies, I offered Lingfield racecourse a few grand to get a front-row pitch. It got them thinking that this was a way to make a few quid, as back then bookmakers just paid five times the entrance fee to bet, which was about £15 per day on the all-weather. The NAB got involved, though, and knocked the idea back. Eventually, though, pitch sales did come about, in 1997. It made sense for everybody: racecourses made more money; older bookmakers who wanted to get out could realise a kind of pension, and upstarts like me could get involved in a more serious way.

'Sandown Park was the venue for the first auction of pitches and it was a place I had waited twenty years to get a pitch. At that time I knew David Johnson, the horse owner, a little bit. Our wives played tennis together and we used to go out to dinner sometimes. I rang him up on the morning of the auction. I was slightly embarrassed but he'd always said if I needed any help to ring him. He told me to go ahead and bid and spend what I needed to spend. We never talked interest rates or amounts. Well, in the end that day I spent over £250,000! I bought top-ten pitches to every racetrack in the South East, finishing up with about 310 days' work in all.' Dennis, clearly, is a gambler at heart.

Dennis has the number seven pitch at Goodwood – that is, he has the seventh best choice. After the bookies have indicated their choices to the NJPC representative, they set up their joints: the upturned box that Sam Grundy stood on is still used, but technology has changed almost everything else. The bookmaker's board, these days, is likely to be electronic (although some, like John Purcell, still use chalk-up boards), tickets will be printed out electronically rather than handwritten and at the back of his joint the bookie will have a computer that allows him to see, at a stroke, how his 'book' is doing. It means that their liabilities on a particular horse no longer have to be calculated mentally. By the side of a horse's name there is a figure in red or green which indicates a bookmaker's liability or otherwise on that particular horse. One thing that has remained unchanged is the satchel which hangs down from the front of the bookmaker's joint. This satchel bears the name of the firm and is used, depending on how the day is going, either to deposit the punters' cash or to pay out.

At least one unfathomable feature of the betting ring has disappeared with the advance of technology: tic-tac men. Tic-tac men used to be a regular feature of the ring, standing at an elevated height and waving their arms and white gloves, passing signals to their particular bookmaker as to where the big money was going. Certain signs were well known – a hand moving in a 'n' shape was William Hill, and a circular motion over the head was the magic sign for Ladbrokes – but often the tic-tac men would deliberately use confusing or conflicting signals to put off rival bookmakers. To the punters it was all a mystery. Now, though, the modern equivalent of the tic-tac man wanders around rather furtively talking into his microphone with his earpieces clamped firmly into his ear.

Once the joints are set up, a bookmaker will start to think about the day's racing. Two down from Barry Dennis's number seven pitch is Andy Smith, who bets under the name of Dick Reynolds. Smith is the antithesis of Dennis: quietly spoken, formally dressed in a mauve suit and trim of build, with the pinched but jowelly look of someone who used to be overweight but is no longer. Like Dennis, Smith has been in racing for years – his father and grandfather were both bookies, albeit at rural point-to-point race-tracks rather than the urban scene that Dennis knows so well. It was the liberation of buying and selling pitches that likewise helped Smith get on in the game, when he also took a chance, buying eighteen good pitches, mostly in the South and South-West.

Once he has set up his joint, Smith is keen to talk to his 'form experts' about the day's action. All over Tatts, bookmakers are now having furtive discussions with their contacts, who will give them information on what horses are fancied and what horses have been backed during the morning either on the exchanges or in the offices (i.e. with the big high-street bookmakers like Ladbrokes or William Hill). Any information that will give the bookmaker an edge over the punter is eagerly sought. Of course, all over England punters are doing the same thing, taking tips from those 'in the know', hoping to sting the eternal enemy. Smith considers himself to be an expert on jump racing, and will not use any outside help, but for flat racing he relies on his contacts.

The conversation between Smith and his contact lasts no more than two or three minutes. The talk is rapid-fire, laced with racing jargon, and, as he talks, Smith makes notes in the day's *Racing Post*, ticking some horses, putting a line through others, circling and querying others. 'Stoute/Spencer combination feared in the first, as well as Nero's Return of Mark Johnston's. OK. The Geezer? Strong money for that? OK. Court Masterpiece and Autumn Glory in the third. Master Blaster, the fourth.' He shoots a look at me. 'Master Blaster? That's more your game, isn't it?' Back to his contact. 'Sergeant Cecil. They fancy the Sergeant, do they? Criminal Act? Hill's fancies that over his other one, does he? And in the last? Selective and Waterside. OK.' (As it happens, only The Geezer and Court Masterpiece win, which suggests that bookmakers' tips are often as useless as those given to the ordinary punter.)

Half an hour before the first race, then, the battleground has been prepared: pitches have been allotted, joints set up and contacts have been squeezed for information. All that is needed now are the punters, their cash and the horses.

On-course bookmakers like Barry Dennis and Andy Smith are the latest of a lineage that stretches back to the early 19th century.

The key impetus towards the introduction of bookmaking was the emergence of the sweepstakes race which came to dominate the racing scene in place of the match race. Owners suddenly realised that they could 'hedge' against their horse losing by backing other horses in the race, so ensuring a profit no matter what the result. This method of insurance could only work, however, if there were other bettors to bet with. This system of an owner hedging against his horse losing by betting on other horses became known as 'betting round'.

(This terminology still exists today, and its explanation is at the heart of understanding what making a book is about. When making a book, bookmakers try to allow themselves a margin of profit – this is called betting 'over round' – that theoretically allows them to profit no matter what the result of a race.

Occasionally, a bookmaker has to bet 'over broke' to attract custom, and in that instance a punter should theoretically be able – provided he can work out the percentages and get his bets on in time – to make a profit by backing every horse in the race. Professional punters will always calculate the 'over round' percentage that a bookmaker is making, and will rarely bet if the 'over round' is ridiculously in the bookmaker's favour.)

Bookmakers came into being by offering this opportunity for owners to bet round. These early layers – men such as William Crockford, John Gully, Dennis O'Kelly and Dick England – appeared on racecourses towards the end of the 18th century. They were not yet bookmakers in the truest sense of the word, as they were as likely to profit from backing as from laying. The final impetus for bookmaking came from the establishment, in the last quarter of the 18th century and first decade of the 19th, of the great classic races which encouraged turfistes to back ante-post at Tattersall's when the horses were still yearlings. With ante-post betting came an opportunity for owners to continually hedge their positions; to do that they needed people prepared to lay odds about every horse in the race.

The father of modern bookmaking is generally accepted to be the Lancastrian William Ogden who, in 1790, became the first man to offer odds on all the horses in a particular race. He was quickly joined by men such as 'Crutch' Robinson and 'Facetious' Jemmy Bland, who recognised that sharp wits, a mathematical brain and some courage to lay long odds were the route to new-found wealth. Men such as Bland had mixed reputations: their success – Bland had a house on Piccadilly – inspired jealousy, and yet it was generally accepted that they were honest payers out. Ogden's faultless reputation was such that he was the only betting man ever admitted to the Jockey Club rooms at Newmarket. By the middle of the 19th century the terms 'the ring', to describe where bookmakers congregated, and 'bookmaker' or 'penciller' were in common use.

It is from these early years, no doubt, that the mixed reputation of modern bookmakers originates. On the one hand, men such as William 'Leviathan' Davies were admired for their mathematical felicity, for their guts in laying large bets and for the alacrity and honesty with which they paid out their losses. Leviathan was prepared to accept huge bets – he laid £50,000 to £1,000 against Lord Exeter's horse winning the 1850 Derby – and his integrity was beyond question. This was the description afforded to him by the *London News*: 'The sole and unassisted architect of his own fortune; gifted with a clear head and quick perception, calculating mind and most retentive memory, he has undoubtedly turned those natural endowments to the very best advantage, and he now shines forth in the sporting hemisphere as a star of no common magnitude; his unassuming deportment and unwavering probity of conduct during his career on the turf . . . have earned him "golden opinions" in every sense of the word.' Leviathan was one of the first bookmakers to post betting lists. He did so in two pubs in London, the Durham Arms in Serle Street and Barr's in Long Acre, and by 1850 his two shops were estimated to turn over somewhere in the region of £300,000 per annum.

Whilst a betting ticket from the Leviathan could be traded like a bank note, the activities of other bookmakers and betting shops gave bookmaking the kind of bad reputation that still exists today. In 1851, the betting shop Dwyer's faced a payout of £25,000 after it laid generous odds against a horse that won the Chester Cup that year. When punters arrived the next day to collect their winnings they found that the shop had been completely gutted. Partly as a result of such swindles, and because, as we have seen, attitudes towards gambling were starting to change, the government moved to make betting houses illegal in 1853 – and off-course cash betting remained illegal for another 107 years.

Bookmakers did not disappear, however. We have seen how working-class gamblers got around the prevailing anti-gambling sentiment and the anti-gambling legislation of the time. In order to bet they needed bookmakers. Street bookmakers began to emerge in the last three or four decades of the 19th century and although they were illegal they largely escaped the clutches of the law. A 'dogger-out' (lookout) would be posted in close proximity to a 'back-entry bookie' who would be working from a back yard of a terraced house. These dogger-outs would have a sophisticated signalling system to forewarn the bookie of an oncoming police raid. Often the bookies were tipped off, and in that case they might employ a so-called 'joey' to take the rap instead. The bookie would pay the joey's fine and the bookie would escape court action.

Street bookies survived partly because the police were unwilling to uphold such unpopular legislation and partly because they were a fundamental and accepted part of the local community. A successful pitch could bring in up to £100 a day and the bookie would be an important source of local employment. He employed a clerk, various runners, a dogger-out and a joey and paid house-wives for the use of a back yard. Many such jobs were given to the local unemployed, and so a street bookie would be seen as a benevolent employer. As we have seen, betting was a fundamental part of working-class existence and the street bookie was sustained by the community that needed him.

It was the introduction of competition, not prohibition, which caused the backstreet bookie to die out. The legalisation of betting shops in 1961 meant the end for many of them. Furtive betting was no longer necessary and those bookies who were not quick enough to recognise, or could not afford, the opportunities in a changed world died out. Gradually, big business came to dominate the off-course bookmaking scene. It is on-course layers like Dennis and Smith – rather than Ladbrokes, William Hill or Coral – who are the true descendants of William Ogden.

A punter wishing to back a horse on the first day of Glorious Goodwood doesn't have to bet in the ring with a bookie. He can bet with the Tote if he so wishes. The Tote was set up in June 1929 as a pool betting system of the type that operates in most other racing countries. As well as being able to place a win bet with the Tote, a punter can also bet a horse to place, or to win and place. He can also, and this is the most useful function of the Tote for serious punters, try his luck at the more exotic bets on offer, such as the Placepot, which pays out when a placed horse in every race is selected, or the Jackpot, when the punter must pick the winner of every race. Once the Tote has made its deductions for overheads and profit margins, then the rest of the money is shared out as a dividend between the number of winning tickets.

No serious punter, however, bets with the Tote, for two reasons: firstly, it works on the basis that the odds of a horse are determined by how much money is placed on that horse. So, at a small track a decent-sized bet on a horse of your fancy could seriously cramp its odds. It is true that on the big race days, when there is a considerable amount of money in the pool, it is less likely to happen, but even so when a punter places his bet with the Tote he has no idea of the odds on offer, as they are in constant flux and are only finally calculated when all the bets have been made. Secondly, most punters see themselves in an eternal battle against the bookie. This is a very personal duel, a matter of honour between the two that is reinforced by the knowledge that gambling debts are still irredeemable at law (the Gambling Act of 2005 recognised gambling debts at law, but this legislation does not come into effect until September 2007). Every punter is looking for an edge in the ring, the slightly better odds offered by Smith or Dennis or Sealey and Son, and it is this hustle and bustle that makes the ring an exciting but sometimes unpleasant place to be. So, because of the cramped conditions and the complete lack of deference in the ring, some small-time punters do prefer to bet with the Tote. It is simply a more comfortable, less stressful way to bet: the queues are smaller and more orderly, and the Tote booths are generally manned by inoffensive-looking pensioners rather than lairy bookies waiting to turn you over the moment your wits are slightly dulled. The ring is a rough, tough, masculine place to be.

And, in the betting ring, you do need your wits about you. For a start, there is a whole new language to contend with. 'Take the bottle out of it!' screams Andy Smith just before the second race of the day (meaning that he wants to reduce a horse from 2-1, pronto). Just before the last race, a representative from Hill's wanders over to Dennis. 'I'll have ten monkeys to five on Another Faux Pas.' Dennis nods. Moments later the man returns to check that Dennis has taken the bet. 'Yeah, ten monkeys to five Another Faux Pas,' Dennis shouts, with a slight note of irritation in his voice, as if to say 'Is my word not good enough?' It clearly is good enough, because ten monkeys represents £5,000 and not a note has changed hands. Dennis attracts much of the action, partly because he is a fearless layer, partly because his overbearing presence dominates the ring and partly because the mug punters have seen him on television and they fancy their chances of putting one over on him. Each punter is greeted with a bon mot. Before the first race, an Australian has £300 each way with Dennis on a horse called Tiger Tiger, and as quick as a flash Dennis announces that 'You know you can't bet each way in Australia, don't you!' The Australian went away chuckling but he didn't come back. Tiger Tiger finished down the field and his £600 finished in Dennis's bulging satchels.

Every mug punter – and 90 per cent of punters at the racetrack are mug punters – is prey for the hungry bookie. As Dennis says, 'There's less money swilling around than there used to be and the margins are much tighter. If a mug punter walks in the ring I want his money. The rest of the bookies don't really like me, they think I'm after all the money. And do you know what, they're right! They are shark-infested waters out there and you have to be ruthless. There's no camaraderie amongst the bookies in the ring. We're all after the same money. My ideal mug is a guy who's at the races with his mates, has a few bevvies and bets in hundreds. He's seen me on television and thinks he can give me a bloody nose. By the end of the day I'm the one usually offering the handkerchief.'

Dennis's lament for the good old days, when bets were bigger and punters numerous, is well illustrated today at Goodwood. Despite it being one of the major flat meetings of the year, the action is desultory. There is no need to fight the queues, because there are no queues. There are simply a few too many pitches chasing too little money. Watching the action and listening to the complaints of the bookies, it's not hard to reason where all the money has gone.

Looking down upon the goings-on in the ring, dry and comfortable and no doubt just a little smug, are Andrew Black and Edward Wray – the men behind the Betfair revolution. Both are dressed formally today, which is usual for Wray but not for Black, and both have the easy and relaxed air of men who have been through the difficulties of a start-up business and are now on the home straight to flotation. Since they are sponsoring the feature races of the afternoon, they have been afforded a large, airy hospitality box in which they are hosting thirty or so of their more important customers. The late Robin Cook is one of them. In the corner of the hospitality box is a cubicle housing three high-speed internet computers, so that if any of their customers want to bet on the racing, or anything else that day, there is no need to brave the outside elements. This is 21st-century betting: cool, clinical, comfortable and completely impersonal.

The irony that the most revolutionary shift in gambling for decades has come from the grandson of a fiercely anti-gambling politician, Sir Cyril Black, is not lost on Andrew Black. Not that he looks or sounds as though he regrets his role in setting up this cyberspace betting exchange; since he owns 15 per cent of the company, he is sitting on a potential fortune of anywhere up to £100 million if and when Betfair floats. Black's background is in mathematics, computers and gambling. He took – but didn't finish – a computer-science degree at Exeter University, and afterwards worked variously as a shelf stacker at B&Q, builder's labourer, derivatives modeller, computer software analyst for the Ministry of Defence and trader for City hedge fund Boxall. Gambling was a constant passion: he played bridge and backgammon semi-professionally and after a big win (£25,000) on the 'spring double' (the Lincoln and the Grand National) in 1992 he punted the horses fiercely. He recognised both that he wasn't good enough as a bridge player and that the horses bored him. 'When I got bored, I started losing money. But in any case, it was only ever about the money and when my father died that didn't seem enough any more. I wasn't creating anything, just starting out with a wad of money and ending up with a bigger or smaller wad.'

The death of Black's father, Tony, from pancreatitis and of his younger brother, Kevin, from a brain haemorrhage at 21 were the catalysts he needed to, as he puts it, 'get off my arse and do something with my life.' And it was whilst he was working at Boxall that the idea of a betting exchange first came to him. 'The impetus came from the New York stock exchange, really. I noticed that, unlike the London stock exchange, New York encouraged short-term trading. In New York you can ring your broker and say I want to buy a certain stock at a certain price and your bid simply gets posted on a board and anyone can come and match it. It was just a really efficient system.' Black's moment of genius was to recognise that such a system could be transplanted onto betting. 'The advent of the internet was crucial because it meant that there were no physical limitations and you could create a completely open marketplace. As soon as I thought of the idea I knew I was on to a winner.'

Even so, it took Black and Wray a considerable time to set up the business. Wray worked on the business plan, Black on the software – and at trying to persuade others that they had a winner. 'The problem was that it was a completely original idea. Venture capitalists like ideas that they can compare to other successful business models, but we had nothing to compare Betfair to. In the end, it was a company called Flutter.com that got all the money, about £36 million, whilst we were left to scrunt around for £1 million from our City mates. They are all glad they invested now.'

The success of the Betfair concept was immediate. 'We managed to double our turnover every month after the start-up. We launched in June 2000 and at the end of the first week we had turned over £35,000 of business. Within six weeks we had done £100,000 worth of business. We didn't have to raise any more capital until November of that year. By the time of our third round of financing in April 2001 we were turning over £1 million a week. By the end of that month it was £2 million. Our only real scare was when our competitor, Flutter.com, relaunched with the aim of knocking us out of the market. Funnily enough, there was an anonymous employee at Flutter, who sent emails under the name of "tin man", who kept us abreast of their moves. Their critical mistake was that they relaunched without "in-play" betting [betting on horses during the running of a race]. Eventually, we merged with them – although it was virtually a takeover on our behalf.' Now, Betfair have just under half a million subscribers; they have modern, sleek offices in Hammersmith with a young, tie-less, suit-less workforce of over 500 people, and business that last year turned over £50 million a week, with revenues of just under £70 million and profits of £13 million, accrued from the small rake they take from winning bets. The boom and bust of the internet has resulted in companies that dominate their particular area of the web: Google is the dominant search engine, eBay the dominant auction house, Amazon the dominant retailer, and Betfair has come to dominate betting on the internet – controlling an estimated 13 per cent of the entire global online betting market. Ironically, the bookmakers themselves tried to follow Betfair's example by setting up an online betting exchange called Betmart, but the greater liquidity in Betfair means that, for punters, there is only one choice.

Betfair is popular with punters for the simple reason that it offers them greater choice, greater flexibility and better value. Logging onto Betfair at the time of writing (October '05) there is a kaleidoscope of activities to bet on: American football, Australian rules, baseball, basketball, boxing, bridge, darts, ice hockey, trotting and volleyball, as well as the traditional range of sports. There are specials: Andrew Flintoff is trading at around 25-1 on to win the BBC Sports Personality of the Year award; you can get 4-1 on it being a white Christmas in London; if you think global warming is an immediate threat, you could put money, at 1000-1, on the October temperature nudging above 90 degrees, and just as unlikely a scenario, it seems, is David Davis for the Tory leadership – a weakening 6-1 shot. Punters can often get up to 20 per cent better prices on Betfair, because there is no bookmaker skimming the cream off the top. Not only that, but punters can also set their own prices. If you think a horse is a 6-1 shot, you can offer to back it at

6-1 or 13-2 if you're greedy, and wait for someone to match it. If it doesn't get matched, no harm done. It is as simple as that. And, of course, the pièce de résistance is that the punter can now play the role of bookie by offering to lay horses. Punters have complained for years that bookmaking is a licence to print money. Well, now they can do it, too. Black knew that his betting exchange, like most good ideas, was devastatingly simple and he could also see that it was the ultimate challenge to the established order. 'I knew it was the most disruptive thing for the betting industry – it drove a horse and cart through the whole bloody lot of it.'

During the first day of Glorious Goodwood, the Betfair effect is obvious. Andy Smith turns over £23,073 during the seven-race card, paying out £23,365 for a loss of £292 on the day. His biggest bet of the day is £800 at 9-4 on Mark Johnston's Prince of Light, which is a bullet dodged because it eventually wins at 7-2; his next biggest bet is £400 on Master Blaster.

The amount traded on Betfair, meanwhile, dwarfs the on-course boards bookmakers: £981,069 is matched for the first race; £19,697.21 for the second; a staggering £1,597,033.30 for the third; £89,677.12 for the fourth and £1,721,358.80 for the fifth. Follow the money, said Deep Throat, and you'll find the story. If you follow the money at the racetrack these days, there is only one conclusion to draw. Betfair is winning the battle.

Both Dennis and Smith are fully aware of the potential problems to their business posed by Betfair. 'Betfair has had a massive effect on our on-course bookmaking,' says Dennis. 'It's the middling punters, the £50 to £100 punters, who have deserted us. They no longer bother to come racing. We still get the big rollers, because there isn't the liquidity in Betfair to stand a big punter a twenty or thirty grand bet. And we still get the guys and families who go racing to enjoy a day out. I hope that we'll get the middling punters back. They might realise that it's more fun to come racing than sit in front of a computer screen, but to be honest they get better value on Betfair, so I'm not hopeful.' Andy Smith is equally pessimistic. 'I wasn't bothered about the exchanges at first because it became easier for us to hedge our prices, but now I'm losing all the money that bookmakers used to hedge with me. For example, if I went a bigger price in the ring, I'd get lots of hedging money from other bookies. I don't get that now – it all goes to Betfair.'

To illustrate Smith's point, a month after the Goodwood meeting William Hill announce that they will no longer hedge with on-course bookmakers, that they will hedge instead through the exchanges, using one of Betfair's competitors called Betdaq. Although little reported outside the *Racing Post*, this is a huge move and one that will have a significant effect on the smaller on-course bookie. Hill's chief executive explained the rationale behind the move: 'Racecourse bookmakers have been allowed to hedge directly into betting exchanges since September 2003 and many traditional bookmakers have been replaced by, or have developed into, operators who, in effect, act as mere commission agents for the exchanges . . . we'll save them the bother by using the exchanges directly.'

The effect of Betfair on Dennis's on-course business has been huge. 'In the glory days, after the liberalisation of the pitches and before the betting exchanges, I used to turn over £50,000 a day at a profit of 5 per cent. Now my average turnover is around £35,000 a day at a profit of 4 per cent.' Andy Smith has seen his business shrink from an annual turnover of £4.5 million to £2.75 million since the advent of the exchanges.

Like most savvy bookmakers, Dennis has not been standing idly by. He turns over a massive amount on Betfair himself – he put £15 million through their books last year alone. Whereas on-course bookmakers used to set the prices for each race, now they react to the morning's movements on Betfair, which means that there is even less good value at the track than there used to be. Dennis has two of his sons, Patrick and Daniel, wired up to Betfair and Betdaq, monitoring the price movements continually, with instant access should he need to 'get on', 'lay off' or simply help move the price in his favour. Because Dennis has such an important influence on course with his front-rank pitches, and because he puts a massive amount through Betfair, he is able to move markets in his favour. 'I use Betfair to hedge and cover my positions. I use it to my advantage. All's fair in love and war, isn't it? I'm not doing anything illegal. You've got to play the game as it confronts you. Betting exchanges have changed the face of betting and I'd be stupid to ignore them.'

Despite William Hill's decision to hedge with the exchanges, they, along with Ladbrokes and Coral, are still vociferously opposed to them. Bleating long and hard is a sure sign that they are worried about the future. Ever since it became clear to the leading bookmakers that Betfair and their ilk were not only here to stay, but to compete, they have launched a series of broadsides against them.

Leaving aside the possibility that the leading bookmakers might just be squealing because their historic monopoly is being challenged, they have three objections to the online betting exchanges: that they are illegal, that they are under-taxed, and that they promote corruption in racing. This is David Stevens, a spokesperson for Coral, in 2003: 'If I were to go into a pub and take bets from people, I'd be breaking the law, but if I do the same thing on the internet via a betting exchange, it's legal. We think this is a massive discrepancy.' Not, Stevens emphasised, that they want to ban betting exchanges, merely that they want a 'level playing field'. In other words, they wanted those who lay horses on the exchanges treated as bookmakers, and taxed as such. As Warwick Bartlett, chairman of the Association of British Bookmakers, said when giving evidence to the Joint Committee on the Draft Gambling Bill in 2004: 'What concerns us is that the people who are on the exchanges are not licensed and people are making a living out of taking bets and laying bets on the exchanges without paying any tax or levy.'

So far, Betfair have won the battle, if not the war. In the 2003 Budget, the Chancellor announced that online betting exchanges would be charged a tax on gross profits of 15 per cent, rather than having the punter's individual profits taxed.

The corruption argument is more blurred. I, for one, imagine that the onset of the exchanges has increased the scope for corruption, now that anybody can make money from a horse losing. That is potential dynamite for owners, trainers and the like. Chris Bell, the spokesperson for Ladbrokes, said last year: 'At least a race a day, if not more, is now being corrupted by the availability of laying horses to lose on betting exchanges.' David Harding, the chief executive of William Hill, called the exchanges 'carte blanche for skulduggery'. The *Racing Post* refused to accept any advertising from Betfair during their first three months because of this concern.

It is obviously true that there is now more scope for profiting by horses losing rather than winning, and that represents an opportunity for some. Betfair's argument is that their trail of bets is much more transparent than that of high-street bookmakers. Anybody can go into a bookmakers and place a large bet and no one would be the wiser where that money has come from. On Betfair, the trail of money can be followed. To that end, Betfair have signed agreements with the Jockey Club and the Football Association to monitor unusual betting patterns and pass them on. Andrew Black says that they willingly pass on information about certain accounts to the Jockey Club. Black is clearly troubled by the accusations of fraud. For that reason he refuses to allow his employees to bet whilst at work: 'I look at us exactly as I would look at the stock exchange. We have to be whiter than white. Sometimes we get privileged information here and so I don't think it is right that we should be taking advantage of that.'

What of the future? The good news for punters, who have been liberated by the Betfair revolution, is that the exchanges are here to stay. Bookmakers continue to bleat, which means it must be hurting. They are a powerful enemy and will continue to lobby against the exchanges. Should they succeed in bringing about more punitive taxation, Betfair will simply move abroad.

The high-street chains of William Hill, Ladbrokes and Coral will continue to flourish, moving as they are into other areas of gambling and other revenue streams. The bigger, smarter on-course bookmakers, like Barry Dennis, will also survive because people still enjoy racing and enjoy the battle of wits that betting with a bookmaker provides. I imagine, though, that over time the ring will continue to contract in size. Smaller on-course book-makers will simply succumb to market forces and to the age of technology. Instead of laying bets at the track they may simply stay at home and lay bets on their computer. If you can't beat 'em, join 'em.

DAVE NEVISON
The Horse Player

Tonbridge Wells – nice, polite, leafy and conservative with a big and small 'c' – is not the place you might expect to find a professional horse player, but in its midst lives one of the best known: Dave Nevison is a forty-something former currency trader who has been living off the horses for thirteen years now. And living off them well. Each year that he has gambled professionally he has made more money than the last, culminating in £250,000 profit (tax-free profit at around 7 per cent of turnover) in 2004. 'It's been going so well,' he says, 'I wondered how it was going to last.' The answer is: it hasn't. This year, although profitable (£80,000 to the good so far), has been a bad year and when I visit in November 2005 he is in the middle of a three-month losing streak. It's the longest losing streak he can remember.

When I first contacted Nevison, back in the early summer of 2005, I envisaged a day out at the track, following his tips, checking out his modus operandi and working out what separated the successful pro from the rest of the mugs. By the time I got back in contact, in the autumn, Nevison had made the decision to abandon the racetrack completely – he has not abandoned betting on horses, you understand, but he is no longer betting on site. He is betting from the front room of his flat in Tonbridge Wells.

For someone who has been addicted to the colour, the noise, the excitement and the buzz of the racetrack for the last thirteen years, it has been a seismic decision. 'It's no longer where the action is,' he explains. 'It's sad, really, because I love going racing. I love the adrenalin and the buzz, but for some time now I've spent most of my time at the racetrack with a phone clamped to my ear. I had virtually stopped betting with the on-course bookmakers.'

Not that Nevison has a bad relationship with the bookies. He is friendly with many of them and there is a high level of mutual trust – although he says he never forgets the fact that they want his money and he wants theirs. It's not even that he struggles to get bets on with them. He uses 'satellite' accounts, that is, accounts under false names. For a while he even managed to piggyback onto a high-rolling, losing punter – 'the perfect combination,' he says, because it enables the pro to camouflage his bets.

Now, he no longer bets with the bookies because, he says, 'The action is on the exchanges.' The irony is not lost on him: thirteen years after welcoming the redundancy package that was offered to him as a currency trader in the City, and thirteen years after making a lifestyle choice to enjoy fresh air rather than an office, he has now swapped one computer terminal for another.

His betting life began when he was four years old. Whilst his father liked an occasional punt on the horses – 'the Grand National, the Derby, that kind of thing' – it was his grandfather who really had the bug and who passed it on to his grandson. 'I remember my grandfather and others sitting around for hours discussing the football pools – it was a ritual in our family and one that involved serious form study. I can't remember my first bet but I reckon virtually every shilling of my pocket money used to go on the horses. If it's not an addiction by now, then it's certainly an affliction – a lifelong affliction. It is my only interest, really. I don't bet on anything else.'

He hated his career in the City, doing all that was possible to ensure that when the redundancies started to hit home, he would be among the first to be offered one. 'At that stage I was a Timeform and Pricewise punter,' he says, doffing his cap towards the 'bible' of form books, set up by the legendary horse-racing form student Phil Bull, and to the influential tipping column in the *Racing Post* that highlights horses at big prices. 'There is obviously a synergy between trading and gambling and I've always been a risk taker. But all the city did was to give me money to punt, and the small successes I had along the way fuelled the dream that I could gamble for a living. When the sack came [11 November 1993], I was determined to give it a go.'

It was a case of learning the ropes of professional gambling as he went along. 'At first I was very selective and very disciplined, because that is what I had always read about the pros. That is how I thought I had to be. It took me a while to realise that the psychology of a gambler is essential to how he must bet. It was no good for me to travel all the way up to Sedgefield for one bet and for my horse to fall at the first fence. Temperamentally I wasn't suited to that kind of gambling and that kind of discipline. Now if I go for half an hour without a bet, I reckon there's something wrong.

'I'm an action junkie. I need to bet. So I worked out a system whereby I could bet on most races, often betting on four or five horses in a race. What I do now [and the similarity to Alan Woods's methods is striking, if less systematic] is price up a race without looking at the odds in the *Racing Post*. I accord every horse what I think is its true probability of winning. Then, when I see a discrepancy in the price that is offered, I have a bet. It's quite indiscriminate and I fire a lot of bullets, many of which miss their target. But as long as my form study is sound I should win eventually. It is punting according to the price of a horse, not according to whether I think it will win or not.'

Does he rely just on his form study, or does he have contacts inside the industry as well? 'To be honest, I ignore everything that those who are "in the know" tell me. For one, they are usually wrong; secondly, if they fancy a horse, then that information is usually built into the price. I do have horses with one stable and I know their horses inside out – but of course I pay for that information through training fees.'

How does he decide how much to bet? 'It's not that systematic. Now that I've been in the game a long time, I rely on gut instinct and feel as much as anything else. I've had as much as £5,000 each way on a horse – although that is about my limit – but I need to bet at a certain level, otherwise it's simply not worth my while. At the end of the day, it's my living: I've got an ex-wife and kids to feed [gambling, like professional sport, seems to take a heavy toll on private lives] and expenses to pay, so it's no good backing a horse to win £100. But ultimately I'm not playing to become a multi-millionaire, I'm playing to be able to stay in the game. I love it.'

Nevison's betting has changed in the last four years since he has started working in partnership with a trader from the spread-betting firm IG Index. 'It's taken me a long time to realise the benefits of a partnership: I guess it's having a shoulder to cry on when that 25-1 shot loses by a short head; it's having a like-minded soul to chat to for those miserable nights in Southwell in the depths of winter; it's good to have someone else to look at my form study dispassionately, and it helps coping with long losing runs. The theory is that we shouldn't both be cold at the same time – although it's happening right now for the first time. Basically, I do the form study and work out the probabilities and he scours the markets for opportunities. We trust each other implicitly, which is of course vital.

'It has also meant that we can pool our resources, which enables us to ply more money into the exotic bets like the Tote Jackpot and the Scoop6. We won a £240,000 Jackpot at Haydock last year. I find those bets offer good value because there is a lot of "mug money" around. As a pro, it pays to play where the mugs play.'

Just as Nevison finishes espousing the benefits of two pairs of eyes instead of one the phone rings and it is his partner asking for the day's probabilities. The racing today is at Southwell (flat) and Warwick (jumps). Nevison gives his odds for the first couple of races. The conversation is short and to the point and devoid of any niceties whatsoever.

It is time to see the pro in action. He has two computer screens set up at his desk, which face a widescreen television built into the wall. The *Racing Post* and form books are scattered on the floor. The racing at Southwell is what is called banded racing – that is, it is the worst-quality racing in Britain. As a result, Nevison is working on betting around £1,000 a race, which, he says, would double or treble on a normal racing day and be even bigger at one of the major meetings like Cheltenham or Ascot. The first race at 1.10 is the 'Bet On Champions League Football @ Betdirect Banded Stakes', worth just over £400 more to the winner than the amount Nevison is planning to stake on the race. 'Jesus Christ,' he says, 'I could pick up the whole of this field for about £600. They're so bad they can hardly pick one foot up in front of the other.' Action is action, though, and Nevison punts around £1000 on four horses called Mind Alert, Beamsley Beacon, Amanda's Lad and Blendon Belle. His computer screen shows those four horses in green (potential profit) and the rest of the field in red (potential losses). A horse called Largs wins from Empress Josephine and Nevison's losing streak continues.

There is little sign of irritation or disappointment, though. As he said, he fires a lot of bullets and not that many hit the target. He is, he says, a good loser and a magnificent winner – one who tends to celebrate a big win in style.

Over to Warwick for the 1.20 where the mounts of Richard Johnson and Tony McCoy are dominating the betting in a seven-runner handicap chase. 'They bet 5-2 and 9-4 and I'm backing both, which means I'm backing to about 7-4 on the two of them combined. I don't like my strategy, but I can't see anything else in the race.' A horse called Romany Dream wins with Jupon Vert second. McCoy and Johnson nowhere. Nevison announces that it is his seventeenth straight losing bet.

Southwell 1.40: another desperate contest full of hopeless horses. Nevison sees five horses whose odds are greater than his calculated probabilities. One horse, Ice and Fire, he thinks should be priced up at around 50-1. The odds at the track are shown at 80-1. On Betfair, Nevison sees that Ice and Fire is offered at 150-1. There is not much liquidity in the market but he manages to put on £30 at 150-1. The other four horses are all potential winners for him, to around £1,500. Around the last bend, Ice and Fire is upsides the favourite and going well. I look towards Nevison, whose eyes are widening as he starts to rise from his chair. Ice and Fire wins at a scarcely believable 150-1. It nets Nevison the best part of £4,500, and ends his seventeen-race losing streak. It is, he says, his second biggest win (in terms of odds) ever. He once had a 300-1 winner.

The purity of the exchanges – man to man betting – means of course that whilst Nevison has won £4,500 somebody else has lost that same amount. Does it bother him? 'I would much prefer to see the whites of someone's eyes when I bet and I'd prefer to be taking that money off a bookie at the track. But what kind of person offers those odds? Why would anyone risk losing £4,500 to win a curry and a couple of pints? No one, I reckon. I think that is money put there by a "robot" to balance out someone's book. And if it's a robot, then I certainly don't have any qualms.'

The presence of robots – computers designed to clean up any discrepancies in the market – has long been a feature of the financial markets. Nevison thinks they are present, or soon will be, on the horse-racing markets. Therein, he says, is the danger of the exchanges. 'There can be no argument against the exchanges. It is the perfect way of betting. I want to bet, you want to bet and we'll meet at a fine margin of around 100 per cent, less Betfair's rake. When the bookies argue against it, it is purely out of self-interest. Having said that, we are very close now to a perfect betting market, where every race is being played out at around 100 per cent [i.e. if you backed every horse in the race, you would neither win nor lose]. I believe the exchanges have the most sophisticated players, robots and all. In a perfect market you should never lose, but you'll find it very difficult to win. I'd much rather be a shareholder in Betfair than a punter right now.'

No doubt, had he been at Southwell, Nevison would have celebrated his 150-1 win long and hard. Instead, as the sun streamed through the windows of his flat in Tonbridge Wells, a phone call to his partner was the only way of sharing his joy and sharing his addiction-cum-affliction. Financially, Nevison has probably made a sound and sensible decision to quit the racetrack. I don't think, though, that it suits his temperament at all – and, as he said himself, understanding your temperament is the key to knowing how to bet. I'd say it's odds on that Dave Nevison will soon be back at the racetrack.

8

SAY IT AIN'T SO, HANSIE

'Everything is spoilt when money puts its ugly nose in.'

Mary Russell Mitford

In 1975, a completely different kind of betting revolutionised the face of gambling – a revolution which, while it had major advantages in the financial field, would come to have grave consequences for a sport that had marketed itself on notions of fair play, honesty and integrity. Stuart Wheeler had been amused by the possibility of becoming a bookmaker, but never expected to be one until, sacked from his merchant banker job for picking too many dud shares, he did indeed become a bookmaker. But Wheeler was no East End barrow boy; he was a bridge- and poker-playing Old Etonian, and the type of bookmaking firm he founded was as far removed from the traditional image as he was from the traditional bookie. (The only similarity was profit. Spread betting, like traditional bookmaking, proved to be a licence to print money: Wheeler sold his shares for nearly £40 million in 2003.) When he set up IG Index in 1974 with £30,000 (only £300 of it his own money), spread betting on financial movements was born. A quarter of a century later, cricket was to face its gravest crisis. The two events were directly linked.

In 1974, due to strict Exchange Control regulations, the buying and selling of bullion in England was prohibited, except on a very disadvantageous basis. Wheeler recognised, however, that there was nothing to prevent anybody from *betting* on its price movements. With that in mind, IG Index (IG stands for 'Investors Gold') was born. Soon, Wheeler widened the net of opportunity for gamblers so that they could bet on the movements of other commodities and, later, stock-market indices.

What Wheeler wasn't offering was a traditional bet, a fixed-odds bet. A fixed-odds bet would offer a punter the chance to bet, for example, 10-11 on the price of gold going up, and even money on it going down. The fixed-odds punter knew his potential profit or loss. What Wheeler was offering was a *spread* bet on the price of gold. So, if IG Index offered gold at, say, 150–155 (actually the dollar price per ounce of gold), a gambler could decide to buy (go long) or sell (go short). If he sold, say, £10 for every movement of 1 on the price at 150, and the price fell to 120, he would have made 30 (150 minus 120) times £10, a profit of £300. If, however, the price rose to 185, then he would have lost 35 units (185 minus 150) times £10, a loss of £350. Simple – but, given the volatility of the markets, far more risky (and potentially far more rewarding) than a fixed-odds bet.

Despite the risks, spread betting offered serious advantages to the financial bettor. Crucially, because this was betting and not trading, any winnings were free of tax. Wheeler had sought clarification from tax counsel before he set up IG Index, to ensure that spread betting was likely to obtain the same tax-free status as normal betting. The Chancellor of the Exchequer's main concern was to make sure that the Exchequer was not a significant loser. It became clear that the punters' losses were likely to exceed their gains and so it suited the Chancellor to maintain the tax-free status of spread betting. Otherwise, if there were more losers than winners, the Exchequer would be faced with too many spread bettors being able to offset their losses against tax. There were other advantages. As bookmakers, IG Index could keep longer hours than the stock exchange; it opened up the market to the smaller punter; and there was far less paperwork floating around than if you were dealing with a traditional broker. But its tax-free status was the main advantage.

Spread betting on financials was initially for the minority. It received more prominence when the price of gold shot up from about $150 an ounce to $850 an ounce during the Iran-Iraq war in 1980. On the back of that, the great stock-market boom of the early to mid-1980s, along with the Conservative policies to deregulate and privatise, encouraged more and more people to invest in the stock market. Spread betting's day had arrived.

Soon, other firms, such as City Index and Cantor Index, joined Wheeler's revolution, and when Sporting Index joined the fray, offering spread betting on sport, it was clear that spread betting had reached the mainstream. Spreads could be offered on various elements of all sports: the number of minutes before the first corner in a football match, or the number of lengths separating the first and second in a horse race, for instance.

One thing, though, is certain: there has never been a better sport for spread betting than cricket. With the number of variables on offer, it is a marriage made in heaven. Traditional win, lose or draw bets are now accompanied by a whole host of alternatives. During the Ashes series in 2005, markets were offered on anything from the number of runs a batsman would score, to the number of wickets a bowler would take, the number of appeals in an innings and the number of boundaries hit. Sporting Index took 123,000 bets during the five-Test series and was thankful for the unexpectedly poor performance of the Australian team, which wrong-footed many punters. 'Overall,' said Sporting Index's spokesman, Wally Pyrah, 'the company made enough money to hire the *QEII*, sail to Australia and have a barbecue on Bondi Beach.'

Now that profits could be made from the performance of

individual players, rather than the performance of the whole team, it also meant that the scope for fraud was dramatically increased. When you add human weakness and greed to the perfect marriage of spread betting and cricket it is a potent mixture.

It is a dictum of a number of gamblers – Richie Benaud amongst them – that you should 'never bet on anything that can talk'. The implication, of course, is that human beings, unlike animals, are inherently crooked and therefore bad betting propositions. But if the history of gambling tells us anything, it is that the maxim should be changed to 'never bet on anything that can be influenced by anything that can talk'. And if you take that to its ultimate conclusion, you would never have a bet at all.

Match-fixing in sport is the ultimate betrayal. In sport, we make assumptions about the players we watch – that they are absolutely committed to give of their best, and we make assumptions about the game – that it begins on a level playing field and that the best team will win out. Even in horse racing, a sport where the great stings are talked of in reverential terms and 'gambling' trainers are looked up to, fixing is regarded as beyond the pale. A number of British jockeys are currently under investigation. If convicted, the punters' reaction will be far removed from the nod-nod-wink-wink type of reaction that accompanies a good old-fashioned sting.

There was no greater betrayal than when Arnold Rothstein paid eight of the Chicago White Sox team to throw the World Series against the Cincinnati Reds in 1919. Has there ever been a more poignant image than the ten-year-old fan who, tears streaming down his face, confronted the great 'Shoeless' Joe Jackson and said to him: 'Say it ain't so, Joe! Please say it ain't so!' It must have been a heart-breaking moment for the young boy, and for Shoeless Joe who, in that instant, must have known the scale of his betrayal. Although the eight White Sox were acquitted, they were banned from baseball for life.

The cricket world faced its own 'Say it ain't so, Joe' moment on Friday, 7 April 2000. I was at Fenner's, Cambridge University's historic cricket ground, playing against my old university, and it just so happened to be the first day of a new season, a day that is usually associated with freshness and optimism. Except this day was to be different – and not just because I had been bowled out for eight by Charlie Pimlott, the son of my local butcher. Sometime during the day, I was approached by Peter Mitchell, the deputy sports editor of the *Sunday Telegraph*, who told me that the Delhi police had released tapes which claimed that the South African captain, Hansie Cronje, and a number of his team-mates were involved in match-fixing. A random phone tap set up by detective Ishwar Singh Redhu, to look into complaints of extortion against certain Delhi businessmen, would eventually reveal the cancer that had been eating away at international cricket for the best part of two decades.

When the Delhi police released the tapes on 7 April, on which Cronje could be heard discussing business with Sanjay Chawla, a well-known bookmaker, the reaction of the cricketing world was generally dismissive. Partly, this was because one South African journalist claimed to have heard the tapes and said that the voice was not that of Cronje. (In fact, the tapes at this stage were under lock and key and the journalist had only heard Indian actors reading transcripts of the tapes.) Mainly, though, it was down to the fact that the allegations were against Hansie Cronje – the upstanding, God-fearing, self-righteous captain of South Africa – who was the embodiment, supposedly, of all that was good in the Rainbow Nation, the recently cleansed South Africa. It struck me at the time that the incredulity of the cricket community said much about the ingrained prejudice of certain parts of the cricketing world. The suspicion was that Indian detectives were about as competent as Inspector Clouseau – although throughout the match-fixing crisis it was the Indian police who proved to be the most thorough and zealous of them all. And as other cricketers had already admitted to taking money from bookmakers for information – notably Mark Waugh and Shane Warne, who themselves had accused Salim Malik, the Pakistan captain, of offering money to fix matches – the allegations against Cronje should not have come as a bolt from the blue. Had the accused been black, coloured, Muslim or Hindu, would the reaction have been so dismissive? I doubt it. The fact is that Cronje was white and middle-class and Christian – with an almost unblemished reputation. (Cronje had, in fact, been up before the cricketing beak on a couple of earlier occasions, when he was accused of being over-zealous in trying to win matches, not trying to throw them.) Cronje and match-fixing? It was like hearing the Pope had been caught in a brothel.

The incredulity was also based on a mythical view of cricket itself: cricket as the noble game, and cricketers as the most noble of sportsmen. This myth was propagated by Victorian writers on the game and none more so than the game's first historian, the Reverend James Pycroft, in his classic *The Cricket Field*, published in 1851. The second chapter of *The Cricket Field* is entitled 'The General Character of Cricket', and it is this chapter that is as responsible as anything for the propagation of the myth of cricket as the epitome of competitive games. Here is a flavour: 'Certainly there is something highly intellectual in our noble and national pastime. But the cricketer must possess other qualifications; not only physical and intellectual, but moral qualifications also.' And: 'Such a national game as cricket will both humanise and harmonise the people. It teaches a love of order, discipline and fair play for the pure honour and glory of victory.' And: 'For the most part, there is little to ruffle the temper, or to cause unpleasant collision, that there is no place so free from temptation – no such happy plains or lands of innocence – as our cricket-fields.'

It was Pycroft's work which gave rise to the phrase 'It's not cricket'. Of the quick bowler Harvey Fellows, Pycroft wrote, 'We will not say that anything he does is not cricket, but certainly it is anything but play.' Soon the phrase 'It's not cricket' had become an accepted part of the lexicon, appearing in the *Oxford English Dictionary* in 1867.

Gradually the myth developed of a game with institutionalised high moral standards. Soon, this extended beyond the boundaries of the game itself, so that cricket became a metaphor for the British way of life itself. By 1921, Lord Harris was able to claim, proudly, that cricket represented the value system of a whole nation: the phrase 'It's not cricket', he said, was 'in constant use on the platform, in the pulpit, parliament, and the press, to dub something as not being fair, not honourable, not noble. What a tribute for a game to have won!'

A dozen years later, the manager of the MCC tour to Australia, Sir Pelham Warner, was quick to espouse these very British notions of fair play: 'The very word "cricket" has become synonymous for all that is true and honest. To say "that is not cricket" is to imply something underhand, something not in keeping with the best ideals . . . The aim of the MCC . . . in sending teams to all parts of the world is to spread the gospel of British fair play as developed in its national sport.' (The 1932–33 tour was, of course, the Bodyline tour – a tour which nearly caused a complete breakdown of diplomatic relations between England and Australia on account of the desire of the England captain, Douglas Jardine, to win at all costs, even if it meant offending the spirit of the game.) This juxtaposition between Victorian-inspired ideals and pre-Victorian (and late 20th century) reality has been a constant source of conflict: the spirit of the game is still the first port of call for some, and an anachronistic irritation to others.

Pycroft's book was written, in fact, as a part-celebration of the fact that cricket had managed to cleanse itself. 'Constant betting,' he complained, 'will take the honesty out of any man.' The second quarter of the 19th century onwards was a period in which gambling was on the retreat in the face or a withering attack by Victorian moralists, and Pycroft's paean was written at a time when cricket had expurgated itself of gamblers, blacklegs, book-makers and match-fixers. But it was the gambling and subsequent match-fixing which came first and then the cleansing, not the other way around.

Cricket developed as a rural game, growing in popularity after the Restoration of 1660, much like other rural pursuits of the time: cockfighting, bear-baiting, dog-fighting and cudgel fighting. All were convenient games to have a bet on and cricket was no different. And yet there are few records of cricket before 1700, partly because it was still a game for the rural poor rather than a game for the aristocracy and the gentry, as it soon became, and partly because the sums staked were so small as to attract little outside interest.

This soon changed when the aristocracy and the gentry took guard in the 18th century. It is no surprise that cricket failed to escape their enthusiasm for a bet. There is some argument amongst the game's historians as to the degree to which the aristocracy got involved out of a desire to gamble. For Derek Birley, author of *A Social History of English Cricket*, aristocratic involvement was down to nothing more than its penchant for gambling; for David Underdown, author of *Start of Play*, the gambling was less im-portant. The aristocracy, he says, actually enjoyed the game for what it was, and in cricket they saw certain characteristics – leadership, manliness and courage – that reflected their own view of themselves. What is certain is that cricket was a perfect vehicle for gambling, that gambling was the dearest enthusiasm of the most important patrons of the game, and that the game would not have spread so far and so quickly had it not been for this happy combination.

We have already seen that weird and wonderful individual wagers were de rigueur for the 18th-century aristocracy, and cricket saw its fair share. The 4th Earl of Tankerville, a man who was as responsible as any for drawing the famous players of Hambledon village into the metropolis of London, once bet £100 that his gardener, the famous bowler 'Lumpy' Stevens, could land a ball on a feather that had been placed upon a length. Lumpy won the wager for his employer. In 1757 the degenerate gambler Lord March bet that he could convey a letter a certain distance in a certain amount of time. He won his bet by enclosing the letter in a cricket ball, which was then despatched by cricketers throwing the ball at fixed distances. The spirit of gaming, then, provided some stimulation to the sport in its early development.

Some of the game's best-known patrons were gamblers of some notoriety. John Sackville, the 3rd Duke of Dorset, was one such. Dorset was a *bon vivant* who spent a considerable amount of time, and considerable sums, in White's and Almack's. He was a close friend of the infamous Duchess of Devonshire, who described him as 'the most dangerous of men'. Given Georgiana's recklessness when it came to gambling, we may assume that Dorset was no shrinking violet himself. Dorset liked to play cricket as well as gamble on it, unlike another gambling aristocratic patron, the Earl of Winchelsea. Winchelsea liked to bet rather than play, and his accounts for 1792 reveal winnings of £218 on various matches that year. Sir Horace Mann completed this triumvirate of aristocratic patrons who were so important to cricket of the Hambledon era. Mann was an inveterate gambler who was forced to sell his estate at Bishopsbourne – where he staged great matches (one such in

1772 between Kent and Hambledon attracted 20,000 spectators and much gambling) – to pay his gambling debts. The size of the stakes between teams was surprisingly large – often the big matches would be played for 500 or 1,000 guineas a side – although it has to be remembered that tales of big bets and their resultant winnings were as prone to exaggeration then as they are today.

This desire to gamble on the game had a clear influence on its development. Before the laws of the game were standardised, most big matches had Articles of Agreement drawn up so that gambling disputes could be easily settled. One such to have survived was the agreement between the Duke of Richmond's XI and Mr A. Brodrick's XI in 1727. The excessive details of the Articles can only be explained by the wagers that were to be staked on the game (although in this case they are relatively small). ''Tis lawful,' the Articles say, 'for the Duke of Richmond to choose any Gamesters who have played in either of his Grace's last two matches with Sir William Gage; and 'tis lawful for Mr Brodrick to choose any Gamesters within three miles of Pepperhowe.' It goes on to say that 'twelve gamesters shall play on either side; that each match should be for twelve guineas of each side.' The description 'gamesters' implied, of itself, that the match was for more than mere pride or honour.

Seventeen years later, in 1744, a number of gentlemen drew up the first version of the laws of the game in the Star and Garter pub in Pall Mall. Individual Articles of Agreement had become redundant. Now there was a common set of laws upon which all gaming disputes could be settled. Such a move was entirely necessary, because of the increasing amount of gambling associated with the game. That same year, the *Morning Chronicle* complained against the 'excessive gaming and public dissipation' and the fact that 'cricket matches are now degenerated into business of importance'. As with cricket, so with prizefighting and horse racing, sports whose first regulations were also drawn up principally with gambling disputes in mind.

The presence of bookmakers at cricket matches was the clearest indication of the public's desire to spice up their entertainment with a bet or two, for bookmakers came into being in response to the public's (and, it later transpired, the players') enthusiasm for gambling, not the other way around. Their presence was also the first warning sign that all might not be what it appeared on the field of play itself. Pycroft tells us that 'Jim and Joe Bland, of turf notoriety' were often to be seen at the big games. 'Silver Billy' Beldham, one of the greatest of early batsmen from Surrey, was surely too naive for his own good when he recalled the presence of those two indefatigable bookmakers-cum-gamblers, William Crockford and John Gully, at Lord's simply enjoying the game. Silver Billy did remember, however, how easy it was to bet on the big games: 'If gentlemen wanted to bet, just under the pavilion sat men ready, with money down, to give and take the current odds.' Mary Russell Mitford complained in 1823 of men who 'make the noble game of cricket an affair of bettings and hedgings and, maybe, of cheatings.'

And so it was, in the last years of the 18th century and the early years of the 19th, that cricket faced its first match-fixing crisis. Recalling the golden years of the Hambledon village team (1750–80), John Nyren was adamant that 'tricking and crossing' were then unknown and that the game was clean. Hambledon players certainly seemed to value their club's high reputation. In a match against Surrey in 1775, two Hambledon supporters bet heavily against their club only for their wager to be lost by a large second-innings partnership between Nyren and another fine Hambledon player, John Small. When the supporters complained of their losses, Nyren was supposed to have said, in some indignation, 'Another time, don't bet your money against such men as we!'

Match-fixing really came to the fore in the early years of the 19th century. In an interview with Pycroft, 'Silver Billy' Beldham recalled those grim years: 'Matches were bought and matches were sold and gentlemen who meant honestly lost large sums of money, till the rogues beat themselves at last.' Beldham even admitted to playing his part in one fixed match in Nottingham because he had lost money in another fixed match just before. 'Of this roguery,' he said, 'nobody ever suspected me.' But he continued, 'Many a time I have been blamed for selling when as innocent as a babe. In those days, when so much money was on matches, every man who lost his money would blame someone.' The game had become institutionally corrupt. Beldham recalled one single-wicket match played at Lord's in which the men on both sides had been got at: the bowler refused to bowl straight and the batsman refused to try to hit the ball. The game ground to a halt. 'Gambling and honesty don't often go together,' he complained.

The high-water mark of cricket's first match-fixing crisis came in 1817, when one of the great players of the day, William Lambert, was found guilty of match-fixing and was banned from ever playing at the home of cricket again. The MCC was forced to act before cricket went the same way as prizefighting, which had declined as a sport under the weight of corruption, and bookmakers were banned from Lord's in the early 1820s, not to return for over 150 years.

Betting and corruption were not removed overnight, but the tide against gambling had turned. The development of cricket mirrored the relationship between gambling and society. It developed so quickly and so widely because of the gambling craze that afflicted 18th-century England. Its very existence was then threatened when corruption, which some would say was the inevitable result of that craze, began to dominate. Its survival, and subsequent makeover into a noble, virtuous game, can only be understood in the wake of the cleansing of the game in the Victorian age, at a time when gambling generally was under attack.

To be fair to the *Sunday Telegraph*'s cricket correspondent, Scyld Berry, he was almost alone in giving the tapes of the Delhi police the credence they deserved. Berry is a brilliant essayist with an aversion to hard news. Suddenly, though, the thought that the game he cherished was corrupt and that he, like the rest of us, had been duped all along transformed him into a journalistic bloodhound who, over the coming months, did as much as any journalist to chase the scent and stench of corruption.

The match that finally exposed the sorry situation was a game I played in. England's last Test match of the 1999 South African tour was, in hindsight, the perfect vehicle for corruption. The series had already been won by South Africa 2–0, and so the final match at Centurion Park was a 'dead' match. Rain had prevented any play for three out of the first four days. When the weather finally relented, the odds on the draw were obviously prohibitively short. Shrewd punters who had seen the forecast were on to a good thing and the bookmakers faced massive liabilities on the draw. Given that the draw was offered at such short odds, the odds on either England or South Africa winning the match were correspondingly long.

It was the thought of such enticing odds that persuaded a South African gambler called Marlon Aronstam to call on the South African captain on the fourth evening of that Test match. Aronstam planned to back both teams to win at large odds, provided that he could persuade Cronje to influence the England captain, Nasser Hussain, to make a game of it. Aronstam's motivation is clear. What about Cronje's? Cronje, we now know, was already caught up in a web of intrigue and deceit that had been going on for the best part of half a decade. He compared his actions to those of an alcoholic who couldn't resist the temptations of one final drink. There was also the added incentive of a bit of ready cash. Aronstam gave Cronje 53,000 rand (about £5,000) plus a leather jacket for his wife. It seems astonishing that Cronje would agree to risk so much for so little money with a man he had only just met. The cash was a mere aperitif, though – a down-payment for later: that evening Cronje agreed with Aronstam to see what he could do to manipulate his team's forthcoming triangular one-day matches against England and Zimbabwe and then on the upcoming tour of India. It was a fortnight later, during a one-day international in Durban against Zimbabwe, that Cronje met Chawla and received, amongst other things, the mobile phone that was to bring about his downfall.

On the fourth evening of the final Test at Centurion, then, the bait had been offered by Aronstam and the trap was set. All that remained was to persuade Hussain to play ball. This proved harder than Cronje might have imagined. Hussain, and England's coach Duncan Fletcher, are naturally conservative by nature. They might also have been suspicious of Cronje, a man who also had a reputation for giving away as little as possible on the cricket field, and worried about the fact that the pitch had been under the covers for the best part of three days. Cronje's initial offering that England should forfeit their first innings and then chase 270 in seventy-three overs was spurned. Cronje's 'generosity' knew no bounds that day, and after protracted negotiations it was agreed that England would chase 249 in seventy-six overs – a remarkably generous offering.

The travelling English fans were ecstatic that they were to be treated to a competitive match when, arriving at the ground, all they might have expected was two teams going through the motions at the end of a long and tiring five-match series. Cronje, a captain long criticised for his negativity, was now lauded in the press as a man who was prepared to put the interests and the spirit of the game before winning and losing.

Cronje would later defend himself by arguing that he did his utmost to try to win the match for South Africa. Indeed, he was trying. But, and this is where the match-fixing is undeniable, if it became obvious that South Africa couldn't win, Cronje was going to do his utmost to ensure that the match would not be drawn. When England lost wickets, and Hussain sent out instructions that we were to play out the draw, Cronje brought on the debutant and part-time spin bowler Pieter Strydom. He set attacking fields and encouraged England's batsmen to go for their shots. In a short space of time, thanks to Cronje's 'generosity', we were back in the game, and in a tense finish Darren Gough hit the boundary that would seal an infamous victory and spark jubilant celebrations in the England dressing room. Cronje, not always known for his tactical imagination on the field, certainly showed his acumen that day: he played his role to perfection, engineering a tight finish so that the only result not possible at the end of the match was a draw. Ironically, the final negotiations took place too late for Aronstam to get his bets on. The only people to make money out of the game were Cronje and the bookmakers, for whom the draw was a huge liability.

What was my reaction? Instinctively, I was troubled. Not that I suspected match-fixing, but the whole episode seemed so odd and Cronje's behaviour seemed so out of character. I had captained England in two full Test series against Cronje and I knew him to be as defensive and cautious as his reputation. The England team went to celebrate the victory over the far side of the ground in front of the travelling fans known as the Barmy Army. I stayed behind. We had lost the series and I couldn't find much in Cronje's strange generosity (for that was the only reason for our victory) to celebrate. Later that evening, after a few drinks in the hotel bar,

I relayed my concerns to the *Sunday Times*'s cricket correspondent, Simon Wilde. Later, Wilde was to write a comprehensive account of the match-fixing crisis, but at that stage he was clearly as oblivious as everyone else. My suspicions warranted only a stinging attack in the following week's paper from Wilde. I was accused of being a killjoy.

My wariness and suspicion of Cronje and the South African team was at the heart of my disquiet. I had long been irritated by the holier-than-thou attitude of many of the South African team. Possibly, it was just a result of a large dose of cynicism, but I felt it was all a sham. Later, during the South African inquiry into match-fixing, Cronje was again to use religion as a convenient crutch. Describing his fall from grace, he said that it was a lesson to be learned and that 'when Satan comes knocking on the door, always keep your eyes on the Lord Jesus Christ and ask him to protect you from any wrong. The moment I took my eyes from Jesus, my whole world turned dark.'

It was three months after this debacle at Centurion Park that the Delhi Police dropped their bombshell. Cronje initially refuted the claims. When one of the employees of the South African Cricket Board, Bronwyn Wilkinson, first told Cronje of the existence of the tapes, he issued a kind of derisive 'snort laugh', although he later admitted to a 'sinking feeling in his stomach'. Initially, Cronje tried to ride out the storm: two days later, in a press conference in Durban, he denied that he had ever taken money from bookmakers, or that he had ever spoken to any colleagues about fixing matches. 'Sports betting,' he claimed piously, 'has no place in sport.' He was supported by Ali Bacher, the chief executive of South African cricket, who described the claims as 'absolute rubbish'.

Two days after Cronje's initial denial, and four days after the tapes had been released, either Cronje's conscience got the better of him, or the realisation hit home that he was bang to rights and there was no escape route, or maybe Jesus reappeared after a brief sojourn. At about 2 a.m. on 11 April 2000, a distraught-looking Cronje knocked on the door of Rory Steyn, one of Nelson Mandela's former personal bodyguards, and a man who was regularly seconded to the South African and touring cricket teams for protection, and indicated that he had not, in fact, been entirely truthful in his denials. It set in train a sequence of public inquiries that exposed the fact that, for a decade or more, cricket had been in the grip of bookmakers.

In May, Pakistan were forced to release the findings of their own internal inquiry into match-fixing, headed by Justice Qayyum. In it, Qayyum accepted that Salim Malik's reign as captain was tainted by match-fixing and that he was guilty of, amongst other things, trying to bribe three Australian cricketers to throw matches. Malik was banned for life, as was Ata-ur-Rehman for perjuring himself in court over allegations surrounding Wasim Akram. Qayyum recommended that Akram never captain Pakistan again and 'be kept under strict vigilance'. Akram was also fined, as were Inzamam-ul-Haq, Mushtaq Ahmed, Waqar Younis and Saeed Anwar – all mainstays of the Pakistan team throughout the 1990s – either for bringing the name of Pakistan cricket into disrepute or, through what Qayyum called 'partial amnesia', for failing to cooperate fully with the inquiry. So whilst Qayyum's inquiry fell short of accusing these great players of match-fixing, his report fuelled rather than banished suspicions. Qayyum later told Reuters, 'I am convinced that some of the Pakistan players are involved in match-fixing.'

In June, a tired and depressed-looking Cronje sat before South Africa's inquiry headed by retired justice Edwin King. In it, the scale of Cronje's descent into corruption and greed was laid bare. During the India tour of 2000, shortly after England had departed from South Africa, Cronje approached six South African players with a view to under-performing. Perhaps the lowest moment of all came when it was revealed that Cronje persuaded two of the youngest and most naive South African players – Herschelle Gibbs and Henry Williams – to accept money to under-perform, whilst at the same time taking a cut for himself. (Gibbs was told to score less than 20, and Williams had to concede more than 50 runs off his overs.) Acting as intermediary, Cronje told his two gullible team-mates that the amount offered for their connivance was $15,000 when in fact it was $25,000. Cronje, it seemed, was taking 40 per cent commission. Nice work – unless you get found out. Overall, Cronje admitted to taking £140,000 from bookmakers over the second half of the 1990s. Cronje was banned from cricket for life. Gibbs and Williams got six months each. Conveniently forgotten is the fact that the South African team came within a whisker of accepting $250,000 to throw a one-day international in 1996.

In November, India's Central Bureau of Investigation revealed the results of their investigation into match-fixing. It was the most thorough and revealing of the inquiries because for the first time bookmakers as well as players were interviewed. It showed that match-fixing was rife, that players had been regularly in contact with, and paid by, bookmakers both for information regarding matches and for under-performing, and that, far from being sporadic, there was a pattern and history of corruption. The CBI report centred on the testimony of a bookmaker called M.K. Gupta. Gupta stated that his first cricketing connection was the Indian cricketer Ajay Sharma, and that in time he built himself a web of contacts that included several Indian internationals and several captains and cricketers from other countries. His closest contacts were the former Indian captain Mohammad Azharuddin, who was duly banned for life, and Cronje, who was shown to be in cahoots with Gupta from about 1996.

The governing body of the game, the International Cricket

Council, was forced to act and it set up an Anti-Corruption Unit, headed by the former head of the Metropolitan Police Paul Condon. In April 2001, Condon's ACU produced its sensational report. It talked of 'at least twenty years of corruption linked to betting on international cricket matches', and declared that 'corrupt practices and deliberate under-performance have permeated all aspects of the game.' Condon was convinced that 'corruption continues to happen', that 'allegations in the public domain were only the tip of the iceberg' and that 'the potential for a resurgence of corruption in cricket remains a real threat.' As if to prove a point, the Kenyan cricketer Maurice Odumbe was found guilty of accepting money from bookmakers three years after Condon's report was published, when no cricketer could plausibly have said, as Inzamam-ul-Haq said to Justice Qayyum, that he had never heard of match-fixing.

The pattern of corruption seemed clear: bookmakers initially approached cricketers offering money for information on such things as pitch conditions and the make-up of the team. Once cricketers had been drawn into this trap, bookmakers started to enquire whether they might not under-perform for greater sums of money. Match-fixing was the logical next step in return for hundreds of thousands of dollars. Those who had been dumb enough to get caught up in the first place said that they felt physically threatened thereafter, and unable to get out of the web they had become entangled in.

England escaped the smears almost completely. Alec Stewart, accused by Gupta of taking cash for information on the tour of India in 1992, was cleared by the England and Wales Cricket Board, whilst nothing came of allegations against three unnamed England cricketers made in 1999 by Chris Lewis (although he was only repeating allegations relayed to him). My only involvement with the whole nonsense was a brief twenty-minute interview with Scotland Yard during the 1999 New Zealand series in relation to the allegations made by Lewis. I'd like to think that England's cricketers were cleaner than the rest, although I'm bound to say that a more plausible explanation is that, by a quirk of the fixture list, we didn't tour the Indian subcontinent between 1992 and 2001.

Fundamental to the spread of match-fixing was the rise of the subcontinent as the dominant force in world cricket. India and Pakistan resumed matches against one another in 1978, partisan games that sparked huge interest. Then, in 1983, India beat the West Indies, the pre-tournament favourites, to win the World Cup, and they could boast, in Sunil Gavaskar and Kapil Dev, genuinely world-class performers. The Indian public embraced the game with renewed passion, a passion that also involved gambling on it. Today, an average one-day international might have a TV audience in India of 300 million, and an average betting turnover of $150 million. Betting in India, apart from on-course horserace betting, is illegal and that made following the money and the bookmakers all the more difficult. Condon's report highlighted the unregulated Indian betting industry as the 'engine room which has powered and driven cricket corruption'.

Two things happened at the same time as this upsurge in interest on the subcontinent: cricket's governing body sanctioned a massive increase in the number of one-day internationals, and spread betting, as we have seen, emerged as a popular new form of gambling. Between 1993 and 2000 there were the same number of ODIs played as between 1971 and 1993, with spurious tournaments breaking out in Sharjah, Singapore and elsewhere. These tournaments, whilst lucrative, had none of the cachet of, say, a World Cup and they came to be viewed as little more than money-making vehicles for players and administrators alike. Spread betting meant that it was no longer necessary to fix the outright result of a match to make money: it was much easier to bribe one player rather than the whole team. One-day cricket in the 1990s, then, resembled little more than a giant casino, in which many of the players acted as the house taking a nice cut.

On two occasions, almost two centuries apart, cricket has faced crises in which betting, under-performing and match-fixing were the essential components. The similarities are striking: gambling was rife in England in the late 1700s and early 1800s, as it was in India in the 1990s; bookmakers were present but not accepted in early 18th-century England, and they were illegal in India; and, finally, there existed a bunch of professional (often underpaid) cricketers who were vulnerable. Silver Billy Beldham said that 'the temptation really was too great for any poor man to be exposed to', and went on to identify the Green Man and Still in Oxford Street as the place where cricketers and bookmakers met to discuss terms. Two centuries later, the cricket world was a much bigger place: bookmakers met Shane Warne in a casino in Columbo and Hansie Cronje in his plush hotel suite in Johannesburg. The motive, though, remained the same.

Since I retired, much has happened to try to prevent a repeat of the 1990s. Players can no longer use their mobile phones in dressing rooms. Security guards accompany the teams at all times and access to the players is strictly limited. Contractually, the players know exactly where they stand: if they bet on any cricket match, receive money from bookmakers or under-perform for financial gain they will be banned for life. And yet. And yet. A casual look back at the history of gambling tells us that corruption and gambling are constant bedfellows. As long as cricket remains the perfect vehicle for gambling, the temptation will always be there. As Condon says, 'Corruption is about greed and opportunity. Neither of these things will ever disappear.'

The resumption of matches between Pakistan and India in 1978, so central to the beginning of the crisis, coincided with the late Kerry Packer's challenge to the established cricketing authorities.

Packer's victory ushered in an era of professionalism for the non-English countries where the game was still largely amateur, and an era of rampant commercialism, of which, it has been argued, match-fixing was the obvious consequence. As the cricket historian Gideon Haigh says, 'Morally void as its habitués are, match-fixing is merely the logical outcome of the concept of sport as business and its leading participants as businessmen, auctioning themselves in the free market of entertainment.' Packer was the highest bidder in 1978; fifteen years later it would be a bookmaker called M.K. Gupta.

If Cronje was simply acting in the commercial spirit of the time, what, then, was his crime? Obviously, sport is about more than simply money. Richie Benaud, a man who has watched more cricket than most, knew as much. He reacted furiously. Never one to be outspoken for the sake of it, Benaud called the match-fixers 'bastards' and wondered how, when he had spent every waking hour as a cricketer trying to work out how to win matches, others could spend just as much time working out how to lose them. Benaud's anger was understandable. But, given his insistence on not betting on anything that can talk, surely he wasn't surprised? And, given the combination of human nature and cricket's murky past, neither should we be. Match-fixing is the natural and inevitable consequence of the commercialisation of gambling, the professionalisation of sport and human nature.

TONY BLOOM
The Sports Bettor

The atrium at the Landmark hotel – one of the grandest in London – is a fitting place to meet Tony Bloom, one of the biggest players on the gambling scene today. Bloom, a thirty-something north Londoner, leads a kind of double life as a gambler. He has a reasonably high profile as a poker player, and an incredibly low profile as a sports bettor. He competes successfully (under the nickname of 'The Lizard') in many of the biggest poker tournaments around the world. The poker, though, is merely for fun, relaxation and recreation, he says. It is his sports betting, particularly on football, and more specifically Asian handicap betting, that has made him the biggest player, certainly in Britain and in Europe, and possibly in the world.

As with many of the gamblers I have spoken to in this book, there was a family influence. His grandfather owned greyhounds and liked the casinos. 'He was a small-time gambler and probably a loser, as 99 per cent of people are, but he loved it, the losing was under control and it never became a problem for him. He passed on his enthusiasm to me.'

Bloom started gambling at an early age himself – at seven or eight – frequenting the arcades in Brighton where he grew up. After the arcades, he found the betting shops in and around Brighton, recalling that, as a fifteen-year-old, he would con the bus drivers into believing that he was really fourteen, so halving his fare, and then a false ID got him access to the betting shops when he was still three years under age. As with the arcades, the betting shops took most of his pocket money without giving much back.

'Early on, I was a hopeless gambler, really,' he says. 'I liked to think that I understood the form and had a strategy, but I was just guessing.' It was at Manchester University that Bloom got involved with sports and spread betting and began to make his hobby pay. He left university to take up a trainee position with the accountancy firm Ernst & Young. Like most gamblers, Bloom's strong subject was maths (his A levels were maths, further maths, statistics and economics, which seems as good an academic grounding for a gambler as it is possible to get). He lasted two and a half years at Ernst & Young, punting successfully in his spare time, so that when he left the firm in 1993 he had accumulated a bankroll of £20,000 from sports and spread betting.

He briefly entered the City, which he says is a natural progression for a gambling enthusiast, learning to trade options on the LIFFE floor. He found that he was making far more from his betting than his job, and the City experiment lasted just six months. It was time to go it alone as a professional gambler.

At this stage, Bloom hadn't really homed in on one area of expertise. He was spread-betting on most sports without a particular staking strategy. Young and single, with no financial commitments, he says he was far more aggressive than he ought to have been. He recalls one England v West Indies Test match in 1994 (I was captain at the time), when he bought West Indies runs firstly at £25 a run, and then again and again until he had £100 a run staked on the West Indies getting more than 350. Spread betting on runs in cricket can be risky: there is the potential to lose 200 points either way, and so Bloom's downside on this bet was almost his whole bankroll. It was, he says, 'ridiculously bullish' and in the end cost him £5,000 – although since at one point the West Indies were 120 for 7 the final reckoning felt like a triumph.

Bloom is a true gambler at heart. He says he likes to take a position, rather than hedging, and he says that once he has taken his position he won't necessarily follow the action closely. 'You've either got value, or you haven't. You've either made a good bet, or you haven't,' he says. 'I believe in betting aggressively and, occasionally, to win big, you have to risk losing.'

Increasingly successful, especially betting on football, Bloom was contacted by Victor Chandler, a bookmaker, in 1997 to help break into the Asian football market, where the sums bet are routinely outrageous. Bloom spent six months in Bangkok, profitable for him and for Chandler's, and it was there that he first started to learn about Asian handicap betting.

Asian handicap betting evens football matches up through offering a handicap on one team, and increasingly it is the dominant form of sports betting in the Far East. Whilst traditional fixed-odds bookmakers might offer odds on, say, Manchester United at home to West Bromwich Albion as: 2-5 (United), 2-1 draw and 4-1 (WBA), Asian handicap betting is designed to even up the match. So, for example, the Asian handicap version of the above match might be United minus 1.5 goals, WBA plus 1.5 goals, with both offered at 10-11. WBA get a handicap start of 1.5 goals as the underdog and the punter either bets on United to win, or WBA, with the draw taken out of the equation. If the punter bets on United then they must win by two clear goals for him to win the bet. The beauty for the punter is that, whilst fixed-odds bookies operate to around 110 per cent on a football market, Asian handicapping works to around 104 per cent because of the absence of the draw. And, with the English Premiership dominated by three or four teams who are far better than the rest, it gives the market a more interesting feel from a betting perspective.

After coming to terms with this relatively unknown (to English punters) form of betting and helping Chandler break into the football market in Asia, Bloom returned to Chandler's operation in Gibraltar for three years, before he left to set up his own book-making firm called Premierbet on the eve of the football World Cup in 2002. Why did the poacher turn gamekeeper? 'Mainly, it was a business decision. I could see that Asian handicap betting was huge, so I decided to set up as a bookmaker to bring that to an English audience. Also, I wanted to move into business and other areas of investment and this seemed to be a good place to start. It did OK, but the market got tougher because of the dotcom downturn and the arrival of Betfair and other low-margin opera-tors, and also I had to position the company very neutrally on Asian handicap betting because people knew it was my company and they would closely follow the markets we were setting.' He sold out, he says, 'for a tiny amount,' which I later discovered to be £1 million.

Since then, Bloom has been concentrating on football and Asian handicap betting. Bloom, like many professional gamblers, keeps his cards extremely close to his chest and is unwilling to divulge too many details of his betting modus operandi. I am told that he has a large team working for him in north London and that he employs an army of analysts, statisticians and researchers. Football is by far the biggest part of his business, although they are moving in-creasingly into cricket as well. Understandably, Bloom is coy about the sums they invest, but various people within the industry have told me that his operation is unequivocally the biggest in the world. Another player in the same business told me it was not unusual for Bloom to bet £250,000 a go on football matches.

At the time of writing, Bloom's operation is no doubt gearing up for a frenzied summer of activity as the football World Cup in Germany looms. Betting operators in Britain said that the 2002 World Cup was by far their biggest ever single betting tournament, even though they were stymied by the unsociable hours in the Far East. Germany is a much more convenient time zone for punters and it threatens to dwarf 2002. Some betting firms have predicted that the British alone will haemorrhage over £1 billion on the tournament. Paddy Power, over two months before kick-off, had already taken £10 million worth of bets. Sports betting is increasingly becoming the big beast of the betting world, and within that jungle, football betting is king.

As with most of the other gamblers I have spoken to, Bloom's gambling takes a toll on his home life. Whereas most of the older gamblers are divorced, Bloom has yet to take the plunge into marriage. I can't imagine that he has much time for such frippery. His relaxation, apart from other business ventures, is poker. He won the 2004 Australasia poker tournament in Melbourne, winning £180,000 in the process, and his earnings to date have passed the $1 million mark. He thinks that it is to his advantage to treat the game as a bit of fun and that he plays better as a result. Last year, he was confident enough to take on the American professional Daniel Negreanu, head to head, in a game of pot-limit Omaha, for $500,000. Bloom lost in Las Vegas, but has already arranged a rematch with Negreanu.

Bloom is, I suppose, the epitome of the high-stakes gambler. His motivation? He seems to me to be both an instinctive and coldly calculating gambler. He recognised early on that he loved gambling and that he has, in his own words, 'an addictive personality'. Since he recognised that he wanted to gamble, he thought he had better get good at it unless he wanted to end up in the gutter. Since university, he has not only found his specialist niche, one that has in-built advantages to the punter provided you know your market, but he has become expert at it.

Money, and the desire to have lots of it, has in the end overridden his desire to gamble constantly. 'Those early losing experiences stood me in good stead. It taught me how not to do it and I had a long, hard look at the losers around me and I promised myself that I wouldn't become one. Some gamblers are addicted to losing and they get a thrill from going from solvent to broke and back again. That never appealed to me. At university I made myself a promise that I would become fiercely disciplined. I wanted to gamble, because I enjoyed it, and therefore I needed to do it properly in order to win. I didn't want to lose my money.'

9

TWISTED REALITY

'This is not a good town for psychedelic drugs. Reality itself
is too twisted.'

Hunter S. Thompson, *Fear and Loathing in Las Vegas*

American sport has never forgotten the 'Black Sox' match-fixing
crisis of 1919. The memory of it, and of college basketball match-
fixing scandals in 1951 and 1961, retains a fierce grip on the
administrators of that most idiosyncratic of sports, American Football. The climax of the American Football season is the Super Bowl
and it is an event that has seen an exponential growth in popularity
over the last four decades. Apart from the quality of the athletes and
the cultural significance of the sport to Americans, the increased
television audience (now estimated at 90 million in America alone)
can be partly explained by sports fans' love of a bet. As Americans
watched the 2006 Super Bowl between the Seattle Seahawks and the
Pittsburgh Steelers, and whilst they gorged themselves on an estimated 113 million pounds of French fries, it was also estimated that
internet betting operators, in tax-free overseas havens like Costa
Rica, took over $600 million – despite the fact that internet betting
remains illegal for Americans – and the Nevada sports books, the
sports betting area in the casinos, for whom Super Bowl weekend is
their busiest of the year, took over $100 million in wagers. Gambling
and the Super Bowl nourish each other.

Despite all this, the administrators of the NFL retain a hostile attitude to gambling, and in particular to Las Vegas. Perhaps they see the NFL's past – the numerous betting scandals and the fact that many franchises were owned by well-known gamblers – as the only possible threat to its future prosperity. As a result, the NFL refuses to broadcast any Las Vegas commercials, it has challenged the right of some of Las Vegas's satellite owners to broadcast the game and, because the NFL own the copyright to the term 'Super Bowl', they have challenged the right of casinos to use that name in advertising their annual 'Super Bowl' parties. Now most casinos do not use the term 'Super Bowl' at all, referring instead to the 'pro football championship game'.

(This puritanical attitude extends beyond gambling. During the interval, it was the turn of the Rolling Stones to offend the NFL's feelings. When Mick Jagger referred to making a 'dead man come' in the song 'Start Me Up', and when he referred to 'cocks' in the song 'Rough Justice', the NFL slyly turned down the microphone to protect the sensibilities of the 72,000 fans in the stadium, and the millions of listeners on the ABC network.)

The attitude of the NFL's administrators towards gambling is a microcosm of America's schizophrenic attitude to gambling in general. State laws govern the status of gambling in America and so the picture is a confused one. Most states allow daily or weekly lotteries and some allow on-course pari-mutuel betting. Historically, Nevada has had a monopoly on casino gambling. But in 1978, New Jersey followed Nevada's lead and more than half the states now allow casino gambling, on steamboats, for example, moored on the Mississippi River, or, following the Indian Gaming Regulatory Act in 1988, on tribal lands. The gambling economy in America is worth over $50 billion annually and increasingly forms an important source of revenues for state legislators. Yet internet gambling remains illegal, according to the terms of the Wire Act of 1961, and in many states betting on sport is illegal. America, like

Britain before it, cannot really come to terms with gambling: they are happy to accept the revenue that accrues from it, and yet it is considered morally indefensible, especially by the religious right.

America's attitude to gambling was summed up by a story that dominated the national media on Super Bowl weekend, the weekend I arrived in Las Vegas. Ralph Reed, the former head of the Christian Coalition, now a Republican strategist running for high office in Georgia, and a man who had once described gambling as a 'cancer', was embroiled in a gambling scandal. It was a story that stank of hypocrisy more than illegality. On leaving the Christian Coalition, Reid set up a PR and lobbying business with close links to the disgraced Washington lobbyist Jack Abramoff. Abramoff had pocketed millions lobbying on behalf of Indian gaming interests and, keen to exploit Reid's connections within the conservative community, he paid Reid's company $2 million to run a lobbying campaign to prevent the spread of gambling on behalf of some of Abramoff's clients. And the identity of these clients? A casino-owning Indian tribe in Louisiana keen to maintain its gambling monopoly by preventing a rival tribe setting up its own casino.

Whilst Reed had not been accused of anything illegal, it might still have been thought that the scandal would affect his position as a defender of the American right's moral values. But no, Reed was unrepentant and continued to propound his anti-gambling message. He assured prospective voters that his fees did not come from gambling revenues and emphasised the good his campaign had achieved. 'We will never know,' he said, 'how many marriages and lives were saved and how many children were spared the consequences of compulsive gambling.' He continued to receive fees from two anti-gambling groups in Alabama to prevent the introduction there of a state lottery and legalised video poker.

The story of Las Vegas – its birth, expansion, development and dazzling success – is the story of a city that stepped into this dichotomy between Americans' desire to gamble and America's puritanical desire to restrict it. The gap between liberty and restraint presented a huge opportunity for a state that was prepared to legalise gambling, especially if that state was so isolated that it offered a negligible threat to mainstream America.

Nevada's decision to legalise gambling in 1931 led to the development of gambling halls on Fremont Street in downtown Las Vegas, an area now known as 'Glitter Gulch'. But whilst Glitter Gulch still offers opportunities to gamblers, the majority of the casino-resorts are now located out of town, on a five-mile-long freeway known as the 'Strip'. The development of the Strip, and therefore the development of Las Vegas as we know it today, must be seen in the context of the suburbanisation of American life in the 1950s, and the power of the anti-gambling movement that was at its height after the Second World War.

The development of giant resort-type casinos in the middle of the desert was the perfect answer to the growing problem of urban gambling. After the Second World War there were increasing concerns over the burgeoning number of slot machines in retail outlets and the close association between organised crime and illegal gambling rackets. What better way to solve the problem than to contain it in the middle of a desert, miles from anywhere else. On the Las Vegas Strip, gambling was exclusive, isolated and therefore safe. Gambling, then, created the Las Vegas that we see today, and Las Vegas helped, in turn, to provide answers for a country torn between the compulsion to gamble and the desire to prevent its spread.

Although, in recent years, Las Vegas has tried to spread its wings, marketing itself firstly as a convention centre, then as a family destination and now as an adult entertainment centre, it is essentially still a city that exists for gambling: one third of its population is employed directly by the gambling industry, one third indirectly, and the other third wouldn't be there without it.

> Glad to be in America
> Where at least I know I'm free
> I won't forget the men who died
> To give their freedom to me
> God Bless the USA!

When I heard those lyrics, I guess I could have been anywhere in George Bush's America, but when the lyrics coincided with a fountain display spurting out of an eleven-acre lake which framed a 5,000-room Tuscan-themed hotel, then there's only one place I could have been. Gambling has resulted in many things throughout history, but none as weird as the Las Vegas Strip. From the Mandalay Bay hotel at the north end, to the Sahara hotel at the south, this is a stretch of real estate that is at once outrageously expensive, kitsch, fake and absurd.

The Strip has undergone many incarnations during the past seven decades: its ersatz Old West/Frontier period, as the first casinos sprang up in the 1940s, thanks to entrepreneurs like Billy Wilkerson, who was the first to conceptualise the idea of the resort-casino; its mob period, when the mafia's criminal activities were bankrolled by skimming the profits from the casinos they had been shrewd enough to buy; simultaneously, there was Hollywood cool in the shape of the Rat Pack; in the late 1960s Howard Hughes brought reclusive genius to the Strip as he holed up on the ninth floor of the Desert Inn and bought up massive tracts of Vegas real estate; a drug-fuelled and bloated Elvis brought a kind of glamour as he filled the 1,600-capacity auditorium at the Hilton for twenty-eight days straight during the spring and summer of the early 1970s; corporate America arrived in the 1980s to clean up the joint as Wall

Street ownership replaced the mob; and now the themed ghastliness of today, which promises to be replaced in time by something more culturally mature.

The man responsible for the Strip in its current guise is Steve Wynn, the son of a local bingo operator, who shattered the boundaries of excess when he opened the $700 million Mirage mega-resort in 1989. The Mirage boasted 3,000 rooms, a casino containing 2,200 slot and video poker machines, a $30 million volcano – the only volcano in Nevada! – which had to be infused with pina colada scent to mask the unwanted fumes from the flames which erupted every half hour. Three thousand exotic plants filled its gardens and five bottle-nosed dolphins cavorted in the 20,000-gallon aquarium. 'It was,' quipped Wynn, 'what God would have done, if He'd had the money.' God might have had a bit more style. The money, though, came from Michael Milken's Wall Street junk bonds, which just about sums up how shallow the Mirage was. Wynn's audacity paid off, however, and the Mirage was soon raking in over $1 million a day, which was just enough to pay off Wynn's debts.

The Mirage set the scene for everything that followed and since then seventeen themed mega-resorts have been built along the Strip. Want to be surrounded by Arthurian legend? No problem; book into the Excalibur, the 4,000-room hotel that opened within six months of the Mirage. Want to see the pyramids of ancient Egypt? Head to the Luxor next door. The Empire State building, Brooklyn Bridge and the Statue of Liberty stare down at you from the New York-New York hotel; the Eiffel Tower from the Paris hotel; the Parthenon from Caesars Palace; whilst outside the Venetian a flotilla of gondolas brings you the romance of Venice. The murals of sky and sunlight that adorn the inside of the Venetian are remarkably lifelike, just in case you don't want to pop outside and see the real thing. Clearly, the best way to entice people to a parched strip of desert land is to convince them they are going somewhere else. Why spend thousands crossing the Atlantic, when you can see it right here on your doorstep! When a city has so little history of its own, the answer is to borrow a little from elsewhere.

The next stage of the Strip's evolution promises a little more class and style. Once again, Steve Wynn is to the fore with his eponymous hotel, the $2.7 billion Wynn Las Vegas, which opened in 2005. Having run out of themes, Wynn erected this themeless chocolate-coloured monolith and simply scrawled his own autograph all over the hotel. It breaks new ground in conspicuous consumption, housing an art gallery for its owner's $300 million art collection and an internal garage to show off his forty Ferraris and Maseratis. Themeless urban chic would appear to be the next stage, as George Clooney recently announced a $3 billion project to open Las Ramblas, which he promised would be more 'Tony Bennett than Britney Spears'.

As gambling profits continue to swell the coffers of developers like Wynn, the Strip will continue to evolve, for Las Vegas has no respect for history or tradition. Sentimentality has no place here. When the next big thing comes along, the town planners simply agree to another implosion. Between 1993 and 2001 there were seven huge implosions. Hundreds of pounds of dynamite are placed at the base of the unloved and unwanted and, by Vegas standards, historic building, which is then brought down rapidly, with minimal impact on the surrounding areas, in front of the thousands who gather to watch. So it was that the last vestiges of the Howard Hughes era disappeared, as the Desert Inn was blasted out of existence, to be replaced by the Wynn.

Whilst the casino-resorts of the Strip dance to various themes, they all have one thing in common: the casino. The casino is the centrifugal force of every mega-resort on the Strip. The only hotel which failed to adhere to this basic principle – the Aladdin – was the only venture which failed. The aim is to ensure that punters spend as much time in the casino as possible. In order to access any of the hotel's other amenities they must walk through or pass by the casino. And once in it, everything is done to ensure that they stay in it: there are no clocks to tell them the time, and no windows tell them whether it is day or night. Gambling in a Las Vegas casino must be one of the most isolated pastimes known to man: an isolated city, in an isolationist country, in a casino where time stands still. A nuclear holocaust could be going on outside and the punter would be none the wiser. Gamblers often talk of time disassociation when gambling – nowhere is this more true than in Las Vegas.

The casinos may vary in size and in the stakes that they offer, but they are essentially formulaic in design. All of them pay homage to the slot machine, thousands of which occupy up to about 70 per cent of the total floor space of the casino. Vegas is the city of slots. The first thing that greets you as you step through the McCarran International airport is row upon row of slot machines, dancing, whirring, sparkling like daleks on drugs. The image of dead-eyed punters playing the slots is a Vegas cliché, and in the Bellagio where I was staying barely more than a tenth of them were being played at any one time. Nevertheless, this is partly a reflection of the sheer number and variety of slot machines that the Vegas casinos offer.

In 1990, even before the arrival of most of the mega-resorts, there were 85,000 slot machines in Las Vegas. That number has now been dwarfed thanks to the giant casinos of the Strip, all of which offer between 2,000 and 4,000 slot machines each. There is a bewildering array of choice – slots called White Ice, Hot Pepper, Ten Times, Jackpot Party, Wild Eights blink and flash their seductive lights and aural come-ons for the sucker punter. They cater for all, from the quarter slots to the special high-stakes slot room which, at the Bellagio, is 'by appointment only'. In this room you can slam $1,000-dollar notes into a machine that offers a $2m jackpot. They are everywhere: go for a drink at the bar, and you will see slots nestled neatly into the bar top. No wonder: the humble slot contributes over 50 per cent of the Strip casinos' profits, and up to as much as 70 per cent in the casinos downtown.

Slots are the perfect profit-making vehicle for casino operators: they guarantee a payout of between 5 and 15 per cent, they have no overheads, and they are the most addictive machines on the gambling scene today. It is an addiction spurred on by the hope of a huge payout for minimal cost (the 'progressive' machines in Las Vegas have paid out a jackpot of more than $30 million). It is an addiction spurred by rapid turnover and instant gratification or, more likely, disappointment. It is an addiction nourished by the con that players can affect their chances by using 'nudge' and 'hold' buttons. And it is an addiction nourished by the 'near miss' psychology whereby machines are calibrated to show enough winning symbols to keep the punter interested. Occasionally, just occasionally, the gong will sound to announce that the jackpot has been won – often enough to encourage the rest to play on.

Craps is another game where the punter is unlikely to win, but the action is fast and loose and the group of African Americans I watched were having much more fun than those on the slots. Craps is the descendant of the medieval dice game called hazard and it has lost none of its potency to bewitch. A Samuel L. Jackson lookalike, all bling and black beret, was holding court and holding the dice. Five translucent red dice, which he was rubbing, caressing, nurturing even, in the hope of choosing the two that would bring him some luck.

It was a highly ritualised performance. Firstly, he rolled all five dice until two threes came up. Then, with one die on top of the other, he swirled them around in a letter 'S'. His companions were getting impatient. 'Come on, will ya. It'll be midnight before you throw!' The thrower didn't take kindly to this intrusion into his ritual. 'Be quiet. I'm shootin' dice. I'm shootin' dice!' Then he threw them high and long with a kind of leg-spin action. All eyes followed the dice. No one seemed happy when they landed.

It was his companion's turn now. He took two dice, added them up to five – a three on top of a two – and tapped one on top of the other twice. 'Yeah, shooter!' the party cried, almost in ecstasy. The throw came low and quick – a short-arm jab – but again there was no luck. I asked him why the superstitions, when clearly they could have no effect on how the dice landed. 'It's just a feel I have. When I feel them right, I get lucky.'

There isn't anything in it, of course. The craps player is as certain to lose in the long run as the slot player, the blackjack player (unless he is a card counter), the baccarat player and the roulette player (especially in Vegas, where the roulette tables have two zeros). The only difference is the degree to which the house holds the edge. Benny Binion, the man who built Binion's casino in downtown Vegas, said, 'If you got talent, Vegas is the land of milk and honey; if you don't, it's a burial ground.' He should have said 'luck' not 'talent'.

The equivalent of craps for the Far Eastern punters is baccarat, not so much a game for them as a religion. The Bellagio high rollers' baccarat pit is tailored exclusively for Far Eastern punters who will happily play for $100,000 a hand. Like craps, it is a highly ritualised event. From the fanning and shuffling of the eight decks of cards, to the fraught moment when the players must decide who places the blank card into the deck to cut, to the play itself when players squeeze and bend their cards to prolong the agony or the ecstasy just a little bit longer.

Ritual or not, high stakes or low stakes, craps, baccarat, black-jack, roulette or poker, there is usually only one outcome. 1970 was the first year that Nevada's casinos grossed profits of $1 billion. That landmark was achieved in a month for the first time in March

2005. The casino-resorts of the Strip contributed just under half that figure, and of that the slots contributed $291 million, blackjack $76 million, baccarat $40 million, craps $33 million, roulette $21 million and the sports books $5 million.

Steve Wynn was right when he said the only way to make money in a casino is to own one.

Las Vegas is known as the playground of the high rollers. The highest of these high rollers are known in the industry as 'whales'. Since they might blow as much as $20 million on a weekend's action, they are eagerly sought by casino executives. All the major casinos employ special 'hosts' to look after current whales and to search the waters for prospective whales, and most of them have permanent employees in the Far East, where many of the biggest and most compulsive gamblers come from. All of the casinos offer serious inducements, and the competition to attract the biggest gamblers is fierce.

The largest bet offered by the Vegas casinos is currently $250,000. There might be upwards of a dozen gamblers worldwide who can stake to such sums. Fifty or so might be able to play to $150,000 limits and double that number to $100,000 limits. The casino-resorts which offer the biggest bets to the biggest gamblers are the MGM Grand, Bellagio, Mirage and the Venetian, as well as, more recently, the downtown Golden Nugget, which has been bought by Tim Poster and Tom Breitling, two thirty-something internet millionaires.

All these casino-resorts offer serious enticements to their most favoured clients. They are likely to be picked up in a private jet and then, once they have landed at McCarron airport, offered a limo or helicopter service to whisk them to the Strip with minimal fuss. They might receive inducements of up to $250,000 just to start playing in a particular casino and then offered around 20 per cent reduction on their eventual losses. Obviously, they are given complimentary drinks and dinner, and, these days, Vegas offers up the finest cuisine and wine. Indeed, such is the pressure on these casino-resorts to provide their best customers with the finest food and wine, that there is now a shortage of prestige wines for restaurants throughout the rest of the United States. Vegas's casino-resorts gobble up the best vintages in huge quantities, paying ridiculously over-the-top prices. Bottles of Château Pétrus have been known to sell for upwards of $25,000 a pop, although the whales would not expect to pay, whilst Vegas sells more Cristal champagne than any other American city. Fifteen master sommeliers, one fifth of the total number in America, work out of Vegas. Casinos entice the most exciting young chefs in America to work in their restaurants. Eat at the Picasso in Bellagio and you can not only gorge yourself on Japanese Kobe beef, but you can also stare at half a dozen genuine works by the master.

Most of all, there is the accommodation. Whales are not put up in any old room, but in the suites that these casino-resorts have had specially built for their most valued guests. It was Steve Wynn who first began to offer the most sumptuous accommodation for his high rollers when he opened the Mirage, and in an effort to keep up with the Joneses, every new casino has attempted to offer ever more lavish suites.

Wynn's latest venture has the grandest that Vegas can offer. All are decorated in neo-classical Palladian style and are something to behold. The elevators up to these suites, on the second floor of the hotel, are made of Indian marble with twelve shades of mother-of-pearl. The smallest suite is 5,000 square feet, the largest is double that. Each villa has a private garden, a pool, a spa, a media room, massage room, exercise room and beauty salon with twelve-foot-high walls providing absolute privacy. Each villa has a butler to attend to the gambler's every need. All this is in stark contrast with most hotel rooms in Las Vegas's casino-resorts, which offer minimal trappings – they don't want to encourage gamblers to spend more time in their rooms (and therefore less time in the casino) than is possible. But the whales are different: every conceivable luxury and whim is catered for – they even put in a karaoke machine for their Far Eastern clients.

Who are the highest of high rollers? The most well known, a gambler who was coveted and feared in equal measure, was the late Kerry Packer. With a fortune estimated in billions, Packer presumably needed to play 'deep' to get his juices going. I say 'presumably', because Packer only ever spoke publicly about his gambling once and that was in response to Mark Latham, the opposition leader in Australia, who was deeply critical of Packer's gambling after a multi-million-dollar loss in Vegas's MGM Grand. 'Notions of public morality and justice,' Latham said, 'are under threat when it is possible for one person to accumulate such extraordinary wealth and then use it in such an extraordinary way.' It wasn't very smart of Latham to attack a man who typified the Australian dream (the Packer family fortune was only two generations old, started, legend has it, when his grandfather stepped on a ten-shilling note and put it on a horse at long odds), and Packer remained unrepentant. 'This was my money and I'm entitled to spend it any way. My father was a gambler, I am a gambler. Every man who ever created anything was a gambler,' he said.

Despite the fact that Packer never spoke about his gambling, there are always enough croupiers, hosts, casino managers to let slip the tales of his extraordinary feats on the tables. Packer, apparently, moved around the casino-resorts of the Strip according to his whim: in the early 1990s it was thought that he had a $5 million credit line at Caesars Palace; in 1995 he played every table in the high-stakes blackjack pit at the MGM Grand, winning, reportedly, $26 million in two hours of ferocious gambling. Shortly afterwards, Kirk Kerkorian, the then owner of the MGM Grand, sent a message that Packer was not welcome to gamble any more in his establishment, proving that occasionally gamblers can beat the house.

Packer was a notoriously good winner, and a good loser. He was tremendously generous to waitresses and croupiers, tipping each croupier $2,500 (over $100,000 in all) after his monstrous win at the MGM Grand. He could make life awkward for casino managers who tried to limit his play, and for wealthy bores who boasted about their wealth. It was rumoured that one day, whilst playing baccarat at the high-stakes pit at the Bellagio, he overheard a Texan bragging about the fact that he was worth $50 million. 'I'll flip you for it,' said Packer.

The vast majority of whales now come from the Far East. China, with its combination of surging capitalism, vast wealth creation and a compulsion to gamble that seems to be greater than in any other race, is the promised land for many Vegas casinos. The rest include the usual combination of billionaire businessmen, sports stars (Michael Jordan is known to punt ferociously in Vegas) and film stars.

The biggest whale swimming in the waters of Las Vegas during my weekend there was not instantly recognisable and he wasn't particularly interested in the benefits to which high rollers are routinely treated. He is publicity-shy and down to earth, usually travelling economy-class and staying in a standard room. But that is where the similarity with you and me ends. In a series of head-to-head matches against the word's best poker players, Andy Beal, a Texan billionaire banker, has gambled staggering sums of money.

The latest instalment of these matches just happened to be taking place on Super Bowl Sunday at table three of the poker room at the Wynn casino. The match was into its fifth straight day and it was scheduled to stop as soon as the Super Bowl kicked off.

The poker room in the Wynn casino is much like any other in Las Vegas. It is small – poker is the least financially attractive game in terms of rake, from a casino operator's point of view – and sparsely decorated. Table three is much like any other table, oval with a green felt top surrounded by eight mahogany chairs. On this day, as for the previous five days, a protective rope had been placed around the table, and a security officer, dressed in purple and looking very self-important and fierce, stood guard.

Beal, pale-faced and wearing a maroon cap and enormous Elvis-style sunglasses, sat bolt upright and was a study in concentration. The room, unlike the rest of the casino where the football game was eagerly anticipated, was quiet, and only the clackety-clack of riffled chips disturbed the silence. There weren't *that* many chips on table three and the casual observer might have wondered why the need for the rope and the security guard. But on closer inspection you would have seen that each chip was what is commonly known as a 'cranberry' (because of its colour) and was worth $25,000. At any one time there was between $20 million and $25 million worth of chips in front of both players.

The story behind the highest-stakes poker game in the world is this: five years ago, very rich and very bored, Beal challenged a group of poker professionals in Las Vegas to a high-stakes game. Whilst the challenge was ostensibly to the poker community, in reality Beal was challenging himself. Could he, an amateur poker player, find a way of beating the best poker players in the world? In a game where professionals insist that money is irrelevant except as a way of keeping score, could Beal, for whom money genuinely is irrelevant, raise the stakes so high that even the professionals would start to worry and make poor decisions. Beal was happy to put $10 million on the table; the group of professionals, who came to be known as 'The Corporation', clubbed together to raise their $10 million, and Beal would play against one of their number until the funds had disappeared or until either called a halt.

The game had been going, on and off, for five years now. Whenever Beal fancied a challenge, he would ring up a member of The Corporation and they would stump up $10 million between them to feed Beal's ego. The identity of The Corporation was fluid and changed according to who had funds available and who was in town, but a core of names cropped up time and again whenever the challenge was thrown down. There was Jennifer Harman, whose petite frame and blonde features belied a nerve that regularly enabled her to play in the highest-stakes game that Las Vegas offered; there was Ted Forrest, who craved action so much that he regularly commuted between Vegas and Los Angeles just to play poker; there was Barry Greenstein, known as the 'Robin Hood' of poker because he donates most of his poker winnings to charity; there was the fiercely intelligent Howard Lederer; and the man who now sat opposite Beal, Todd Brunson, a huge bear of a man and son of one of the world's best poker players, Doyle 'Texas Dolly' Brunson.

Beal left no stone unturned in his quest to beat these players. His instinct told him that the professionals' strength lay in their vast experience and that the number of hands they had played over time had given them a remarkable feel for the game. He could replicate that experience by developing a computer program and by doing so he could give himself an edge on the pure mathematics. His computer program played upwards of two million games, so that by the end he knew the absolute odds of success or failure for various combinations. For example, the computer told Beal that 9-6 suited was the lowest suited hand that would win more than 50 per cent of the time, and that 10-8 off-suit was the lowest unpaired, unsuited hand that would win more than 50 per cent of the time. The pros might have a feel for the odds. Beal knew. Priceless information.

The computer furnished him with cold analysis. It didn't protect him against the professionals' uncanny ability to read an opponent. Beal set about building a protective wall around himself so that the pros would find it hard, if not impossible, to read him. Hence the Elvis-like sunglasses, the cap, the iPod, which played bland elevator music, and the buzzer he attached to one sock which gave him a gentle electric shock every eight seconds. He hoped that by making his decisions every eight seconds he could camouflage both his cards and his mood.

Beal's biggest advantage was his billionaire status. He out-bankrolled The Corporation a thousand times over and he hoped that by continually raising the stakes he could send the pros 'on tilt'. The game was limit Texas hold'em. The early games in 2001 were played for $10,000/$20,000 limits, which meant that the opening bets and subsequent bets for the first two rounds would be in increments of $10,000, and then $20,000 for the last two rounds. Until then, the highest game anyone had ever heard of in Vegas was $4,000/$8,000. By 2003, Beal had persuaded the pros to raise the game to $50,000/$100,000. During the World Series of 2004, he had finally got his wish to play a $100,000/$200,000 game, during which he won $12 million in a single day and proved that if you raise the stakes high enough even the pros can be affected.

Between 2001 and the 2004 World Series, Beal had made ten separate trips to Las Vegas to test himself against the pros. Since then, there had been a 619-day hiatus. My trip to Vegas coincided with the resumption of a $50,000/£100,000 game. On the Wednesday before I arrived, Beal lost $1.9 million to Todd Brunson; on Thursday he won $100,000 off Ted Forrest and Jennifer Harman;

on the Friday he lost $4 million to Forrest, winning $500,000 the next day; and now, on Sunday, he faced Brunson again.

What was it like, this game involving sums that most people would find obscene? In truth, it was a joyless, dispiriting game. There was no animation and no conversation, and it looked like a complete endurance test. Brunson, slumped over his chair, occasionally tapped his cards and tried to start a conversation; Beal was having none of it. A waitress in the shortest of short skirts passed occasionally. Neither player looked up. After a while a dealer would be replaced. I asked one of them how it was going: 'Back and forth like a tennis match,' he said. 'It's as boring as hell. The whole point of poker is to have fun. This is just a business for these two guys.' He was right. Poker players say the game is not about money. This was only about money. And as with many things in life, more does not necessarily mean better.

By the time both players called a halt to proceedings, just before the Super Bowl began, Brunson was a shade over $1 million to the good. Over the five days, The Corporation were up $3.2 million overall, a 30 per cent return on their investment. Beal and the rotating group of pros had played close to 2,000 hands in all and had contested pots totalling $600 million, with Beal having won $298.4 million and the pros $301.6 million. It was a staggering amount of money, but it didn't seem like a hell of a lot of fun.

Away from the themed excess of the Strip and the high rollers who gamble obscene amounts of money, there is plenty of grit beneath the glitter. To see it you have to take the short bus ride downtown. As you pass the Sahara hotel, suddenly the buildings start to get less tall and less wacky. For a short time, as you pass the discount markets, burger joints, 7-Elevens, All Star Donuts and low-grade motels, you could be in any Midwest town in America. For the first time you sense that Las Vegas is a place where people live normal lives, where they work, shop, go to school and do their laundry.

And then, as you continue south, the slots parlours suddenly start to spring up again and the neon returns and before you know it you are on Fremont Street, which, as it proudly boats, is 'the street that started it all.' Tourists and gamblers are still attracted here, although in far fewer numbers than on the Strip, but it is generally at the low-staking punter that Glitter Gulch aims its fire. Ten years ago a $90 million canopy, which produces a dazzling light show at night, was erected above five blocks of Fremont Street in an attempt to lift the downtown area out of the doldrums. Despite the best efforts of the municipality, it is an area that reeks of seediness, from the bars offering strip shows, to the Las Vegas Club, which openly promises it has 'the most liberal "21" in the world' as its door policy.

Head west out of Fremont Street and you begin to see the underbelly of Las Vegas, and the side of the city that rarely gets publicised. A couple of blocks out of town on the right, amongst low-rise shabby motels, low-income housing and trailer parks, is the Western hotel-casino. You can get a room for less than thirty bucks a night and you can, of course, gamble. The Western's casino is designed on pretty much the same lines as those on the Strip, with a central block of slots off which sprout the table games. But here the players feed the slots with nickels and quarters, rather than dollars, and the blackjack tables, replete with cigarette burns and beer stains, cater for the $1 and $2 punters. It is a sad place.

This is an area of crumbling infrastructure, of few community amenities and of drugs and crime and violence, home to the Vegas underclass who sweep the floors of the Strip's casinos in the early hours of the morning and creep back to bed before dawn, home to a population that feels acute social dislocation and isolation – one of the reasons, no doubt, why Vegas has the fourth highest suicide rate in America. It is also home to the Gambler's Book Shop, a mecca for those interested in gambling literature. Howard Schwartz, who has run the book store for the last five years, but who has lived in Vegas for decades, confirms my worst fears when he asks me how I got to his shop. When I said I had walked there from Fremont Street, he told me I was lucky I hadn't been shot.

The Las Vegas story has some relevance for Britain today. For, just as Las Vegas provided a solution to America's attitude to gambling in the second half of the 20th century, so Britain is looking to the Las Vegas model for a solution at the beginning of the 21st. The Gambling Act, which received Royal assent in 2005, and which will come into full force in 2007, allowed for, amongst other things, a single Las Vegas-style casino to be built in an area ripe for regeneration. Around thirty municipal councils have applied, although it is thought that Blackpool is the destination most likely to win this guinea pig contract.[10] Opposition to the government's Bill watered the proposals down to a single giant casino, but few doubt that, should the experiment prove to be a success, more will follow. The aim is to use gambling to help regenerate decaying urban areas, but if the American example tells us anything, it is that casino-resorts and urban generation do not go together.

Las Vegas, remember, was America's answer to the problem of urban gambling. The development of the Strip went hand in hand with the suburbanisation of American life in the 1950s and the desire to place gambling in an isolated, non-threatening environment. As the Strip prospered, so downtown Las Vegas, Glitter

[10] By May 2006, the shortlist had been narrowed down to eight: Blackpool, Brent, Cardiff, Glasgow, Greenwich, Manchester, Newcastle and Sheffield. A decision is expected in Sheffield.

Gulch, decayed and declined. With casino-resorts offering everything a visitor could wish for, there were precious few reasons to leave its environs. As David Schwartz, author of *Suburban Xanadu*, says, 'as single nodes in a larger metropolitan system, casino-resorts can work spectacularly well, but they are not effective anchors for urban development.'[11]

More recently, the spectacular success of Indian tribal gaming shows what can be achieved when casino-resorts spring up on marginal, isolated and desolate ground. There are now twenty-seven states which allow gaming on tribal lands, following the passage of the Indian Gaming Regulatory Act in 1988. The beacon example of what casino gambling can do on marginal land is in Connecticut, on the land of the Mashantucket Pequot tribe. Their enormous Foxwoods Casino (320,000 square feet, 5,800 slot machines), now nearly fifteen years old, employs over eight thousand people, earning revenues well in excess of $1 billion per annum. The profits from gambling have enabled the tribe to build a community centre and a child development centre, and each member of the tribe receives about $400,000 income every year. Gaming on tribal land has proved to be a perfect answer to endemic economic backwardness and social deprivation, and, like Las Vegas, the casinos are isolated enough for the rank whiff of gambling not to be smelt by mainstream America.

For a better parallel with Blackpool we should look to what

---

[11] Shortly after this chapter was written, a study by consultancy group Hall Aitken concluded much the same thing. They reckoned that casino construction would provide a temporary shot in the arm for jobs in, say, Blackpool but that the potential costs would outweigh the benefits. These costs included the loss of jobs and money from other businesses to gambling, the number of problem gamblers increasing exponentially and profits from regional casinos simply disappearing into the pockets of overseas investors. Their detailed analysis can be downloaded in full at www.hallaitken.co.uk.

casino gambling has done for Atlantic City. Like Blackpool, Atlantic City had a long history as a seaside destination, and like Blackpool it was a favoured resort until the 1960s, when a combination of its own decaying infrastructure and cheap air travel caused its decline. The Casino Control Act, which legalised gambling in Atlantic City in 1978, announced that gambling was 'a unique tool for urban redevelopment'. It also dictated that the casinos had to incorporate extensive leisure and convention facilities, thus paving the way for the resort-style casinos of Las Vegas, rather than stand-alone casinos.

The move did give a shot in the arm to the tourist industry, creating thousands of new jobs and providing millions of dollars' worth of investment. But Atlantic City did not benefit from urban renewal. If anything, the urban decay continued apace: homelessness increased, as did crime; unemployment remained high; and rampant land speculation led to soaring property prices and rents which forced out many local businesses. The New Jersey Governor's Advisory Commission on Gambling in 1988 could not have been clearer 'that retail businesses and retail employment in Atlantic City have continued to decline despite the presence of gambling.'

Now Atlantic City is essentially a gambling-only destination. The very fact that the casino-resorts had to offer everything to their customers meant that those same customers found few reasons to leave the casinos and plough their money into non-gambling businesses. Casinos are bad neighbours to have in a business environment. Unlike Las Vegas, Atlantic City's tourists are also less likely to stay overnight, it being less isolated. It is not hard to predict that visitors to Blackpool from cities like Manchester and Liverpool will do the same. Not so much tourists as gambling commuters.

Las Vegas is a unique answer to an American problem. It won't necessarily transplant successfully.

10

DEAD MONEY

'In order to play high-stakes poker, you need to have a total disregard for money. The only time you notice is when you run out.'

Doyle Brunson, poker professional

Las Vegas was the city that put poker on the map. Although a bastardised form of the game had been played from the early 19th century in New Orleans – the earliest recorded game was in 1829 when an Englishman, Joseph Cowell, witnessed a rigged game on a Mississippi steamboat – it was the arrival in Las Vegas in 1946 of a bootlegger called Benny Binion that led eventually to poker becoming the discerning gambler's game of choice. Binion had a police record as long as the trip he undertook from his native Dallas to Nevada in order to escape the clutches of the law. Vegas, with its legalised gambling and whiff of crime, proved to be his ideal resting place and casino ownership, in the shape of Binion's Horseshoe, proved to be his perfect metier. When it came to poker, Binion was a man of vision: despite the fact that it was an unfashionable game in casinos because of the relatively poor house rake, Binion's Horseshoe was marketed as the venue for the world's highest-limit poker games. In time, it became the spiritual home of the game.

It was in an attempt to re-create the buzz and excitement of a legendary five-month game of poker between Johnny Moss and Nick 'the Greek' Dandolos twenty-one years earlier that Binion brought into existence the World Series of Poker in 1970. He invited the world's best players to compete in games of their choosing, for stakes of their choosing, with the winner to be declared the World Champion. The tournament lasted a week, seven professionals took part and Johnny Moss was declared the inaugural winner. In 2005, the tournament lasted three weeks in May, there were more than thirty tournaments within the main tournament – with games ranging from hold'em to Omaha, from draw to stud, from pot-limit to no-limit. Just short of six thousand people made the journey to Vegas in order to take part and try and win the $7.5 million pot – a first prize that dwarfs virtually every other sporting tournament.

Binion's Horseshoe, along with the Golden Nugget, still dominates the downtown area of Las Vegas, although, relative to the casino-resorts of the Strip, it is a small-stake player in today's game. The poker room is still the grandest of any of the casinos, with forty-five oval-shaped poker tables, and a photo gallery of previous World Champions adorning one wall. Nevertheless, the atmosphere of faded glory is unmistakable. When I visited there were only two poker tables in use, the hollow clacking of chips mournfully filling a near-empty room. Harrah's, the casino group, now owns the rights to the World Series of Poker, with the result that the tournament is no longer played at Binion's. Across the street from his casino a statue of Benny Binion on horseback looks on in disgruntlement. Binion's statue faces due south, towards the casino-resorts of the Strip five miles away, where the grandest action now takes place.

John Duthie, a big-boned, floppy-haired forty-something, is no Benny Binion – as an independent television producer, his background is far more respectable than Binion's ever was – but he is to European poker what Binion was to the World Series. Despite having won the first ever Poker Million in the Isle of Man, Duthie describes himself as a recreational player. What he means by that is poker is no longer all-consuming. 'The game was everything to me for a while,' he told me over dinner at a casino in London, 'and I didn't like what it was doing to me as a person. To be really good at poker you have to be, at the table at least, a bit of a shit. You have to be aggressive and nasty, you have to be completely deceitful, and it is addictive to the point where everything else suffers – if not financially then certainly emotionally.'

It was Duthie who had the idea of instigating a European Poker Tour, to try and feed off the frenzy of interest in the televised World Series of Poker and the burgeoning internet poker market. It was Duthie who was also responsible for putting a poker tyro (me) up against the cream of European poker talent.

The tournament: the European Masters. The venue: the Grosvenor Victoria Casino. The game: Texas hold'em.

The Poker world, like the county cricket circuit, or any other chummy fraternity-cum-closed shop, has a lexicon all of its own. Knowing and speaking the lingo is paraded as a badge of honour, as proof of belonging. Whereas cricketers talk of 'bunsens' (spinning pitches), 'taking the gas' (bottling it), 'arse-nippers' (close games), 'good wheels' (quick bowling) and 'pulling the ladder up' (bottling it, again), poker players have their own, to outsiders, baffling language.

Listen to any poker conversation and you might hear a liberal sprinkling of the following terms: 'the nuts' (best hand), 'bad beat' (unlucky defeat), 'bullet' (an ace), 'the flop' (community cards), 'in the hole' (a concealed card), 'kicker' (side card to a pair, say), 'on tilt' (playing badly), 'rags' (shit cards), 'rock' (conservative player), 'trips' (three of a kind), 'all in' (to bet everything), 'under the gun' (first to bet) and 'wired' (a pair in the hole). 'I was playing against a rock and had been having rags all night. Suddenly, under the gun, I was aces wired. The flop produced another bullet and I had the nuts. I went all in.' You get the drift.

Mostly, the language is a constant. Phrases go into folklore and become part of the vernacular. 'Dead man's hand' – aces and eights paired – is perhaps the most famous example. It became so on 2 August 1876, when Jack McCall walked into Carl Mann's saloon in Deadwood, Dakota, and shot Wild Bill Hickok in the back of the head. Hickok was playing poker at the time and holding aces and eights when the moment arrived to go and meet his maker.

Occasionally, a new phrase pops up and instantly catches on. 'Dead money' is one such phrase. What does it mean? Basically, it means a sucker player, a player so useless, so out of his depth, that the other players have already mentally split the money between them. Even before a card has been dealt, before a bet has been called or raised, or a flop checked, that player, and his money, are lost. Finished. Dead. As stiff as a gentleman's collar.

It was a phrase that perfectly summed me up as I queued for the draw for the second European Tour Event of 2005 in London on Friday, 30 September. Actually, I never intended to play. The tournament was being held in my local casino, the Grosvenor Victoria – the 'Vic' – on Edgware Road, a couple of hundred yards from Marble Arch, and I wanted to go down and observe a tournament and get a feel for this strange game, which has exploded into the mainstream in recent years. Digital television channels show poker most evenings; internet poker companies advertise liberally (you will have seen the one which asks 'Have you got a bad poker face?'); people with established and steady jobs have been known to jack everything in to pursue a dream of making a living on the turn of a card; and semi-respectable people, like the journalist and biographer Tony Holden, have written bestselling books about the game.

I entered the casino and went up to the third floor where the draw was being held. I made myself known to the organisers to make sure that I was allowed to move around freely, to observe, to ask questions and generally make a royal nuisance of myself. 'Well, do you want to play?' asked Duthie and the marketing wizard from PokerStars.com, the company that was sponsoring the tournament. (The tie-up with PokerStars.com is a shrewd one, cashing in, as it does, on the internet poker boom.) Apart from wearing a lurid top with the PokerStars.com logo, there were no obvious drawbacks. My entry fee, £3,000, would be paid for me and I could play for the first prize of close on a hundred times that amount. It seemed a no-brainer. It certainly wasn't a gamble.

And yet I hesitated. Their assumption, since I was at the event, was that I could play. 'How many tournaments have you played?' Duthie asked casually. How about none. How about I've only ever played the game twice in my life: once in Georgetown, Guyana, on a particularly wet day when the only thing we could think of doing with the inflated and worthless Guyanese dollar was to play seven-card stud; and one evening before the last Ashes series began in a celebrity Ashes poker challenge against the former Australian fast bowler Merv Hughes, whose expertise at Texas hold'em was such that he thought you had to use the cards in the hole for every hand. That, gentlemen, I felt like saying but didn't, was it. Instead, I swallowed hard and thanked them for their generosity. Dead money, for sure. At least it wasn't my dead money.

I felt at home in the crowd. At just before four in the afternoon, there were about 250 players milling around. A melting pot of human existence – white, black, Asian, young, old, male, female – but I could see only one player in a suit, who I later found out was called 'Gentleman' Liam Flood. The rest were pretty dishevelled, which, since I have never felt at home amongst the sharp suits, was exactly my type of crowd. I sensed a disgruntled air: the Vic is too

small to house all the players at once and they had to play the first
stage of the tournament over two days: one half playing on Friday,
one half on Saturday, until the final twenty-four players were left to
play on the Sunday. It meant, though, that half the players had
come to London on a Friday, with the extra cost of travel and
accommodation and so on, but wouldn't be playing until the
following day.

Each evening the play lasted either until twelve players were left,
or until the casino closed at around 4 a.m. There was one, one-
hour, break for dinner, although players could get up and leave the
table at any time for a fag break or a piss if they so wished. Stamina
is a definite necessity for a poker player. Each table had eight or
nine players and, after eliminations, the organisers moved players
around to ensure that the optimum number was maintained at all
times. There were four card rooms, spread over two floors of the
casino, with the main feature table – the televised table – on the
third floor. Each player had paid a £3,000 buy-in (which gives you a
starting pot of £10,000 worth of chips to play with), so there was
just shy of three quarters of a million pounds in prize money to be
shared out. The winner would take home £280,000, with the prizes
reduced incrementally, so that places seventeen to twenty-four
would take home £4,000 each.

I approached the table where the draw was made, praying hard
that I would be in the following day's half of the draw. I needed a
day's grace to find my feet, ask a few questions and acquaint
myself with the nuances of the game. I knew the basics – like, yes,
there are four aces in a pack, and that, yes, a flush beats a straight
– but not much else. At 3.58, two minutes before the scheduled
start of the first day's play, I reached into the green bag to draw
out my table number. F5. 'You'll be playing tomorrow, Mike.'
Thank Christ for that. 'Most of the good players are playing
tomorrow, actually. There's Chris Moneymaker, a former World

Series champion, and Isabelle "No Mercy" Mercier.' Oh Fuck. Fuckity Fuck.

The game is no-limit Texas hold'em, regarded as the daddy of all poker games – a simple enough game to learn but an enduringly complex one to master. Each player is dealt two cards face down, called pocket cards. On the strength of these first two cards a player must decide whether to enter the hand. Then the flop is dealt – that is, three cards face up that everyone can see. Then come two more community cards dealt face up – the turn card (fourth card) and the river (fifth card) – and from these seven cards (two down, five up) a player must make his best five-card poker hand. In descending order, the best hands are: royal straight flush, straight flush, four of a kind, full house, flush, straight, three of a kind, two pair, pair and finally a lowly high card – with the ace being, obviously the highest. So far, so easy.

Then there is the betting structure. The tournament game is no-limit, which means that you can, at any time, bet all your chips. The first round of betting comes after the first two cards have been drawn. The betting begins with the person to the left of the big blind. Small and big blinds are the rotating mandatory amounts which must be paid before each game begins. These are to prevent conservative players from just sitting and waiting for a good hand, and to ensure that there is something in the pot before the cards are dealt. The blinds, in this tournament, start at £25 for the small blind and £50 the big blind, and they double every hour. The first person to bet – the person 'under the gun' – can match the big blind, raise the bet or fold. The rest then bet accordingly. The next round of betting comes after the flop has been dealt. The options are to check (no bet), raise (increase the bet), call (match the bet) or fold. Then there is a round of betting after the turn and river cards.

Then the pocket cards are revealed and the best hand scoops the chips.

All this much I know. What I don't know is the strategy, the tactics, the nuances of the game. What are good hands to play with? Are there dangerous hands? Is there a good position to bet from? What constitutes a big bet? Is it best to play aggressively or conservatively? Is it good to play chancily, to gamble? Is poker gambling at all? I had twenty-four hours to find out.

The first person I bump into after the draw is Neil 'Bad Beat' Channing, an established player on the British scene – the only British player to have finished in the top 200 of the World Series in consecutive years. He has, in fact, just returned from an eight-week stay in Vegas, where he had won $33,000. He looks like a fish that has been lying doggo for months – totally listless and lifeless. All pokered out. Nevertheless, he isn't about to miss a tournament on his home patch and he's simultaneously entered into another one at the Gutshot club in London's East End. When I say hello he is trying to negotiate selling off his place at the Gutshot to someone else.

He sums up player 'types' for me: the first, the 'rock' or conservative player, the player who has plenty of time and patience and who sits and waits for a good hand, and will only play a good hand; the second, the more aggressive player who tries to make things happen by taking risks, the type for whom bluffing is an integral part of the game; and the third, who doesn't really know what he is doing but, by dint of that fact, can be just as dangerous as the other two. I knew which category I belonged in. Which was he?

'I'm arrogant enough to think I'm in the second group. The best hold'em players play aggressively. Your best bet,' he adds, 'is to get yourself from the third group into the first group as quick as you can. Take your time to suss out the table.'

Channing points out what looks to be a table with some good players. There is a young, good-looking, hip-looking Asian with dark shades perched on the top of his head. This is Ram 'Crazy Horse' Vaswani of the 'Hendon Mob' – a group of four poker nuts who travel the world playing poker and bring us news of their progress on their site TheHendonMob.com.

Then there is a sallow-faced Chinese man, Willie Tann, who last year topped the rankings on the European tour and is one of the few Europeans to be in possession of a World Series gold bracelet. If body language counts for anything in poker, then Tann is having a miserable time of it. He sits slumped, head permanently bowed as if the poker gods have been constantly dealing him bad beats. It turns out they have.

Channing looks around the room and points out other well-known faces to me: there's Lawrence Gosney, who won a $2,000 no-limit hold'em tournament at Vegas in 1994, winning a gold bracelet – the ultimate poker trophy – in the process; there's Iwan Jones, who was working for Sky Sports six weeks ago when he was persuaded by his mates to enter the World Poker Exchange London Open and walked away with £750,000. He doesn't work for Sky Sports any more. There's 'Smokin' Steve Vladar, who fell in love at the poker table with Xuyen Pham, spent two years teaching her the poker ropes, after which she entered the world pot-limit championship in Ireland and walked away with $300,000. They are now married and she's known as 'Bad Girl' Pham. There's Dave 'El Blondie' Colclough (he has peroxide-bleached hair), one of the best players on the European circuit, one of the few, says Neil, to really make it pay. He's sitting next to Richard Gryko, an up-and-coming young player, and the player whom Colclough said recently in an interview he most respected.

What is it, I ask Neil, about these nicknames? 'Most players have one. Usually they are given to you by your opponents as a mark of respect. But see him there,' he says, pointing to a large, shaven-headed player on El Blondie's table, 'he's called Simon Trumper and he gave himself his nickname. Simon "Aces" Trumper.' Neil snorts and repeats incredulously, 'Simon "Aces" Trumper! No one takes him seriously.'

Suddenly, Neil nudges me and points to Crazy Horse's table. 'This is a big hand.' Willie Tann is sitting opposite an avuncular-looking, white-haired man (in a different place, you might think of him as a retired grandfather) called Frank Callaghan. Callaghan has gone all in, having seen the flop fall A-K-Q. Willie sits motionless, deciding whether to call or fold. One mistake here and he's gone and forgotten. Three grand up in smoke. Frank fixes Willie with a stare and repeatedly twists a commemorative World Masters disk that all the players have been given. As Willie contemplates the continuing cruelty of the poker gods – why am I on *this* table of all tables, and why have they dealt me *this* hand? – Neil whispers his analysis of the hand to me: 'This is a huge hand. Willie knows that Frank is a conservative player. Willie's probably got a bullet in his own hand, and therefore the best pair. But Frank's gone all in so soon in the tournament, which must mean he's got something big, pocket aces, kings or queens, I should think. Willie should pass.'

Willie hasn't moved. Crazy Horse is getting irritated and starts flicking his chips forward with backspin motion, so that they roll forward and then spin back towards his pile, a bit like a golf ball spinning back on a green. Very cool.

'Jesus, it's a good job you don't play speed poker, Willie,' says Crazy Horse. Willie looks up to the heavens. He looks around the table. He raises both arms and places them behind the back of his head. Finally, he folds but does so by turning his cards upwards. He has A-K. He looks pleadingly to Frank to show his cards. Frank obliges. Pocket aces. Willie, momentarily, sits up a fraction in his seat. 'Dodged a bullet there,' he says, before collapsing back into a slump.

I wander off to elicit some more advice. 'Gentleman' Liam Flood lives up to his nickname and gives freely of his time. (In fact, throughout the tournament I found the older, experienced tournament players absolutely charming. It was the young, internet players who were less forthcoming. Maybe that's the result of sitting in front of a computer screen all day long.) The Gentleman's advice is this: 'Play tight around the button and around the blinds. And more expansively away from the blinds.'

'What's the button?'

He raises his eyebrows quizzically but calmly adds, with no discernible sense of condescension, 'That's the position where the cards are dealt from.'

The Gentleman is advising me on the basics of positional play. 'If you are first to play, or "under the gun", then you are at a disadvantage, as the other players get to see what you do first. Consequently, when you are furthest away from the blinds, you are amongst the last to play, and as some players will have already folded you can often sneak into hands with less good cards in an attempt to "steal" the blinds.'

'You have three options,' he says, 'you can call, raise or fold. Use only two of them. Raise or fold, don't call. Twos through tens are small pairs – don't play them. Aces with sevens, eights or nines don't win many hands, either – don't play them. And most of all, don't try bluffing.'

I ask him whether he is an aggressive or conservative player. 'Aggressive. Definitely aggressive. All the best players are.'

Why, then, are all the aggressive players telling me to play conservatively?

I'm introduced to the grand old man of British poker, Colin Kennedy, a softly spoken, professorial-type Irishman. 'Play solidly,' he says. 'It's almost impossible to play too tightly. But when you bet, make large bets. A small bet is a bit like fishing outside the off stump – it can only get you into trouble. It's an easy game to learn the basics of, but it's extremely complex psychologically. A combination of skill, luck and courage is essential. Of those, courage is the most essential. And remember, it takes courage to fold a good hand. In a funny way, though, stupidity can be an advantage. Even stupid people can learn the basics and that gives them a tremendous feeling of confidence, which makes them extremely dangerous.' I don't know whether this last insight is aimed at me, but I take it as a positive.

Willie's table is no longer Willie's table, as Willie is no longer there. His place has been taken by a much younger Chinese man, with a wild mop of raven-black hair, whose style of play, I'm told, matches it. Sure enough, he soon causes consternation. He doesn't realise that one of the players on the table has gone all in, and he attempts to raise. His chips have crossed the line, but when he realises that his opponent is all in, he withdraws his chips. One of the organisers is called for and the ruling is that the Chinese man must call and show his hand. He has 3-4 and his opponent has gone all in with A-K. Unbelievably the flop comes 2-5-6 to give the Chinese man a straight. Suddenly, he's the chip leader on his table. What was Colin saying about courage being more important than luck? He was right about stupidity, though. The Chinese man is not deterred: soon enough he calls £10,000 with 10-2; then he loses A-J to Crazy Horse's Q-Q; and then goes all in with A-6 and loses to Crazy Horse's A-J. The Chinese man stands and without a hint of emotion departs the scene. He goes straight to the roulette tables. Crazy Horse is the new chip leader. Whoah, boy!

The wild Chinese man is clearly an impulsive and compulsive gambler and probably a loser on the poker table. Most poker players are uncertain when you ask them whether poker is gambling at all. For whilst luck accounts for anything up to 20 per cent of the game, courage, skill and mastery of psychology count for far more. The best cards don't often, in fact they rarely, win the most money. The best players often do. Poker, unlike other forms of gambling such as roulette or dice, is all about wagering at favourable rather than unfavourable odds. Players who consistently rely on the turn cards to get them out of jail will, in the long run, be losing players.

Even so, the need to take risks, to bluff bad hands, which is essential to success at the tables, fits in with the profile of a typical gambler. And, in fact, some of the poker players I bump into at the Vic are what is known as 'leak' players – that is, whatever they win at poker they tend to lose at other forms of gambling. Willie Tann is one of the biggest leak players on the circuit. He knows it, too. 'Mike, it's a sickness. I've lost so much over the years on horses and dice. I'm trying to cut back now, but it's difficult. About the only good thing I've done in my life is to put my boy through Westminster School and Oxford. He's now a successful lawyer. Last Christmas we had a pact that if he stopped smoking I'd put an end to my "leaks". He doesn't smoke any more.'

The most shocking example of a leak player in the history of poker is Stu 'The Kid' Ungar. He was an almost impossibly brilliant poker player, with a photographic memory, razor-sharp mind and balls of steel, who won the World Series three times: at the first time of asking in 1980, then in 1981 and again, in his last appearance, in 1997. He was also an almost impossibly terrible gambler. He craved action no matter what the action was or for how much. He was the ultimate sick gambler for whom money was simply a means to an end. When he was found dead of a drug overdose in 1998 he had $800 to his name.

When I find Willie he is not leaking but replenishing – alone at the bar, nursing a drink. I ask his advice for tomorrow. 'Stay alive,' he says slowly, staring into his drink. 'Staying alive is the most important thing. Play consistently. Last the distance. Accumulate slowly. Don't commit your chips. Play the small and medium-sized pots.' Was this advice for me or a mournful review of his own play that evening? Suddenly, he brightens up. 'The five Ps are essential. Position. Psychology. Perseverence. Practice. What's the fifth P? Shit, I can't remember. Look at my website tonight and find out the fifth P. Good Luck.'

Willie Tann's was the last voice I heard from the poker world before I went to bed that evening and the first voice I hear the next morning. 'Hi, it's Willie Tann speaking,' the voice message on my phone says. 'Could you give me a ring, please.' The message was left at 2.42 a.m. Clearly, after his exit from the tournament Willie had continued to play the tables. I don't have his number, but since I will see him at the Vic I think little more about it.

What am I feeling this morning? Nervous? A little. Excited? Certainly. Confident? Absolutely not. But, who knows, maybe this story has the prefect ending.

I want to get to the Vic in good time to settle my nerves and find out a little about my opponents. When I arrive all the talk is of the previous evening's play and the bad beats handed out to El Blondie and Greg 'The Fossilman' Raymer (so named after the fossils which he uses to guard his cards). The Fossilman was last year's World Champion and was ousted in this tournament just before the cut-off point of twelve players was reached. Only Crazy Horse, of those that I had watched the previous evening, had survived the cut, with £89,500 in chips.

Once the playing list has been posted I ask around for some information on my opponents. The most renowned, apparently, is Noah 'Exclusive' Boeken, a thrusting young player from

Holland who already has a European Tour event to his name. Not only had he won last year's tournament in Copenhagen, and finished seventeenth on the money list with 170,000 euros, but he had finished third in the first event of this year's tour in Barcelona only a fortnight before. A man – a boy – in form. He was described to me as an 'alpha male' of European poker. Others who are well known enough to merit respect are Anthony Mackay – three top-ten finishes in 2004 – and an old-school tournament professional called Dave Barnes, who 'Gentleman' Liam Flood tells me has 'already forgotten more than you'll ever know about poker.'

It is time for a last-minute piece of advice. Cue Des Wilson, one time President of the Liberal Democrats, environmental campaigner and former cricket administrator, who was now trawling the poker circuit researching a book. 'Above all else,' he cautions, 'don't show any sign of weakness. The moment they know you're a novice, they'll eat you alive.' Great.

At 2.50 p.m., ten minutes before the scheduled start, I wander over to table F and take up the number five position – that is, five from the dealer moving in a clockwise direction. I am the first to arrive. Anthony Mackay is next: mid-forties, relatively smartly dressed by the standards of the tournament, with slacks, an open-necked blue shirt and a jacket. Worryingly, he has a sponsor's cap on his head, and a flashy-looking silver watch. After the first day, a player's watch, and how he handles his chips, were my own particular clues as to how competent a player might be. Crazy Horse was proof enough of the chip-riffling, whilst all the decent players seemed to want to show off their timekeeping wares. Greg Raymer had the biggest, juiciest most diamond-encrusted watch I had ever seen. Mackay's watch is thick, silver and sparkling and he moves his chips effortlessly between the fingers of one hand. I introduce myself. We shake hands. 'You should be good at this,' he says; 'both sports are essentially battles of the mind.' Not much chance of anonymity, then.

Stewart 'Stoogster' Brown sits down next, in the number one seat. Younger than Mackay, it turns out that Stoogster is an inexperienced tournament player who has qualified via a number of home games in Scotland that PokerStars.com have sponsored. He has short, black stubbly hair and is suitably unshaven – as if he is trying to forget the fact that in real life he is a solicitor. He introduces himself to me in a broad Scottish accent: 'This is not your usual bag.' Nor his, I suspect, from the dismal-looking watch (sober-coloured and leather-strapped) that he wears on his wrist.

A young, outrageously young, almost prepubescent American sits down next to the Stoogster. He has greased-down black hair, combed straight forward, which is gelled upwards at the furthest point from the crown of his head. He has the pasty-faced look of someone who has not seen the sun for six months. An internet player, clearly. Flashy watch, though, and a silver neck chain displayed prominently. He goes by the name of Tom Dwan. Tom 'Holdem_nl' Dwan, I later discovered.

Rhea Clevenger from San Jose, California, sits down in seat number seven, two to my left. Short, broad-beamed, leathery features and a blue (sponsor's!) cap pulled down over her straggly ginger hair. A long sports top prevents me from checking out her watch, but in between the thumb and forefinger of her right hand is a small tattoo of a cross. Carefully, she places a number of items behind her chips: a purple precious stone, a family photograph, a silver coin and a silver cross. She'll be the superstitious one, then.

Opposite me, at number eight, Dave Barnes is the oldest member of the group by some distance. He has short iron-grey hair and a bulbous nose. His red-tinted glasses are perched on top of his head and his short-sleeved polo shirt betrays a menacing-looking tattoo and a chunky gold watch. A gold watch! He introduces himself in a rasping East End drawl – the voice of a thousand late-night card rooms.

Three minutes before the off, Liam Barker, a pale, pointy-nosed Irishman, squeezes into the number six seat on my left. Like everyone else on the table, he must fill out a release form for the television company that will broadcast the event. They require every player to give away permission for the tournament organisers to be able to show the programme throughout the universe. 'That's just in case they find life out there between now and the feckin' programme going to air,' says Liam. Mackay complains about the air-conditioning unit, which is wafting out cold streams of air from directly above our heads. Liam agrees: 'It's like sitting under the tail end of feckin' Hurricane Rita.' Then he pulls up the collar of his green sweatshirt and snuggles down into his seat, to make his point. 'If I start shakin' when I want to bet, it doesn't mean I'm nervous, OK? It just means that I'm feckin' freezin'.'

It's 3.01, one minute past start time, and still there is no sign of Noah 'Exclusive' Boeken. About five seconds before the organiser announces the off, a young, spotty teenager sidles into seat number four, directly to my right. In another place you might take him to be a skateboarder, as he wears baggy jeans, trainers and a white hooded sweat top. He sits down, looks at no one, and speaks to no one. He produces a small white iPod, and two earpieces, one of which is inserted into each ear. Exclusive is wired for action. I can't see his watch. I don't need to. He oozes confidence.

Yours truly makes up the table of eight. Jeans. Deck shoes. Awful black polo shirt with sponsor's logo (will it fool them?). Cheap Timex 'Ironman' watch with velcro strap.

I quickly do a mental check list of my tactics: play tight around the button and the blinds, play tight generally; don't bluff; raise or fold but don't call; fold small pairs and anything less than A-10. Shit, I'm feeling so cautious and low on confidence that I'm praying for crap cards so that I don't have to play any hands for a while.

The dealer turns over the cards, which have been pre-arranged in their suits, and begins to shuffle. Soon enough he sends the cards skimming out over the table, two to each player, and decision time is upon me. Like a pro, I cross my right hand over my left and use my left thumb to lift the top corner of my two cards to take a peek. It doesn't do to look at the whole card, I have gathered, just the top corner – enough to know the number and suit. Two little threes are staring back at me. Pocket threes! Shit! A pair on my very first hand. To my right, Exclusive folds, and remembering Gentleman's advice on small pairs I nonchalantly send my pocket threes skimming back to the dealer. Dave Barnes wins the hand with a king high. 'It's never good to win the first hand, Barnsey!' hollers Anthony Mackay.

For the most part the atmosphere is good-humoured. Good hands are appreciated and shrewd folds are generally well received. Whilst the pace of play is quick, the action is slow. With the blinds at just £25 and £50, it means that you can effectively play eight hands and lose just £75 if you play tight. With £10,000 chips to start with, even a duffer should be able to last three or four hours if he wants to.

But, of course, continually looking at the pocket cards and folding is boring. That at least must have been going through my mind when, with everyone else having folded, I call the big blind with 4-8 suited. Dave Barnes is on the big blind and isn't prepared to let me steal it. The flop comes Q-4-7. He checks. I check. The turn comes 9. He checks. I check. The river comes A. He raises. Remembering not to call, I have two options: fold or raise. I should have folded, instead I reraise £500. £500! Normally, I'd no more bet £500 than I would wear a string vest in public. What was I doing? But this seems to throw Barnes a little. He pauses and looks me in the eye. 'What are you doing, Mikey?' he muses for the benefit of the whole table. 'Are you bluffing, have you been slow-playing me, or are you flushing?' All the time he looks me in the eye. Is this poker's form of sledging? Well, I think, I've been here before, pal. I stare straight back. The longer he talks, the more I think he is going to fold. In the end, he didn't want to let this novice steal his blind in front of the whole table. He calls. My tiny pair of fours is no match for his A-A-Q-Q. 'You were bluffing me, Mikey! Nice try!'

'Gentleman' Liam Flood is on the table behind me and has been following proceedings. 'You weren't listening to me,' he shouts out in the general direction of my table so that I could hear but so that it wasn't obviously aimed at me. Des Wilson wanders over before the next hand is dealt. 'You still in, then?' he says, pointing at me, laughing. So much for not showing any weakness.

With my confidence draining fast, I win a hand – A-J to Liam Barker's A-10. At this point, fifty minutes into play, neither Exclusive nor Holdem_nl has yet to twitch a muscle, let alone play a hand. The main action is from Rhea Clevenger. Even I can recognise an aggressive player when I see one. Her actions are decisive, from the moment she places her silver coin and cross on each of her pocket cards, to the moment she scoops the pot, she is all aggression. Forty minutes later, I find myself head to head with her. I have A-K in the hole – the type of hand that even 'Gentleman' Liam Flood would be happy if I played. The superstitious one raises pre-flop £500. I call before I remember that I shouldn't be calling. The flop is no help to me. She raises £1,000. Oh God! My victory over Liam Barker has given me enough confidence to be able to take some time out to think about what to do. I feel this penetrating stare from Clevenger. Allan Donald eat your heart out, you had nothing on this girl. 'I can feel your heat,' I say. She stares. I hear Colin Kennedy in my head: 'Courage, boy, courage.' I fold.

Tic-tac men have now largely disappeared from the racing scene, replaced by mobile phones. The character of on-course bookmaking is set to change even more dramatically as betting exchanges become more dominant.

Kicking King's victory in the 2005 Gold Cup proved expensive for nine anonymous punters. For thousands of Irish, though, Cheltenham 2005 was well worth the wait and the expense.

Barry Geraghty keeps his balance as Kicking King jumps the last in the 2005 Gold Cup. His victory was enough to prove the old adage that 'there's no such thing as a free bet'. Layers who thought he would not even compete are still licking their wounds.

On the first day of the Centurion Park Test match in 2000 both teams were trying to win. Four days later, thanks to Hansie Cronje's greed, the fixer was in.

Darren Gough, Chris Silverwood, Jacques Kallis and Shaun Pollock would not have known of Hansie Cronje's deception, and nor did the general public until much later. It just shows how powerful the captain can be in cricket, and how the advent of spread betting made it much easier for the unscrupulous to target individual players rather than the whole team.

'The moment I took my eyes from Jesus my whole world turned dark' – Hansie Cronje's testimony to the King Commission in Cape Town, April 2000. He looks as though the full impact of his betrayal has finally dawned on him.

Mohammad Azharuddin leaves the Central Bureau of Investigation in New Delhi, June 2000. The CBI report was the most thorough of all the match-fixing reports because it took account of bookmakers and players. Azharuddin was one of a number of high-profile players whom a bookie called M.K. Gupta accused of being crooked.

Inset: The gambling tendencies Nick Leeson, here wearing his Barings trader's jacket, brought down one of the oldest names i British banking. That experienc hasn't stopped him gambling – regularly plays internet poker. A least this time he is gambling with his own rather than the bank's money.

Left: The red letters on the display terminal say that Japan considering suspending Barings business. Leeson's fraud, and th bank's negligence, was about to become apparent to the rest of the world.

Below: A multitude of slot machines tempt the punter in L Vegas. Clint Eastwood pays homage to one called 'a fistful o dollars' – those dollars usually end up in the casino owners' pockets. Slots account for anywhere between 50 and 70 pe cent of the total casino rake in Las Vegas.

Greg 'The Fossilman' Raymer takes home the 2004 World Series poker title and US$5 million. His nickname comes from the fossils he brings to the table when he plays. More off-putting for his opponents are the reflective snake-eye glasses that he routinely wears.

Have you got a bad poker face? On this evidence, I'm afraid I have. I also have a disturbingly small pile of chips, which means my exit from the European Masters is nigh – and no self-respecting poker player would be seen dead at the table with such a feeble watch.

By the time Australian Joe Hachem won the World Series in 2005, it was worth US$7.5 million – one of the biggest first prizes in sport.

Left: The Oasis Casino in Jericho in May 2001, some seven months after it was forced to close. Its future looks bleak in the wake of Hamas's election victory. Gambling, of course, is illegal under Muslim law.

Below: Neon, neon and more neon – the Tropicana Casino on the Las Vegas Strip. Once you've seen one casino, you've seen them all.

uart Wheeler revolutionised the face of gambling when he introduced spread betting on the ice of gold. He is also a mean poker player, having competed in the World Series in Las gas on a number of occasions. Here he relaxes at Binion's Horseshoe, contemplating a yal flush, among other things…

mo wrestlers, in town for the Grand Sumo Championship, enjoy a game of punto banco at e Mandalay Bay Casino on the Las Vegas Strip in 2005. The Far East produces the most natical punters, no matter what shape or size.

Andrew Black and Edward Wray took the gamble of their lives when they introduced betting exchanges to the market in 2000. Now Betfair is reckoned to be worth in the region of £1 billion, but whether betting exchanges will bring about the bookies' demise, as the Betfair launch predicted, is doubtful.

It has never been easier to win or lose your money. The living room is the perfect gambling destination and internet poker – this example is from Victor Chandler Poker – is the latest gambling craze. Internet poker entrepreneurs Anurag Dikshit, Russell DeLeon and Ruth Parasol featured heavily in the latest *Sunday Times* Rich List.

'That's how girls play!' she says, scooping the chips.

'Why d'ya say that?' asks Dave Barnes.

'Because I'm a girl.'

Barnes almost jumps out of his seat. He lifts his sunglasses and looks Clevenger up and down. 'Jesus. Can you prove it?'

A five-minute break is called. I wander away from the table to clear my head. Except that a low-hung fug of smoke has suddenly developed as seemingly all the players use the break to light up. Leaning against the one-armed bandits is Isabelle 'No Mercy' Mercier – a feminine female poker player if ever there was one: tight jeans and tight black top advertising both her website and her charms. I chat with the Stoogster. 'What do you think of the American girl?' I venture. 'She scares the shit out of me.'

'Yep. She wants to wear the penis, that's for sure.'

Annie Duke, brother of two-time World Series bracelet winner Howard Lederer, and World Series bracelet winner herself, believes that women have an innate advantage at the poker table. 'There is an interesting thing that happens when you put a woman at a poker table,' she has said, 'and all you men out there should be paying close attention to this: some men become unhinged – they forget they are playing a ruthless game in which emotion should be separated from strategy – they forget that the gender of your opponent should make no difference in how you play the game. And that is a good thing for all us girls.'

Duke identifies two types of male reaction. First, the flirter, the guy who immediately starts to think with the wrong part of his body. He sees a conquest not an opponent. Duke's advice is to profit from this, even flirt back if comfortable, because deep down this man doesn't want to take money from a lady. Then there is the male chauvinist pig. The man who goes to his weekly poker game to escape the missus, not play poker with her. He's affronted that she's even there. He'll try to show her who's boss, will bluff too often and call too often. Easy money, reckons Duke – although it helps that she's a damn good poker player herself and that she majored in psychology at Columbia University. And she doesn't look like Rhea Clevenger. The question is: is Dave Barnes the flirter or the chauvinist? Odds on, he doesn't flirt with Clevenger.

Two and half hours after the start of play, Noah 'Exclusive' Boeken deigns to join in the action and he calls the big blind. Clevenger raises pre-flop £5,000. Exclusive sits bolt upright, as if the wires from his iPod have suddenly sent 10,000 volts through his body. Exclusive folds.

Next, it's Holdem_nl's turn to feel the Clevenger heat. The flop is 9-K-A and both Clevenger and Dave Barnes are in for £1,500 each. Holdem_nl suddenly looks even younger than his tender years, as if he'd rather be anywhere else except the Vic card room. He calls. Further checks bring a 5 and an 8 on the turn and the river. Barnes has the pot with A-A-9-9. Holdem_nl throws his cards away with a leg-spinner's action. His pale cheeks begin to flush. Yes, they definitely turn red! Bless! I guess no one can see *that* in front of the computer screen. His discomfort increases my confidence. We're three and a half hours in and I still have £8,000 chips or so.

Little was I to know that the end was near. For the second time that day, I get a pair in the hole on the small blind. Pocket kings! Anthony Mackay and Clevenger call the blind. The flop brings A-10-4. The presence of the bullet, and of Clevenger, causes me untold grief. I now have a pair of kings with an ace kicker. I should be raising, but what if either has an ace? What if I raise, and the bitch reraises? Everyone checks. The turn card comes J. The fact that Mackay and Clevenger have checked should be my cue to play aggressively: if either had an ace they probably wouldn't have checked initially (unless they were check-raising, but we're getting technical now). Timidly, I check along with the other two. The river comes 3. Another round of checking and we turn over the cards. My K-K stands out like a bishop in a brothel and I take home a small pot that amounts to little more than the blinds. I'm just relieved to have won a pot against Clevenger.

Next hand: I'm on the big blind, and I get K-J suited (diamonds). The only other person to call is Holdem_nl. Ha! He raises pre-flop £500. I call and then remember that I shouldn't. The flop comes 10-Q-K (Q-10 matching my diamonds). I have top pair, possible royal flush, possible straight flush, two possible straights and a possible flush. And I'm playing against a prepubescent with a tendency to blush at the slightest discomfort. He raises £1,000. I reraise £2,500. £2,500! He goes all in. I turn over my K-J. Holdem_nl turns over J-9. He has a pre-made straight: 9-10-J-Q-K. I need another diamond, or a nine or an ace. I reckon I've about a one in four chance of getting out of the hole I suddenly find myself in. I get no help on the turn or the river. One minute all in, the next minute all out. Holdem_nl lets out a sigh. Etiquette demands that I should have stood up once I went all in, in preparation to leave, since I was the second favourite before the draw. I simply sit there numb. It is time to go. Clevenger shakes my hand – firm grip. I stand slowly and say my goodbyes and wander off to the bar. Dead money.

Eight thousand pounds lost in two hands, in about five minutes' play! There is no getting away from the fact that the essence of poker, as with all gambling, is money. In this case, though, money is both everything to do with poker and nothing. Without money, and the feeling that you are playing for just that bit more than you can afford, the game is irrelevant. And yet there is no way a player can be thinking about money – the mortgage, rent, repayments on the car, for example – when he calls, raises or goes all in. What normal human being can bet thousands, hundreds of thousands, even millions, on the turn of a card? No, the professional poker player, or even the recreational player who plays in a decent hand, must have a supreme indifference to money. For them it is simply a means of keeping score.

For the older tournament players, it seems to me that poker is less about money and more about a lifestyle choice – an attempt to escape the daily grind and the dull nine-to-five existence that most of us lead. These old pros see themselves as bucking the system, reliant on nobody else but themselves. Living on their luck and instinct, often living a hand-to-mouth existence, but at least it is *their* hand-to-mouth existence. 'I'm a sick man, Mike,' said Colin Kennedy, 'but at least it's my sickness. I'm not answerable to anybody and I've led the life I wanted to lead, not the life that other people wanted me to lead.' No surprise, then, that as with many professional sportsmen, the divorce rate amongst professional poker players is alarming. 'It is a refuge from the world,' continued Kennedy. 'A retreat into a bubble where the only thing that can go wrong is that you can lose your dough.' For the amateur, the once-a-week player, the motivation is often the same: it is the one evening where the boring lawyer, accountant or doctor can bluff and bet and bullshit and believe that he is, however momentarily, as cool as the Cincinnati Kid.

For the internet players, though, it seems to me that money is a greater motivation to play than for the older tournament players. Many of the internet players look to the example of Chris Money-maker as an inspiration: the internet qualifier who started with $40 and who went on to scoop millions in Las Vegas. For them it is less about lifestyle – the smoke and grit of the card rooms – and more about clean living and cash.

Poker, like cricket, seems to be one of those games that messes with your head. And so after I got dumped I spent the next couple of hours mulling over what I did right – not a lot – and what I did wrong – plenty. Specifically, I beat myself up over my exit. Not so much the hand that I had played. The experts seemed of mixed opinion whether I should have called Holdem_nl's all in – Dave Barnes said I ought to have definitely folded, the Stoogster thought I made the right call, whilst, later, Holdem_nl thought himself 'a little lucky'. No, I beat myself up over the fact that I was guilty of what, in cricket, we call playing the man and not the ball. After his blushing episode earlier, I had mentally poured scorn on Holdem_nl and discounted him. It took me a while to work out that the one player I ought to have been taking on was the one player who tried her best to intimidate me, Rhea Clevenger. Bitch.

After that I did what most poker players seem to do once they have been eliminated: I bored other poker players with my bad beat stories. I also kept my eye on how far my table companions were progressing. 'Exclusive' Boeken departed about ten minutes after me to another rapier-like thrust from Clevenger. 'She scared me, too,' Exclusive revealed, letting his mask drop for an instant. Dave Barnes was the next to go and when I saw him last he was bemoaning the presence of so many internet players. 'Some of them are fucking clueless,' he complained, 'and it fucks it up for all the good players!' Mackay went shortly after being moved to another table, as did the Irishman Liam Barker. Clevenger found her way onto the feature table where Neil 'Bad Beat' Channing became another victim. Channing wandered past me, chuntering, 'I fucked up. I didn't have a big ace. I shoulda raised her before the flop.'

Clevenger didn't last, though: all in with a pair of sevens, and getting another seven on the flop, she came up against three queens. Six titties as they say in the trade. Ha! Two players from my table did get through to the final day: Stewart 'Stoogster' Brown went through with £72,500 chips and was duly eliminated the next day in twenty-second place; Tom 'Holdem_nl' Dwan blushed (bluffed?)

his way through with £115,900 and was going well on the final day until his A-K met another A-K – unfortunately, the board made his opponent a flush. Holdem_nl's tournament, like mine, was over. At least I could say I'd been knocked out by the player who came twelfth in the European Masters.

My brief flirtation with the poker world over, it was time to go home. On the way out, Willie Tann came running over, excited. 'Mike, I've remembered the fifth P! I've remembered the fifth P! It's patience. You gotta have patience in this game.' Go well, Willie.

JEFF DUVALL
The Poker Player

As his mother started having her contractions whilst enjoying a night out at the dogs, it is no surprise that gambling has been the central force in 56-year-old Jeff Duvall's life. Indeed, for most of his childhood, gambling was ever present: his family lived virtually next to a dog track and they gambled on anything and everything. 'Dogs, horses, cards – you name it, we gambled on it.'

He can always remember a biggish card school going on at home. Mother and father were keen players, as were both his brothers and a large contingent of uncles and aunties. 'The games were Newmarket sevens, chase the ace, brag and solo – but never poker, funnily enough.'

He left school at 16 with two O levels – in art and maths. He went straight into the betting-shop business which was booming on the back of the 1960 Betting and Gaming Act, which legalised off-course cash betting. Technically he was still under age, although it didn't seem to bother A. and P. Williams, the firm that employed him as a trainee manager. By 17, he was managing a betting shop in Oxford Street.

'I was a bit of a sick gambler then. I'd go to the dogs most nights, punt on horses during the day and generally be happy to have a go at anything. In fact, my brother had a serious problem and became a secretary of Gamblers Anonymous. It caused a bit of a falling-out between us: he wanted me to join the group, whereas I was too pigheaded and thought I could control it. My brother was a seriously good boxer whose only professional defeat came in his last fight.

The trouble was that he was a hopeless gambler and would often have gambled away his ticket money before the fight began, so that often he was fighting for nothing.

'I went into the pub business briefly, owning pubs in Blackfriars and Finsbury, and around my mid-twenties I started playing blackjack seriously. I'd been a member of the Vic casino for a good number of years already and knew a little about card counting. Thorp's card counting is the basis of the system we used, but we – and I worked in a team of three – we moved it on a stage further by moving into sequential tracking and shuffle tracking. Essentially, we looked for blackjack games with dealers who were poor shufflers [this was before mechanised shuffling] and we looked for sequences of cards before aces. Often those sequences would repeat themselves after a bad shuffle and we gave ourselves a much bigger edge than you would get through simple card counting. I began to get banned from everywhere – I've been barred from the Vic on four occasions – so earnings kind of ebbed and flowed. It was a good living when we found a good game, but things could be quiet for too long.

'By this stage I was married with two children. My wife later ran off with one of my good friends, although we – the wife and I, that is – get on better now than ever before. But my gambling lifestyle made things tough between us for a while. It was tougher than it should have been, because I was still a leak gambler at this stage. I'd throw a lot of money away on the horses and on sports betting, which was then in its infancy. I guess it was difficult for my kids. I know that one of them used to say I was a fireman when she was asked what her father did. Funnily enough, now that the four of them have grown up they are rather proud of the fact that they have a professional gambler for a dad. Beats saying he's an accountant, I guess. It's a sign of the times.

'In the early 1980s we moved to the States. A good friend of mine called Mike Svobodny is a very famous backgammon player over there. I knew him well from frequent trips to Vegas and in 1986 he mentioned to me that he thought I would do well to go to New York and learn about options trading. The backgammon and blackjack were drying up a bit and so I agreed. I knew nothing about the financial markets, but a firm looking for people to manage risk trained me up. Essentially, options trading is a combination of managing risk and gambling – there wasn't much difference to what I'd been doing all along. In the first year things went really well: I was making good money (about $20,000 to $30,000 a week). Then came the crash in '87. I lost virtually everything in that week. I was half a million dollars up before the crash, and half a million down after it. The impact on the markets was huge: a seat to trade options cost $6,000 the week before the crash; it cost $200 after it. There were two real problems in New York: one, I didn't really know what I was doing; second, I was betting too big. I was over-betting and exposing myself to risks that were crazy, in hindsight. After the crash, I was broke and we had to leave town.

'I gave the wife the choice between returning to England and going back to Vegas. She chose Vegas. We stayed with friends for a while and got back on our feet. I found some nice blackjack and backgammon games. But the same thing started happening again: I started to get banned from casinos and the games dried up. I couldn't walk into a casino without being hassled. I was arrested twice but never charged. That's why I gave up blackjack and took up poker. That was in about 1989.

'I bought a couple of poker books and chatted with friends who had already made the transition. I had two or three years' grounding, playing low-stakes poker. I wasn't really making enough from poker and I couldn't get any blackjack games, so we decided to come home in 1992. I stopped gambling professionally for a couple of years. I worked for Canon, selling photocopiers. The job was going fine from a financial point of view: I had a company car and a couple of big accounts, but I hated the lifestyle. The kids couldn't recognise me any more. It was so hard coming home at six, putting on the television and having dinner. The only gambling I did was to take roulette numbers for someone who was looking for biased wheels.

'In the end I couldn't stand it any more, so I went back to poker full time. Between '95 and '98 I struggled on, just about paying the bills, but it was a struggle. Since then, things have gone OK. I've rarely had long losing streaks, I've made decent money year on year, making a six-figure sum last year. My best performance was finishing fifth in a World Series tournament of high-low Omaha, which netted me $70,000. It was mixing a bit of business and pleasure, 'cos I have two daughters and two granddaughters in Vegas now.'

The lifestyle of the professional poker player is clearly a key reason for Duvall's choice of career. 'I do pretty well financially now. My hourly rate is good – I work out an hourly rate at the end of each month – but the money is not why I play. I don't have any responsibility to anyone. These days, there are so many tournaments and so many options on the internet that I can absolutely pick and choose when and where I want to play. I play when I feel right, and often I combine it with a short break in the particular city I'm going to play in.

'You can't worry about money when you are playing. You can worry about it beforehand, and afterwards, but never during a game. If you start thinking about the value of money rather than thinking of simply the chips in front of you, then you have a problem. We've all done it, I guess, but you won't play well if you're thinking about paying the bills or the school fees. Most of the good players have a little bit of a carefree attitude, a couldn't-care-less attitude

'But we've all been broke at some stage. There's a lot of borrowing that goes on in the tournaments. You ask a guy for a few quid and you have no idea how you are going to pay him back. I'm quite an easy touch on the lending front, and I try to help if I think it's genuine – because I've been there.'

Duvall has, in fact, just come off a reasonably successful cash game when we speak at the Vic casino. He got down to the last four, at which point they all decided to do a deal and split the winnings (£22,000). Duvall says that money is nice, but he feels especially good because he knows that he played well and made the right calls.

What attributes does a good poker player need? 'First of all, he needs to be playing in the right game. Most people go broke because they are simply under-bankrolled [i.e. they don't have a big enough starting pot relative to the size of the game]. If I said to you we'll flip a coin and every time you win you get 1.05 and every time I win I get even money, you're going to win. But if I said that every time you bet, you've got to bet your whole bankroll, then you're going to go broke because sooner or later you're going to hit the two or three times it comes up in my favour. Basically, that's what happens to a poker player who is under-bankrolled. He has to over-bet, and that is fatal. If you're over-betting you can't stand the deviations, so no matter how good you are relative to the other players, you might always have that short-term run of bad luck which finishes you off. So, most important, find your correct financial level – don't play in games too big for you.

'Most of the top players on the circuit now play pretty much as well as each other. People think that some players have got better reading skills or better mathematical skills – that's all bullshit. The biggest difference is how the good players play when they are losing, when they've been dealt a couple of bad beats. You need to still make the right decisions even when it's all going against you, and that's not easy. Most people, when they are losing, start playing hands they shouldn't, or start bluffing, or whatever, it's called "steaming". The very good players don't do that – they stay calm and play according to the probabilities.

'I would say that the internet has had a bad effect in this regard. I reckon people play a lot looser on the internet. I know I certainly do. If you're in a tournament and you're surrounded by your peers, it has a sort of policing effect – you don't want to be seen to be screwing up. But the internet has no such restrictions. People lose their inhibitions because it is so anonymous. There are lots of people who will go potless playing on the internet.

'Strategy is the next most important thing. I find it pretty easy now to adjust my game according to the table I'm playing on. It's no good being known as an aggressive player or a defensive player – you have to adapt accordingly. These days it's very unusual for me to turn a game down. I always feel I'm going to have some sort of edge, no matter who I play. If you're on a table with a load of lunatics, you can't play aggressively. In some games, as the table has changed, I've gone from being the most aggressive player to a total rock; you have to be adaptable.'

And how long can a poker player expect to be on top of his game? 'That's a bit of a worry now, to be honest. I don't have a pension scheme and I'm 56. I see top class players in their 60s and they have definitely lost some of their edge. I think your mind probably goes a little bit and you lose your balls as well. You become more conservative. I'm thinking what the hell is going to happen in ten years' time. At least I know I'm not a gambler now. My philosophy has completely changed: now it's all black and white, and that came with blackjack. I won't play anything now unless I know I've got an edge. I very rarely do anything now except play poker, so the gamble has gone. I would say I'm a professional poker player now, not a gambler, and a pretty conservative one at that.'

Has it been a good life? 'Listen, we're parasites. Same as stock-market traders. We don't contribute anything worthwhile to the world. We don't help anybody. Poker players are probably lazy people. I know I am – that's why I do it. It's a hard way to make an easy living. It's a strange world we move in: I have lots of good friends in poker but I wouldn't trust many of them. You don't want to be made to look a fool. Poker players are liars, aren't they? Dave Ulliott is a great liar. Willie Tann is the best. Deception is the game. But, yes, I've had a great life. Good family, and that's the most important thing. I've raised four good children, got lovely grand-children and, touch wood, they're all healthy.'

11
THE INTERNET REVOLUTION

'We view internet gambling to be in violation of federal law.
Those that conduct this business do so at their own risk.'
USA Dept. of Justice Spokesperson

The hardest thing is coming up with a pseudonym. Two of my cricket nicknames simply aren't suitable. One, 'Athers', is too close to reality – and what is gambling in cyberspace if it is not an escape from reality? The other, 'Iron Mike', is now so far removed from reality – the only competitive exercise I take these days is to race my three-year-old son to school – as to be, frankly, ridiculous. There is a third, though, from the dim and distant past that was the Lancashire dressing room of the late 1980s: 'Mikey Dread' or 'Dready'. Who knows the provenance of that one? 'Dready' it has to be.

The only other difficulty is deciding which internet poker site to choose. Google lists just over 44 million entries for poker – 44 million! – and 19 million entries for internet poker, which is reduced to just under 7 million when I add 'site' to 'internet poker'. Gambling is now the king of the internet: greater than pornography, which gets only 43.6 million results on Google.

Conveniently, PokerListings.com is a website dedicated to offering the punter advice on which online poker company to use. It offers a wealth of choice – 122 poker-playing sites listed in descending order of popularity, from PartyPoker.com at number one (30,000 players at peak times, it says), to EuroSuperPoker.com at number 122 — as well as a comment on the punter-friendly nature, or otherwise, of each site.

I trawl through the list. At number thirty-seven is an intriguing entry: Victor Chandler Poker. Victor Chandler, a fourth-generation English bookmaker, is in charge of a firm that has been in business for nearly sixty years. Billy Chandler, Victor's grandfather, was a fearless layer in the pre- and post-Second World War eras, and Victor senior, the father, added a chain of betting shops around east London to the business, as well as Brighton and Walthamstow dog tracks. When Victor junior took over the firm in 1975, they were a decent-sized credit bookmaker with over forty shops in and around London. Chandler, though, is nothing if not a shrewd businessman – one who keeps abreast of the times and who adapts to the technological challenges of the age. Victor Chandler now has a telephone and internet service that is the envy of many. Indeed, in 1999 he became the first major British-based bookmaker to move his whole operation abroad – to Gibraltar – in order to avoid the punitive tax levy that then existed on British punters. His foray into the world of internet poker, the biggest growth area in gambling in the 21st century so far, is further testament to his adaptability and nous. His reputation, despite the wholesale changes to his business, is still that of the traditional gentleman bookmaker, who will accept the kind of wagers his grandfather was famous for. I rather fancy giving my money to this East End family made good, rather than some faceless internet company. VCPoker.com it is.

There are other advantages, too: a 25 per cent reduction on your start-up amount; PokerListings.com indicates that the site is user-friendly, a key concern for a luddite like me; it caters for low- to medium-level stakes; there is plenty of action (around 15,000 players at prime time); it has a free download; it has top marks for financial security; and, crucially, US citizens cannot play. Not that I am xenophobic, or a patriotic gambler, you understand, but the memories of Tom 'Holdem_nl' Dwan and Rhea Clevenger are still etched on my mind. Victor Chandler's concern, no doubt, is more to do with the fact that US citizens cannot gamble on the internet by law.

VCPoker.com is not short on marketing chutzpah. On entering the site you are immediately greeted by photos of shiny happy people: there's Josh 'The Tooting Tiger' Kennedy ('No matter what time I log on, I can always find a game I want without having to wait,' he says), and there's the blonde bombshell called Alison 'The Lady Killer' Churchill, who extols the virtue of the site's security ('It's my money, so I'm glad it's in safe hands') and the camaraderie of it all ('Join the poker revolution, everyone's doing it'). Josh and Alison look suspiciously like models from the local agency: I suspect most of the players are sad, ugly bastards just like me.

If you do find yourself playing against the Lady Killer you obviously don't know that the Lady Killer is not short and fat and ugly, or even if the she is not a he. Anonymity, of course, is everything in internet gambling. The data collected from internet firms, however, indicates that there has been a massive take-up of internet poker from female players – as many as 40 per cent of the players on some sites are said to be female. Possibly, they have been inspired by the examples of Annie Duke and Isabelle 'No Mercy' Mercier, who have both shown that it is absolutely possible for girls to mix it with the boys over the green felt top tables. The more likely reason for the surge of female players is that internet poker is so easy and accessible, and so less menacing. No need to fight the rain and the snow and have to enter the still-threatening environs of a casino and then sit down around a smoky table with a few hairy-arsed blokes. Two hours in the morning while the kids are at school? No problem. And, of course, the anonymity of it all is crucial. 'Got a bad poker face?' screams the advertising for PartyPoker.com. Well, if you have, and if your 'tells' are obvious, then it doesn't matter in cyberspace: nobody can see the whites of your eyes. There's no need to even play under a female moniker if you don't wish to. In fact, most online players say that whenever you come up against an apparently female player, you can be assured that she is a he.

No doubt, this anonymity is a big reason behind the popularity of gambling (and pornography) on the internet. People who are too embarrassed or scared to purchase pornography, go into a betting shop or enter a casino have no such fears on the net. Not only are the social constraints removed, but so are the physical: playing with virtual chips or typing in your credit card details is far easier mentally and, worryingly, far less inhibiting than handing over ready cash

Once I have downloaded the actual software – less than three minutes, if you have a broadband connection – it's time to go to the users' register where monikers can be chosen, and the all-important data is collected. Unfortunately, the name 'Dread' already exists, so I have to come up with something else. 'Dreadnought' it shall be. Then it's time to choose an avatar, which my dictionary tells me is an icon used to represent a person in cyberspace. I guess it's to make the game feel more real, more sociable somehow, although this is totally alien to the concept of sitting in your front room playing poker on your own. Anyway, the avatars range from those that have gaming connotations (dice, horseshoes) to photos of women and men, to cartoons, to different countries' flags to signs of the zodiac. I choose a shady-looking Oriental girl. Clevenger, eat your heart out!

This, I think, is another reason for the dominance of poker over other forms of gambling on the internet such as blackjack or roulette. People still crave a little competition against human beings even in the comfort of their living room – a chance to test their skill and nerve against fellow players, rather than playing against the house or a preset computer.

Then it's time to choose your game and your table. The options include Texas hold'em, Omaha and Omaha high/low. The highest stakes are $150/$300 games with an average pot of over $1,000 dollars a game; the lowest are 2 cent/4 cent games with an average pot of 22 cents a game. The choice is wide-ranging: around eighty tables, not including those playing tournaments, and on this Sunday evening, the website says, there are just under 8,000 people playing poker on VCPoker.com. Since it is the thirty-seventh most popular site out of 122 there are thirty-six other sites around the globe with more than an average of 8,000 players. The top thirty-seven sites, therefore, must have around 300,000 poker players around the world at any one time. All told, there must be a minimum of double that.

The sensible option, it seems to me, is to start low and get to grips with the process, although VCPoker.com conveniently offers a virtual game with pretend money as a way of dipping your toes in the water. I play one game, but poker for 'play' money is like playing cards for matchsticks: no fun at all.

I choose a table that calls itself 'Around the World in 40 Days' which has a limit of nine players, playing limit Texas hold'em for 2 cents/4 cents a game. It's about as low risk as it is possible to get. Then you are transported to your virtual table – an oval green table with the moniker VCPoker.com scrawled across the middle just in case you'd forgotten where you were. Your virtual opponents are in situ and your virtual chips are soon placed in front of your avatar.

The table is well named: playing against me are 'Sainth' from Strasbourg; 'FulhamFan' from, obviously, London; 'Hardrock' from Idaho (what happened to the non-American policy?); 'Fordy' from Ontario; 'Baldmick' from Kent (if he is, surely he'd want to disguise the fact?), and 'Cagedwoman' from Vancouver, whose chosen avatar is a Melinda Messenger-type blonde. Must be a man.

Speaking as a seasoned tournament player – a European Masters entrant, no less – it takes me a little time to adjust to the pace of play. There is a twenty-second time limit for every decision. You can choose to automatically muck losing hands and automatically post your blinds, which speeds up the whole process considerably. There is, at first, a bewildering speed to it all. But, in truth, it could not be more user-friendly: every time the play comes around, helpful boxes that indicate your options (fold, call, check or raise for certain amounts), pop up on your screen. And this, I think, is another reason why so many virgin poker players have been seduced by the internet: it is far less intimidating. It doesn't matter if you make a mistake, because nobody can see you making a mistake; there is no Dave Barnes or Rhea Clevenger to put you under the microscope as your confused mind tries to remember whether a flush beats a straight, or whether you really should be folding on the big blind. And if you do fold prematurely, when all you have to do is check, then another helpful box pops up reminding you of the fact. Of course, the lack of human contact and psychological battles make the game, ultimately, less interesting. There is no opportunity to look for tells, and bluffing is largely irrelevant because internet players seem to play far more aggressively anyway, but for the uninitiated this can be a definite advantage. There is even a pop-up box in the lower right-hand corner that tells you what your best hand is.

The whole operation is geared to the novice. There are helpful coaching tips that scroll across the bottom of your screen: 'Never criticise a weak opponent for bad plays, it makes them feel uncomfortable and motivates them to play better!' And, 'Sit to the left of loose players'. And, 'When a frequent bluffer checks you, don't bluff!' And, rather philosophically, 'In the beginning, every-thing was even money.'

There is a message board, should you want to converse with your fellow players (although the pace of play is so fast, you'd have to be a courtroom stenographer to use it) and, should you want to go and make a coffee, open another bottle of wine, have (quick) sex, whatever, there is a box to tick indicating that you'd like to sit out the next hand.

Players come and go with bewildering speed. There is the occasional snappy web chat, which is a clue to the fact that, as in 'real' live poker, these are real people out there playing with real money. At one stage on my table, Cagedwoman won a hand against Baldmick with a lucky last-card draw.

'River rat!' wailed Baldmick.

'You're a dreamer,' replied Cagedwoman.

'I had the best hand until the river,' sniffed Baldmick.

'You raise every stinking hand, no matter what you have . . . you're a dreamer,' said Cagedwoman, with a hint of masculine nastiness, I thought.

The next hand, Baldmick is all in, and then out with a pathetic Q high. You can still go 'on tilt' even in cyberspace. Baldmick disappears.

My own demise, once I step up into a bigger $5/$10 game, comes when four nines is posted to my all-in full house of sevens on sixes. It was a pleasant couple of hours, on a dull Sunday evening. Two hours, I have to say, that passed remarkably quickly, confirming what many users refer to as 'time disassociation'. I can believe people just while away hours at a time, almost unaware that they are doing so. In that sense, internet poker conforms exactly to the trend that sociologists call 'cocooning', whereby families are increasingly restricting themselves to their houses without the need to venture outside. Everything you could possibly want – except, that is, human contact – is readily available now without having to leave the house: home entertainment, for example, and shopping that gets delivered. Internet gambling is simply an extension of that.

As I attempted to log out, VCPoker.com asked me 'Do you really want to leave VCPoker?' Not, note, 'Do you want to leave?' but 'Do you *really* want to leave?', as if I was doing something so stupid as to invite ridicule. I did leave, and on doing so I put the download into my trashcan so that the temptation of internet poker would not be in front of me every time I sat at my desk. On leaving, you are invited to send Victor Chandler your thoughts: Vic, old boy, it's never been so easy to lose money to you.

I have no doubt that there are some serious, experienced players who are making a killing from internet poker. The good players, apparently, wait until the pubs have shut, log on and skin those who've imbibed too much; they have internet portals already open that allow them to work out the probabilities of any particular hand in a flash; and some have as many as eight screens going at once. A licence to print money, if you're good enough, smart enough and prepared to sit for hours at a time in front of a computer screen.

Equally, I have no doubt there are thousands of people who are losing amounts that they simply cannot afford to lose, playing a game they are not much good at (although the privacy of your front room and a bottle of wine or two can convince you otherwise), to which they are drawn time and again by the convenience and simplicity of it all.

For most of the second half of the 20th century, Las Vegas was considered the ultimate gambling destination. Everything a gambler could possibly want within the confines of a desert city. No longer. Now, provided that you are wired up to the net, you don't have to leave the comfort of your front room. Poker, roulette, blackjack, fruit machines, lottery tickets – they are all there. The ultimate gambling destination is right at your fingertips.

* * *

The public have not been slow to latch on to this fact. The online poker market has been growing at an astonishing rate. The daily global turnover for online poker was estimated at £5.3 million in 2003, growing to £32 million in 2004 and £95 million in 2005. All told, the global online market was worth £5.25 billion to those companies offering internet gambling.

The online poker companies have started to trade some serious numbers. In the two years to 2004, PartyGaming, the owners of PartyPoker.com, saw their revenues climb from $30.1 million to $602 million. In three months to April 2005, an average of 121,570 people played poker on the PartyPoker.com site, with 1,737,700 playing in April alone. The main competitor to PartyPoker.com is ParadisePoker.com, who had an average of fourteen games a second being played on their site. They had close on one million registered users, all of whom contributed to Sportingbet's (the owner of Paradise Poker) earnings rising threefold in the first three months of 2005.

Internet poker sites have been quick to spot that the combination of money, television and celebrity is an alluring one for many. In England, the likes of Ricky Gervais, Stephen Fry, Nigella Lawson and Charles Saatchi were seen regularly on programmes such as Channel 4's *Late Night Poker*. In America, Ben Affleck, Nicole Kidman, Matt Damon and Toby Maguire played regularly in televised tournaments. PartyGaming made the shrewd decision to sponsor the World Poker Tour and their share of the online market grew from 20 per cent to 50 per cent within three months. Within three years the World Poker Tour boasted $100 million worth of prize money – a level that it took the USPGA thirty years to reach. The ultimate boost to online poker came when Chris Moneymaker, an internet qualifier from a game that cost just $40 to join, won the World Series, pocketing $2.4 million in the process.

Internet entrepreneurs were quick to realise that this glamorous combination, and the relative ease and low-cost nature of the operations, added up to a potential cash cow. All a site does is bring together players and take a rake, or cut, of the turnover. Although the software is complex, once it is up and running the costs and overheads are minimal. There is no need to provide champagne and caviar, or beer and nibbles like a traditional gambling house. Even more shrewdly, companies like Empire Online simply act as 'skinners', taking a cut from redirecting poker players to other online poker sites. Given that most analysts reckon 60 per cent of internet poker players to be losers, it is the house, as always, which holds the whip hand over the punter.

In particular, it was the owners of the house who were quick to appreciate the concept and who were now looking to cash in. It was PartyGaming which gained most column inches over the summer of 2005 as a float was mooted. This was partly because it was the biggest of the internet poker companies – a projected value of somewhere in the region of £5 billion would have catapulted it into the FTSE 100 over the heads of some great and traditional British companies like British Airways, Boots and Sainsbury's – but also because the owners themselves were an interesting story.

Ruth Parasol and her husband Russ DeLeon owned just under a third of the PartyGaming shares between them, and Anurag Dikshit owned a further slice of 31.6 per cent. A graduate of the famous Institute of Technology in India, Dikshit provided the technological knowledge to set up the software. This quiet, shy 34-year-old, married with one son and living in Gibraltar, is the epitome of the modern internet entrepreneur.

Parasol, by contrast, provides the glamour and the mystery. She is the daughter of a holocaust survivor, Richard Parasol, who put his wartime experiences firmly behind him when he forayed into the sex industry in the US. Initially he owned a string of massage parlours in Tenderloin, the red-light district of San Francisco, before relocating his family to California. He stayed in sex, though, running a number of sex-chat lines. By 1994, his daughter, who had graduated from Western State University as a lawyer, was running a couple of sex-chat lines of her own, having been gifted them, according to legend, by her father as a highly unorthodox birthday present. Later, father and daughter invested in the online porn industry in the shape of the Internet Entertainment Group, which provided fourteen girls working on rotation, performing special acts on demand for punters. By 1996, she severed her connections with the porn industry and moved into gambling when she asked Dikshit to come up with the computer software to accommodate online gaming. Porn, gambling and the internet – a cash-generating marriage made in heaven. Parasol keeps the kind of low profile that makes Greta Garbo look like an exhibitionist. She never gives interviews and there has only ever been one photograph published of her. It shows an attractive, dark-haired college girl flashing the enamel-toothed smile of someone who knows that riches of which Croesus would be envious would be coming her way.

Those riches came to pass in the summer of 2005, when PartyGaming finally floated after months of speculation. Parasol and her husband took out £218 million each and retained shares of £810 million each, whilst Dikshit saw his computer program come home to roost to the tune of £420 million, retaining £1.5 billion in shares. All three became paper billionaires overnight. Had there ever been a quicker rise to billionaire status?

So much for the house, what about the investors? Was there any merit to be had in gambling on gambling? The dangers of investing in PartyGaming were obvious from the start. The prospectus didn't try to hide the warning signs and included thirty pages of risk factors. Mainly, they concerned the legal status of online gaming in the US, where PartyGaming rakes in 85 per cent of its revenue. The company was open about the risk and its prospectus warned investors of the bearish noises emanating from the Department of Justice in the US: 'The US Department of Justice considers that companies offering online gaming to US residents are in violation of existing US federal laws,' it said, and added that any action from US authorities could 'result in investors losing all or a very substantial part of their investment.' The US Department of Justice based its concerns on the 1961 Wire Act, whilst PartyGaming's defence was based on a federal case in 2002 when the Wire Act was deemed to be only relevant for sports bets. It seems to boil down to whether poker is considered a sport or not – a risky bet even for speculative investors, never mind some of Britain's biggest pension funds.

There were other potential problems. Jon Kyl, a Republican Senator, was proposing a bill to prevent banks and credit-card companies from allowing US customers using their accounts to place online bets. Analysts also wondered why, if the company was so successful and cash rich, the owners wanted to float in the first place. They wondered, in particular, whether they didn't want to cash in their chips before the bubble burst and the market slowed down. Moreover, analysts showed that the turnover of players – the churn – was huge, with over 70 per cent of players leaving the site and not returning within the first year.

Richard Segal, PartyGaming's chief executive officer, tried to downplay the fears of another dotcom boom-and-bust situation. 'We are,' he said, 'a real company, with real customers, generating real profits.' And of the situation in the US he said, 'We have a high visibility in the US . . . several members of the management team go in and out of the US on a regular basis . . . I have no reason not to go to the US and will go without question.' Nevertheless, it seemed that buying PartyGaming's shares was a risk: investing in gambling was a huge gamble.

Two of Britain's biggest investment companies refused to invest, with one indicating that they felt PartyGaming was not fit to be a part of the FTSE 100. The *Guardian*, in a business editorial, warned its readers that 'in the long term PartyGaming is an investment accident waiting to happen.' Plenty of institutional and private investors ignored the warnings, however. The Initial Public Offering was oversubscribed threefold. PartyGaming floated at 116p, which rose, after the first day, to 129p, so valuing the company at £5.1 billion, which did indeed dwarf the market capitalisation of the likes of Sainsbury's, Rolls-Royce, British Airways, ICI and EMI. Cantor Index, just prior to the float, offered its spread-betting customers a chance to gamble on the gamble on gambling by offering a spread on its share price of 111p–116p.

With the profits already in the bank and generating interest for the founders, punters soon realised that they had made a bad bet. When the fall came it was spectacular. On 6 September, ten weeks after the float, the company announced a fall in player-retention rates and player yield and, crucially, that the increase in the number of newcomers to online poker had slowed in the third quarter to 1 July, to just 4 per cent of the total (down from 26 per cent in the corresponding quarter the year before). The timing of the float looked perfect for the owners, but less good for the investors. The market's reaction was brutal: £2 billion was knocked off the value of the company in a single day as shares plunged from 157p to 105p, a single day fall of 33 per cent. There was similar pain elsewhere in the sector as Empire Online's shares fell 16 per cent and Sporting-bet's fell 11 per cent. Investors were livid. One in the *Sunday Times* said, 'For me, the collapse of this stock has been the most shocking thing that has happened to the stock market in the past decade. We went into this with our eyes wide open about the regulatory risks. But never did we think about a revenue risk. I am angry. There were a lot of smashed telephones on Tuesday, put it that way.' The punters – and surely investing in such a risky stock was a simple punt – had their fingers burnt.

And the future? Are online gambling companies worth a flutter? Here's the verdict on PartyGaming from two of the City's top analysts in September 2005. Andy Brough, fund manager at Schroder, advised those that were holding PartyGaming stock that they had made a bad punt: 'The main cost is that of customer acquisition and retention, with most sites offering incentives in the form of free bets or bonus cash. The problem is that there is an incentive for players to keep switching sites. With margins this high, there is room to offer more incentives and still be profitable. But the trend for margins is down.' He warned that 'the sword of Damocles hangs over the whole industry in the form of the fact that nobody in the industry is sure if it is legal under the 1961 Wire Act to operate gaming over the internet in America. At some point the American Government will have to do something about the huge amount of untaxed money leaving the country. Online gaming could be declared illegal or made legal, but both would be bad results for PartyGaming.' He concluded, 'I've always been keen to act as an investor rather than a player in a casino. I didn't buy shares at the float and I'm not tempted by them now.' His judgement: avoid.

Tim Steer of the fund manager New Star was even more forthright: 'It's a simple model – there are a small number of sharks (winners) who take a large number of plankton (losers) to the cleaners. The question is how much customer-acquisition costs need to be in order to replenish the tables with new, eager plankton happy to be fleeced. My belief is that there is enough plankton around, but it will not be the same quality plankton, which means that returns will deteriorate . . . The original investors in PartyGaming have seen the best of the company, as the quality of the plankton falls and the competition for punters rises. Also the shares are very volatile, as those who invest in them have similar interests to the punters who play online poker – hedge funds and retail speculators dominate trading in the shares.' His judgement: don't be a plankton.

As ever, it seems that the house is winning and the punters are losing.[12]

If the history of gambling in Britain, and elsewhere, tells us anything, it is that there will always be a portion of society who wants to gamble, and who, regardless of the regulations of the time or the risks, will find the means and the wherewithal to do so: where there is a will, there will always be a way.

Gambling in modern Britain has tended to be cyclical in nature: waves of enthusiasm have receded in the face of public opprobrium and state legislation. To recap: the hundred years or so following the Restoration, in 1660, saw an explosion of gambling, so that the 18th century became synonymous with aristocratic indulgence and gambling to excess. The Victorian reaction was to legislate against gaming, with acts such as the Gaming Act of 1845, which made gambling debts unenforceable at law, and the 1853 Betting Houses Act, which made betting houses illegal. The end of the 19th century again saw betting on the rise. The increase in leisure time, improving working wages and a nascent sporting press saw sports, especially racing, flourish, at the same time offering the ordinary working man greater opportunity to gamble. In response, the anti-gambling crusade again found its voice and was at its strongest in the last decade of the 19th century and the first decade of the 20th. The Street Betting Act of 1906, which made betting on the street and in other public places illegal, proved to be the high point of anti-gambling legislation and the anti-gambling crusade. Ever

---

[12] At the time of printing, PartyGaming's shares stood at 87.25p; Empire Online's were 68.5p and Sportingbet's were 174.75p

since, there has been a gradual retreat from that position, and the voice of the anti-gambling movement has steadily been drowned out by those of a more liberal persuasion. The Betting and Gaming Act of 1960 overturned a century of prohibition, although the principle that gambling should not be encouraged was still at the heart of the legislation. That Act, and the 1968 Act which followed, was the basis upon which gambling in this country was governed for almost five decades. Even so, the intervening period saw further liberalisation and deregulation of the industry, mostly in response to the advent of the National Lottery in 1994. A government that both sponsored and profited from gambling, through the Lottery, was hardly in a position to do otherwise. This approach went hand in hand with the Thatcherite policies of economic laissez-faire which replaced the paternal attitudes that had dominated politics until the late 1970s.

But legislation that was forty years old, that had been drawn up before Microsoft was a twinkle in Bill Gates's eye, was ill-equipped to deal with the challenges of this dramatic technological age. And it was in this climate of growing liberalisation and technological revolution that the government asked Sir Alan Budd, a noted deregulator and free-marketeer, to chair, in 1999, the Gambling Review Body, with the remit to point the way ahead for the government and gambling as the 21st century dawned.

At the heart of the dilemma for the Review Body was the dichotomy between allowing punters the freedom to play whatever, wherever and whenever they liked and the need to keep the British gambling industry free of crime and exploitation. As Budd said in a speech to a Salford University seminar on gambling in June 2002, 'We correctly identified the central dilemma – the age-old question of freedom versus protection.'

Two years later, the Review Body announced how it had dealt with that dilemma. It recommended four things: that gambling (except for spread betting, which is regulated by the Financial

Services Authority, and the Lottery, which is regulated by the Lottery Commission) be put under the control of a single regulatory body – the Gambling Commission; that 'remote' gambling (i.e. internet gambling, telephone gambling, mobile phone gambling and any other technology-inspired gambling) be licensed and regulated; that the rest of the industry undergo serious liberalisation and deregulation; and that problem gambling be recognised and the outlets for problem gamblers be funded by the rest of the industry. Liberalisation was at the heart of the report. Budd again: 'A liberal approach would suggest that the present controls cause unnecessary restriction of a basically harmless activity and that they cannot be justified in their present form.'

Not surprisingly, the gambling industry broadly welcomed the report. Casino operators gave it a mixed reception. They were thrilled that the requirement for membership was to be removed, as was the twenty-four-hour 'cooling off' rule, whereby a punter had to be a member for twenty-four hours before he could cross the threshold of a casino. Now you could simply walk off the street straight into one. They welcomed the removal of restrictions on advertising and on the use of credit cards (except in gaming machines).

Local casino operators were less happy about the prospect of huge Las Vegas-style casinos springing up all over the country. Initially, the government paved the way for around thirty of these to be built, and it was foreign casino operators, such as the South African Sol Kerzner (the owner of Sun City, the Las Vegas of South Africa), who were queuing up to invest. American casino owners reportedly spent £100 million on simply preparing the ground for their bids.[13]

---

[13] At the time of publication, the deputy prime minster was embroiled in a scandal over the nature of his relationship with Philip Anschutz, an American billionaire whose sights were set on turning the Millennium Dome into a Las Vegas-style casino.

Broadly, however, it was a report that was welcomed by the gambling industry, and, in anticipation of the forthcoming windfall, the gambling sector was the best performing sector on a bearish FTSE in 2003.

A year after the Review Body published its conclusions, the Department of Culture, Media and Sport followed with its white paper, 'A Safe Bet for Success.' That it was the DCMS, rather than the Home Office, who were now responsible for gambling offered an obvious clue as to the government's position. Gambling had been moved from a department that regulates, to a department that exploits. And here was the rationale behind the efforts to reform the gambling industry. No one doubted that internet gambling needed regulating, but there was little public desire for greater numbers of casinos. The government felt that centres like Blackpool needed urgent regeneration, and that casinos were the best bet to achieve that. And, of course, if gambling turnover increased, then so would government revenues.

'A Safe Bet for Success' accepted nearly all of the Review Body's recommendations. Indeed, where the DCMS disagreed with the Review Body, the alterations were almost entirely in favour of further liberalisation. So whereas Budd recommended local authorities have the power to impose a ban on gambling sites in their area, the DCMS disagreed; whereas Budd recommended that jackpot machines be removed from private clubs, the DCMS disagreed; and whereas Budd recommended category D machines (amusement with prizes machines) be removed from cafés and fish and chip shops to protect the under-age, the DCMS disagreed. Only one proposal, the refusal to allow bookmakers to offer odds on the National Lottery, showed the DCMS to be less liberal than the Review Body

The overall impression, once the double act of Budd and Tessa Jowell had completed its work, was of a traditional industry freed of its shackles, and an online industry that was about to receive its coronation, by dint of the fact that it was to be licensed and accepted, for the first time, as a legitimate business.

Jowell was crystal clear on the implications of her White Paper. Analysing the climate around which this new framework should be based, she said: 'Laws were enacted . . . in an era when gambling was regarded as an activity which was at best morally questionable . . . Since that framework was put in place, the social climate has changed. Almost three-quarters of the adult population participate in gambling in one form or another. It has become part of the mainstream leisure activity.' And so, she continued, 'there is a powerful case for lifting the regulatory borders on an industry that has built a world reputation for integrity.' The result? 'We will remove unnecessary barriers to customer access to gambling. We will abolish the legal requirement that bookmakers, casinos and bingo operators must demonstrate unmet local demand for their product.' In other words, the basic premise that had been at the heart of gambling legislation for nearly half a century, namely that gambling should be tolerated but not encouraged or stimulated, was stripped away.

The ultimate volte-face came with the announcement that gambling contracts will be recognised at law once the Gambling Act comes into force in 2007. It is almost as if gambling is a long-lost son being welcomed back into the fold. It is to be legitimised again after 160 years in the legal wilderness. It is recognition that gamblers and gambling have won the day.

The journey from the 'A Safe Bet for Success' to the statute books took three tortuous, and sometimes tumultuous, years. The government was initially taken aback by the fury of the reaction. The anti-gambling movement found its voice again and allied itself with those who feared that a flood of Las Vegas-style casinos would sweep the country. The Evangelical Alliance printed a booklet entitled 'Help – there's a casino coming!' The Salvation

Army said, 'There are only two winners that will benefit from the new gambling legislation: the gambling industry through massively increased profits and the government through increased taxation. The big losers will be the vulnerable people whose lives are ruined by gambling addiction.' Max Hastings, in the *Guardian*, accused the government of losing 'its social and moral compass'.

In what must be an unprecedented alliance, the *Daily Mail* and the *Guardian* colluded in an investigation which accused government ministers of being too cosy with the leading players from America's giant casino operations. It led to a stormy parliamentary session, in which the Tory shadow to Tessa Jowell, Theresa May, said, 'Huge question marks in the relationship between foreign casino operators and the government remain.' Gambling, it seems, has still not lost its capacity to divide public opinion. Surely only as emotive a subject as gambling could get the Tories, the *Daily Mail*, Max Hastings and the Salvation Army in bed together.

In response to this onslaught, Jowell and the government started to backtrack. When the bill went to the Lords it had been watered down to include only eight super Las Vegas-style casinos. By the time it made the statute book this had been reduced to just one. The existing casino industry was happy that swathes of foreign competitors would not now be coming, although those foreign gambling interests who had spent vast sums of money lobbying and entertaining the government were incandescent. Jowell found herself caught in an uncomfortable position between the rock of public opinion and the hard place of foreign casino operators whose promised £2 billion worth of investment was suddenly looking less secure. *Private Eye* gleefully monitored Jowell's discomfort: 'Do you suffer from Irritable Jowell Syndrome?' they crowed.

Eventually, a slightly watered-down bill, but one that still unfettered the gambling industry, received royal assent on 7 April

2005, four years after Sir Alan Budd began his consultations and a month before Tony Blair was returned to office for a third term. The four main tenets of the Budd report form the heart of the legislation: that gambling will be regulated by the Gambling Commission; that online gambling will be regulated and licensed; that the gambling industry should fund research and help into addiction; and that the industry, generally, would undergo profound liberalisation. Casinos were the cause célèbre of the bill: in the end, it was agreed that there should be just one regional casino (a 5,000 square-metre space allowing 1,250 unlimited jackpot gaming machines), eight large casinos (1500 square-metre space, 150 gaming machines with a jackpot of £4,000) and eight small casinos (750 square-metre space allowing eighty gaming machines with a jackpot of £4,000).

The least contentious aspects of the bill – the need for a single regulator and the desire to license and regulate online gambling – went through unscathed. Nobody could argue with the fact that a worldwide online industry that had increased exponentially in value over a five-year period, with over 1,700 sites that offered gambling opportunities, needed licensing and regulating. Otherwise, the risk to the public was that opportunistic, untrustworthy operators would have the potential to rig games and pass laundered monies through their books. The risk to the government was that great swathes of potential tax would disappear off-shore.

Between 2005 and September 2007, when the Gambling Act is due to come into full force, the Gambling Commission is charged with setting out the regulatory framework for 'remote' gambling. Quite how it will combine internet gambling with its stated aim of protecting children and the vulnerable is unclear. How do you stop children using their parents' credit cards to bet online? How do you prevent people from gambling at work? How can you prevent people from mixing gambling at home with drugs like alcohol which would reduce inhibitions when it comes to betting? Bluntly, short of a Big Brother scenario, how do you control what people do in their own front rooms? How do you stop unscrupulous operators going out of their way to trap unwary punters with dubious practices? Practices like 'embedding', where a company hides its website within other websites – so that someone looking up a compulsive-gambling helpline on the internet suddenly finds a pop-up box advertising a poker site. Practices like 'circle jerking', where a punter trying to exit a certain site is suddenly confronted with pop-up boxes offering similar services, and the only way to get out of this never-ending loop is to click on that box, so entering another gambling site, or shut down completely.

Peter Dean, the chairman of the Commission, voiced his opinions on regulating internet gambling when he spoke to the Remote Gambling Forum in June 2005. He recognised the difficulties of a 100 per cent failsafe system of preventing children gambling on the net. As regards those with problem gambling tendencies, he outlined the potential measures that the Commission will consider: they include warning notices for players; so-called 'reality checks' like clocks, timers and enforced breaks; facilities for players to place self-limits on losses on a per-session, per-week and per-month basis; and self-exclusion systems. Despite Dean's comments, all the academic literature states that increased opportunities to gamble invariably lead to more problem gamblers.

As well as a major consultation with all the industry partners, which will form the basis for the regulatory framework, the Gambling Commission is charged with undertaking the first Gambling Prevalence study since 1999. My guess is that the study will show that we are in the midst of another gambling craze, that there has been a significant increase in gambling amongst the population generally since 1999. All the anecdotal evidence seems to suggest so, largely because of the ease and availability of gambling as a result of technological advances of the last decade.

In January 2006, Peter Dean summed up the Gambling Commission's role, and his own attitude, when he described it as a 'laissez-faire' regulator. His remarks incensed the Department of Culture and Media, who, all along, had tried to water down the effect of the Gambling Bill with public pronouncements saying that the vulnerable would still be fiercely protected. They were so annoyed that they tracked Dean down on the last day of his skiing holiday. But Dean was only expressing honestly the sea-change that had swept over the gambling industry since the inception of the National Lottery in 1994. The National Lottery revolutionised the gambling landscape. The ultimate liberalisation of the industry, through the Gambling Act of 2005, was the inevitable conclusion.

For the first time in modern British history an increase in gambling, due to the internet, has gone hand in hand with government-inspired deregulation and liberalisation. It is a dangerous combination.

RAY JOSEPH
The Internet Gambler

If Alan Woods, the probability-based gambler we met in chapter two, is the Rolls-Royce of professional gamblers, then Ray Joseph is the Skoda. That is not to pour scorn on a man who has gambled successfully enough to avoid a nine-to-five job throughout his adult life, but to spend two hours in Joseph's one-bedroom flat in Charlton is to realise that professional gambling is not necessarily glamorous or overly profitable. And yet Joseph has made punting pay, and he continues to do so through adapting to the opportunities offered by the internet. To describe a sixty-something man as the classic 21st-century gambler might be stretching a point, but Joseph's gambling milieu, and his life seemingly, is played out wholly in cyberspace and as far removed from reality proper as it is possible to be.

Even his flat seems to hold no interest for him, except as a space from which he can gamble. The single light bulb that hangs from the ceiling lacks any adornments and the walls hold just a solitary, nondescript drawing. The plaster on the ceiling is cracked and loose and the only furniture in the room is a purple-coloured sofa and a long oak table. Two crates of French wine indicate an interest in something other than gambling. The centres of attention, though, are the two high-powered computers, flickering constantly in the background – one already tuned into Betfair and the other showing a spreadsheet full of figures and percentages – and a television set.

Before the arrival of the World Wide Web, Joseph led a typical gambler's existence. He dropped out of both Manchester Grammar

School and the London School of Economics before he had completed his studies and opted instead for the professional poker circuit. He played on the pro circuit, in clubs like En Passant, the Vic and the Cromwellian, for the best part of two decades – from the 1960s until the late 1970s – always holding his own until he came up against the top-rank players. From about 1975 he stopped winning and started to lose. 'I cracked,' is how he explains it, saying that, as in professional sport, 'once you start expecting to lose, it becomes a self-fulfilling prophesy.'

The end of his poker career heralded a change of scene. Sports betting had just started to take off and, in particular, Joseph was attracted to the world of football betting, which had expanded after William Hill and Ladbrokes began to offer bets on individual football matches. Joseph, and by this time he was working in a team, began to look for instances where bookmakers were 'over-broke' about certain matches. Bookmakers at opposite ends of the country, for example, might take a completely different view about a team's chances in one particular match and on such discrepancies can the professional gambler find his edge.

Eventually, most of the bookmakers got wise and tightened up and homogenised their books. Joseph turned to horse racing next. Specifically, to a system whereby he would look for the place value in non-handicap races: that is, looking for horses that were almost certain to place and including them in multiple bets – doubles and trebles. In those days, bookmakers paid a quarter of the odds for a place, rather than, as now, a fifth of the odds. Even now, at a fifth of the odds, three horses that place at 5-1 combined in an each-way treble pays 8-1, a large payout for a bet that doesn't include a winner. By this time, Joseph was betting in large hundreds, occasionally small thousands, and coming across some decent-sized ten- to twenty-grand winning days. 'It was great for a while, but eventually it became harder to get bets on. Bookmakers are not stupid, and when they see you betting successfully they tend to discourage your custom.'

And so, in the mid-1990s, Joseph turned to spread betting. In particular he looked for arbitrages – that is, taking advantage of different prices for the same asset. Essentially, it was an extension of his football betting when he found bookmakers who were 'over-broke'. For example, if one spread betting firm, Sporting Index, say, offer a spread on Michael Vaughan's runs at 30–35, and Cantor Index offer 36–40 you can buy at 35 with Sporting and sell at 36 with Cantor and make a profit either way. (If Vaughan scores 10, you make 26 points with Cantor, and lose 25 with Sporting. If Vaughan scores 50, you win 15 with Sporting and lose 14 with Cantor. Either way, you are guaranteed one point profit.) Joseph also quickly realised that punters couldn't afford to be sellers because of the unlimited downside, and so the spreads were almost always artificially high. (Again, with Vaughan's theoretical 36–40 spread, there is a limit downside of 36 points when you buy, but if you sell then your liabilities are potentially unlimited – there being no ceiling on how many runs a batsman might score.) As a general rule, therefore, spread bettors should always sell.

It should be reasonably obvious by now that Joseph's idea of a good bet is one where you can't lose – or at least one where the odds are heavily stacked in your favour. In that sense, he is a gambler only to a limited extent. With the exception of playing low-ball poker for a short spell ('a crap shoot' is his description of the game), Joseph gambles only when he feels he has a considerable edge. 'Listen, the idea of pure chance is anathema to me. I've bought two lottery tickets in my life – for relatives. If I don't have an edge, I don't bet. It's as simple as that. I'm cautious and that means that sometimes I don't give myself a chance to win big, but at least I win. I bet high turnover, low risk. My profit margins are small as a percentage of my turnover, but high as a percentage of risk.'

Joseph's friends had told him that the internet would be a perfect vehicle for his betting strategy, but until 2000 he had never used a computer before. 'My friends were right, you know. They know I'm the laziest bastard alive and for the first few months I found I hardly had to get out of bed. Betting nirvana right in my front room!' Betfair was Joseph's first point of call – he calls it the 'promised land, the eldorado and Aladdin's cave' of betting – followed by all the bookmakers who operated online, and then the spread betting firms. There is even something called Spreadfair which is the spread betting version of Betfair, where punters set their own spreads. If Joseph's flat still resembles a student's digs, he makes sure that his betting equipment is state of the art. Whereas most computers update the Betfair odds every twenty seconds or so, Joseph's is programmed to update every half a second, so that at peak times the screen is a blur of changing prices.

Joseph's main internet markets are the number of bookings in a football match; other side markets on football such as the number of corners and total goals, and Test cricket, which he describes as the 'finest sport known to man ... for betting'. He tried the financial markets for a while and found it great fun and profitable until the advent of 'robots' took away his edge.

The beauty of the internet for Joseph is the range of betting opportunities and the ability to trade or hedge his positions constantly. He gives an example: 'During the last Test of the 2004 series between England and the West Indies, I found myself £300 down on the penultimate evening. I traded all night so that by the following morning I had turned that into £1,000 profit.' How? 'Well, England were about 1-25 on Betfair (which they decimalise as 1.04. That is, £1 wins you fourpence, or £100 wins you £4) so I laid England (that is backed them to lose) at that price to the tune of £400 (to win £10,000). After that I simply bet in tranches of £10,000 or so, hedging my position all the time. My turnover was massive – £250,000 in one evening. My eventual profit was pitiful as a percentage of turnover but it was almost entirely risk free.' Here, the lines between trading and gambling are obviously blurred. Joseph calls it 'scalping the market'.

Such a betting strategy is not time efficient and requires long hours in front of the computer screen. If Joseph is not a sick gambler, in the sense that he only bets when he sees an edge, then it is questionable whether he hasn't become addicted to the internet. It is something he happily admits to. He calls himself an 'internet junkie' and admits to fingering his mouse whenever the computer screen goes blank due to a period of inactivity. His typical day: wake early; switch on Betfair; make coffee; check Betfair's market; trawl through other bookmakers' odds and the spread-betting market; more coffee; log onto his betting forum; chat to fellow forum-ites; nip out to get the *Racing Post*; look for each-way bets in the *Racing Post*; establish a battle plan for the day's football; work 'hard and well' up until lunch; lunch at his desk with half a bottle of Bordeaux; poker for two hours online to relax and to build self-esteem by doing well in small single-table tournaments; strike his bets on Betfair and the spreads, which are his springboard for the day's action; more chat on the forum; check Betfair again to see if there is any need to trade his positions; fiddle around to try and make his positions safe prior to the football ('make the losing numbers less threatening and the winning ones potentially so'); and then settle down to watch two games of football simultaneously – one on the television, one on his computer. Bed.

His only real contact with the outside world is his betting forum, on which he has contact with some cyberspace mates – none of whom he knows personally. His cybermates are called 'Franz Kafka', 'Ricardo', 'Hank Sumatra', 'Duncan Disorderly' and what he calls the love of his life, '36'. How does he know '36' is a woman? 'I don't. She might be Rab C. Nesbitt for all I know, but I've got a feeling.

We correspond quite passionately.' Joseph calls the betting forum – where ideas and betting strategies are openly discussed – 'sustaining' to him, 'almost my life-support machine.'

Whilst internet betting has provided Joseph with five years of constant profit, it has also resulted in him becoming completely withdrawn from the outside world. He says that he has always felt something of an outsider – a common trait amongst many professional gamblers that I've spoken to. He uses phrases such as a 'social outcast' and supposes that gambling came first and then the exclusion afterwards. But in the past, poker tournaments, betting shops and the racetrack at least provided some interaction with the world outside. Now, he says, 'my contact with the real world is becoming increasingly peripheral.'

Not that Joseph seems to mind one bit. He seems perfectly content with his lot. As I make my farewells, though, he recognises the potential problems for others who are less experienced and less wise, in gambling terms, than himself. 'The internet has been great for me, you know, but it's a mixed blessing. Anyone who has sick tendencies as a gambler will get found out by the internet. They will get destroyed by it. Betfair is dangerous because it is such a beautiful product and so seductive, but it is a bit of a spider's web and if you don't know what you're doing, you'll get caught up in it.'

12

ONE DAY AT A TIME

'Some say he was born with cards in his hands, others that
he will die so, but certainly it is all his life, and whether he
sleeps or wakes, he thinks of nothing else.'

Charles Cotton, *The Compleat Gamester*, 1674

A tall, well-built man in his mid-twenties, with close-cropped dark
hair and a straggly beard, walks to the desk at the front of the room
and sits down with a sigh. He is pale. He pauses for a moment,
blinking at the bright lights, as if he is building up willpower, and
then he begins to speak.

'Hi, my name's Andy.[14] I'm a compulsive gambler.'

The assembled group are ready to respond: 'Hello, Andy.'

'I've had a couple of horrific months recently. I've known Rick
[the leader of the group who is sitting at the desk with him],
through these meetings, for ten years now and up until two months
ago I had not gambled for five years. I felt strong. I didn't have the
urge. Four months ago I changed jobs. Last month I lost my new
job and it threw me out of sync. I went back into my old job. Just
after I'd restarted there, I overheard two fellas going on and on
about an unbeatable system they have on Betfair. They were going
on and on about it. They wouldn't shut up. I knew it was bullshit

[14] GA obviously do not use surnames, but out of respect for the gamblers who let
me sit in on their evening on the basis of anonymity, I've changed their forenames
as well.

and I kept telling myself it was bullshit. In the end I tried it. In the last two weeks I've lost two years' worth of savings. I'd put a block on my computer at home, but at work I can't and I haven't been able to help myself. I've been chasing my tail for the last two weeks, getting in deeper and deeper and deeper. I've taken out five loans. Yesterday was just heinous. I sat at the computer all day and lost a thousand pounds. I was playing poker online – and I don't even know how to play fuckin' poker. Other guys must just have creamed me off. At the end of it all I was so angry.'

Andy pauses for a moment, as his voice has started to crack. He cannot face his audience – a group of fourteen fellow addicts – even though they know exactly what he is going through. He is staring at the floor, with his head in his hands.

'I've been living a lie these past two weeks. My girlfriend didn't know. I didn't tell my family. I just kept getting deeper and deeper, reliving a nightmare I thought I'd awoken from. I told my girlfriend everything last night at 11.30 p.m. It was like she'd been hit by a train. I called up my family – they came around at 2 a.m. It was hardcore ugly. I feel so humiliated.'

The tears are coming now.

'I've been trying to think of the positives I can take out of it – I'm going to throw myself back into meetings. I've been happy for the last five years, but now I'm as low as I've been for ten. I don't feel like I want to gamble any more. I know that if I come to the meetings I can get my life back on track. That's why I'm here. My name's Andy and I'm a compulsive gambler.'

One of the few studies into the incidence of gambling and addiction in Britain – the Gambling Prevalence Survey in 1999 – was commissioned by the addiction helpline GamCare. Of those that took part (7,000 adults aged 16 and over), 72 per cent admitted to gambling within the last year, and 53 per cent within the last week. That equates, nationwide, to around 33 million adults gambling in any one year and 24 million in any one week. The questions were designed to measure the prevalence of addiction and the study concluded that between 0.5 per cent and 1.0 per cent of the adult population were addicted to gambling – that is around 250,000 to 400,000 people. To put that figure into some kind of perspective, it is estimated that problem drug users in this country number somewhere between 250,000 and 300,000.

It is a delicious irony that the offices of GamCare are situated just behind Guy's' hospital on the south bank of the Thames – an institution that was built on the back of Thomas Guy's gambling gains (he was one of the lucky ones) from his punt on the South Sea Bubble. Adrian Scarfe – a wiry, thin-faced man – is Gam-Care's chief clinician. He and his staff see around seventy to eighty people every week and the average indebtedness is about £25,000 per patient. I asked him how he reacted to the new Gambling Act. 'GamCare's position is gambling-neutral,' he said. 'We recognise that gambling is not an illegal activity and that people have a right to choose their recreational pastimes. We want to see gambling that is responsible and we want to be there to pick up the pieces for those who get into trouble. We've been consulted extensively on the new bill and we are happy that, at last, the funding in helping addiction is now part of the regulatory framework. It is enlightened self-interest on the part of the gambling industry to help look after the sick. I have to tell you, though, that our clients are both angry and terrified about the new legislation: angry because they can see something that can now be widely advertised that has ruined their life; terrified because they recognise that it will make their attempts to break free from their addiction more difficult.'

Scarfe reckons that the Gambling Prevalence Survey is now well out of date. 'Our evidence is only anecdotal, of course, but my impression is that the gambling scene has changed dramatically since 1999, that it is a growing problem because of the increasingly complex nature of gambling. Originally, people would ring up and say they had a problem with one thing, whether it was the dogs, horses, fruit machines, whatever. Now we find that things are much more interchangeable – people have multiple problems. I have a client at the moment who bets at the bookies between business meetings, at a casino in the evening and then on the internet when he gets home late at night. That's a general pattern of what we are seeing now. The internet is a huge risk area. It's perfect for gamblers. If you think of the psychology of gamblers, they want instant gratification, round-the-clock availability; they are risk takers, therefore will happily try out new technology; and they like anonymity and secrecy. The internet has been shown to have addictive properties of its own, anyway – you lose track of time whilst you are surfing the internet – so that and gambling present a double-whammy effect. You also use virtual money, not ready cash, so people find it easier to bet large sums. They lose track of where they are and they can win fast and lose fast. It's beautiful for chasing losses. Ultimately, online poker and betting exchanges are the biggest long-term problems that we face. The next thing will be gambling on mobiles and all of a sudden you have gambling on the move.'

Addicts have three main choices in Britain today. As well as contacting GamCare, they can contact Gordon House, a residential home for the addicted, or they can go to their local meeting of Gamblers Anonymous. It is ironic, given the Church's historical antipathy to gambling, that GA was set up in this country in 1964 by the Reverend Gordon Moody. Its relatively late start-up must be explained by the fact that off-course cash gambling remained illegal until 1961 – there could be no effective treatment of gambling addiction until the law recognised that many working people gambled. Although GA's success rate is disappointingly low (only about one in ten first-time visitors return to GA meetings), it remains the starting point for addicts. By the turn of the 21st century there were about 200 meetings of GA each week in Britain and Ireland. Scarfe says that GamCare has a good relationship with GA, but he disagrees with two of their assumptions: 'I don't believe that once a gambler, always a gambler, and I don't believe that you have to hit rock bottom before you can get better.'

The West London branch of GA meets in a nondescript community centre in a quiet residential area of Hammersmith. Here, every Wednesday between 8 and 10 p.m., the most heart-wrenching, brutal, but also, in a strange kind of way, uplifting stories can be heard.

I arrived ten minutes before the scheduled start of one particular meeting in May 2005 feeling as apprehensive as an addict turning up for the first time. I asked three guys in the foyer if this was where the gamblers met. I explained my situation and I asked if I could sit in on their meeting. I was told to ask Rick, who ran their meetings, and who would be turning up any minute.

Rick arrived. I popped the question. He told me to wait outside whilst he discussed it with the group. There were no objections. 'This sickness needs all the publicity it can get,' he said, 'just don't use any names.' Before we sat down, one of the addicts came up to me and said, 'I hope you're going to deal with online gambling in your book. It's a huge problem. It's the anonymity of it all that is the crucial thing.' It was anonymity that had got him hooked; it was now anonymity that was going to help cure him. Except that GA doesn't believe in cures, as such. Like Alcoholics Anonymous, the organisation on which it is based, it believes that once an addict, always an addict. It is a problem that can be controlled, but not cured.

Rick sat behind a wooden desk, near the front of the room. The fifteen addicts formed a semicircle around him. There were fourteen men, aged between 21 and 65, and one woman. They were mainly English, but there was representation from Ireland (2), Australia (1) and France (1) as well. Most were dressed casually, except for the woman, who was dressed in a business suit, and one man, who was also suited.

Rick began by welcoming the newcomers, of whom there were four. He told them that they had shown 'guts and brains' in turning up and that these meetings could give them their lives back if they persevered. 'Our philosophy,' he said, 'is one day at a time. That way the days become weeks, the weeks become months and the months become years.' He talked with a slight slur and he explained that this was the result of a car accident years ago – just in case anybody was wondering whether he was attending the wrong meeting. In fact, there was a steady stream of self-deprecating, gallows-type humour throughout the evening. At one point the buzzer rang. An old Irishman got up to answer the door. 'Is it for us?' someone shouted. 'She's far too good-looking for us,' he replied, to general laughter. These guys were not in the business of kidding themselves.

Each of the addicts, except a young, fair-haired man in the corner who remained silent, introduced themselves by their first name and announced the date on which they had last gambled. The length of abstinence ranged from nineteen years to one day. Rick passed around an orange GA booklet – the addicts' bible. He asked everyone to read aloud one of the twenty questions that was intended to indicate the strength of addiction and then answer that question with a 'yes' or a 'no'. The twenty questions are virtually the same as those asked by the Gambling Prevalence

Survey. One question asked: 'Have you ever sold anything to pay for your gambling?' 'Yes,' replied one of the addicts, and then he added 'my soul.' Again, the fair-haired youth refused to join in.

'If you answered yes to seven of those questions,' said Rick, 'then you're in the right place. If not, say goodbye, and we'll see you later.' (I made a mental check to ensure that I ought not to be putting down my notepad and joining in, but only two of the questions defeated me.) Rick recounted that the first time he came to a meeting he answered yes to only five; a week later he realised he was kidding himself, and he answered yes to nineteen of the twenty questions. He's been coming to GA every week since then.

Each of the addicts was then asked to read out a paragraph from the 'Just for Today' page in their bible. 'JUST FOR TODAY, I will try to live through this day only and not tackle my whole life problem at once. I can do something for twelve hours that would appal me if I felt that I had to keep it up for a lifetime.' After ten such paragraphs were read out aloud, the regular attendees chanted in unison: 'JUST FOR TODAY, I will not gamble.'

Then, the stories began. Following the tearful Andy, an old Irishman shuffled up to the desk.

'Hi, my name's Brendan, and I'm a compulsive gambler.'

'Hello, Brendan.'

'I've been coming here nineteen years and I'd like to pass some of my knowledge to the newcomers. I realise that I suffer from a progressive illness. It's that first bet that I try to avoid. I try to protect myself: today I didn't buy a paper so I couldn't look at the horses; I don't have a computer because I know what I'm like; I don't carry credit cards around with me. I only carry an amount of cash that I need for essentials. This is an illness that gets your soul, so that all you can see when you're in its grip is the next bet. When I look back at some of the things I've done, I realise that I've been a fuckin' lunatic. I'm not me when I gamble. It's not about money, it's about the buzz, the adrenalin – but when you come down, it's humiliating.'

Brendan turned to the Australian in the room. 'They call it the adrenalin bet over there, don't they?'

'Where else has a national holiday for a fuckin' horse race?' was the reply.

'I wish you new guys all the best. I'm Brendan and I'm a compulsive gambler.'

Brendan, like Andy, was applauded all the way back to his seat – another ritual in what was becoming a highly ritualised meeting. But I sensed that Brendan struggled to articulate his problem and was reduced occasionally to reciting clichés from the booklet – perhaps he had being going to the meetings for so long now that it was like trotting out lines that had no meaning. The difficulty most people have in articulating their addiction is, perhaps, one of the reasons why people have turned to literature for a better under-standing of what it is like to be an addict, and of the kind of overwhelming passion that grips them. Maybe literature is the best way to translate an experience that is otherwise beyond conven-tional forms of communication.

The most compelling psychological insight into addiction is to be found in Fyodor Dostoevsky's novella The Gambler. It tells the story of a young impoverished aristocrat, Aleksei Ivanovich, who is obsessed with both gambling at the roulette tables and a young woman called Polina, the stepdaughter of his employer. Polina refuses to be with Aleksei because his love for the roulette table is stronger than his love for her, or anything else.

In the final chapter, the reader sees Aleksei, an empty husk of a man, trawling the tables in Homburg, living a hand-to-mouth existence, chancing every last rouble on the spin of the wheel. He tells us how he spent time in prison as a debtor, how he earned enough on his release to start gambling again, how he looked upon 'the streams of gold as they issued from the croupiers' hands and piled themselves up into heaps of gold, scintillating as fire', and as he did so, how he nearly fell 'into convulsions'. Inevitably, Aleksei loses everything. We see a man out of control, trapped in a vortex that is sucking him down ever deeper into debt, until he admits to losing his sense of reality and feeling as though he were just 'whirling and whirling and whirling around'.

Throughout the story, the gamblers are portrayed as people completely out of their minds; as people in the midst of the most uncontrollable passion. Halfway through the novel we are introduced to an ageing grandmother who makes her first ever visit to a casino. She becomes hooked as surely as if she had stuck heroin in her veins. 'The wheel whirled around and around with the grandmother simply quaking as she watched its revolutions.' She wins heavily on her first visit by betting her chips on the zero. On her next visit, she bets on zero seventeen times, only to lose faith on the eighteenth spin of the wheel, which is when the zero finally comes up. At first the old lady failed to understand the situation. When she did, 'she fell to cursing it and throwing herself about and wailing and gesticulating at the company at large.' She made the classic mistake of trying to chase her losses, and the last time we see her she has lost everything. Dostoevsky's grandmother was based on the real-life character of Countess Sophie Kisseleff, who reputedly lost 500,000 florins on one trip to the Homburg casino. The management reacted by renaming the street, on which the casino stood, in her honour.

Dostoevsky gives us the clearest sense of the kind of heightened emotional response that gambling brings. 'It was as in a fever,' Aleksei recounts, 'that I moved the pile, en bloc, to red. "Rouge!" called the croupier. I drew a long breath and hot shivers went coursing through my body.' At the precise moment that the grandmother's ball lands on zero during her first winning streak, Aleksei shares her excitement: 'At that moment . . . my hands and knees were shaking and the blood was beating in my brain.' This heightened emotional response results in the gambler being oblivious to his surroundings, or indeed to time, so that he is able to play on and on and on. Observing one such gambler, Aleksei recalls that 'the player in question was dead to all besides.'

As with any drug, though, the come-down is hard. By the end of the novel, through the eyes of an Englishman called Astley, we see Aleksei as he does not see himself. 'You have ruined yourself beyond redemption,' Astley tells him. 'Once upon a time you had a certain amount of talent and you were of a lively disposition and your good looks were not to be despised . . . but you remained here and now your life is over.' With that Astley throws Aleksei ten sovereigns to fuel the addiction for one more evening. Aleksei gratefully accepts the offering, still believing that one big win will change everything.

The apparent similarity between the effects of gambling and the physical effects of drug-taking was striking. It was noted by Colin, the next to shuffle up to the desk at the front of the room.

'This is my first time here. I need to take control. I've listened to all these stories and I feel exactly the same thing. I'm glad I've come now. I really want to quit. I'm sick of doing my bollocks day after day after day. I'm sick of the lying, the debts and all the shit that goes with it. My mate's an ex-crack cocaine addict. He told me I had as bad a problem as he did. I didn't believe him, but he's right. The only difference is that you can see the damage it is doing to him. I thought I was smart and in control and that I didn't need to come here. I thought I could kick the habit whenever I wanted. I was wrong. The other day was my first glimmer of hope. I went into the bookies with money in my pocket. I stayed in, didn't gamble and came out for the first time ever with money in my pocket. Now I'm here. Thanks for listening.'

Derek was next to unburden himself.

'It's been one hell of a week. Last week was my first meeting. I got through to Sunday fine. I felt strong. On Monday I arranged a one-to-one chat with GamCare. I find that it's really good to talk. On Tuesday I'm at work and I hear they're making 500 people redundant. Half of my department is going – including me. Today I got an email from my girlfriend saying it was finished between us, because of the lies that I told her. She doesn't trust me any more, basically. I'd been gambling badly for eighteen months before she found out. So today my job and girlfriend have gone and I've just realised that after this meeting I need to find somewhere to live.' The group laughed sympathetically along with Derek, who was shaking his head ruefully.

'I've banned myself from my local betting shop and I've told the manager there that he mustn't accept any more bets from me. I now walk the long way home from work so that I don't pass any betting shops. Today, coming here, I found myself outside the betting shop where it all started. I didn't go in. I didn't want to. I stopped for a while and looked at the entrance. I couldn't believe how dumb I've been. There have been a few highs along the way, but so many lows. At the moment I don't feel the need to gamble and I haven't done so for a week. We'll see how we go tomorrow. My name's Derek, and I'm a compulsive gambler.'

The next addict, Steve, was the first to address the fundamentals of the financial ruin that addicts face.

'It's been eleven weeks now since I've had a bet. It's not been a good week, though. The problems of gambling have to be faced and I've got large debts that are starting to bite. I realise now that

40 per cent of my salary over the next five years will go on repaying debts. The scariest thing is facing up to the debts and I did this today. My mortgage is up for renewal – I'm trying to persuade my wife to remortgage to pay off my debts. I looked at my credit report today. Everything is there, and there is no hiding away from it. There is full disclosure: like how many times you've asked for a loan, or the fact that I was blacklisted by Orange six years ago. I'd forgotten that. I've got a truly awful credit rating. I'd encourage everyone here to check it out. It forces you to address your financial situation, and that is the key to getting out of this mess. Looking at it, it's mind-boggling what I've thrown away on gambling. Life is hard enough without all that shit on top. The greatest thing for me is that my wife is going to stick by me. She said to me this weekend, "You haven't told me everything. We've been married for eighteen years and I didn't know until ten weeks ago that you gambled. What else have you got to tell me?"

' "Christ," I thought, "I've lied, cheated, stolen from her. I even remortgaged the house and she didn't know about it." This weekend I told her everything. The senselessness of it all – I'd lose thousands in a day and wouldn't give her a hundred quid for the housekeeping. Most of my life has been a lie – and when you're in your mid-forties that's a painful truth to accept. She listened to it all and then she said, "Right, we'll start again now." I couldn't believe it. "Are you sure?" I said. "Yes, it's gone now. We'll start again." I said to her the next morning that I'm not sure I would have done the same thing if the roles had been reversed. I think I would have walked out of the front door. So I thank God for my wife. I feel strong now that I know she's going to stay with me. I feel happy. I realise that these are early days but I feel good. I know I can't treat this problem with contempt – you have to treat it like the animal it is. I'd like to finish with this story: in 1998 one of the first roulette machine companies turned over profits of £32,000.

Today it's worth £330 million and this year it has been named business of the year. It was set up by two independent bookmakers. I'm Steve and I'm a compulsive gambler.'

Rick sprang into action for the first time in a while. 'We have no policy on gambling here. We're not here to campaign against gambling. We're only here to help the sick.'

Anthony took over from Derek and got the meeting back on track, albeit with a stream-of-conscious rambling.

'My wife came with me to another meeting last night [there is a branch of GA called Gam-Anon which encourages the wives, friends and family of addicts to attend]. She was shattered by the end of the night. I looked through the GA literature this morning. I started crying. Is that really me?

'It's been my life for thirty-odd years. It's only in the last four weeks that I've started coming back here. My wife didn't know the person she married. I used to live near Haydock Park racecourse. I remember the day there was an almighty punt on a horse called Captain Christy. I remember a priest unloading his collection box with one bookie. The horse fell close to the finishing line. There was an almighty cheer from the bookies and silence from the punters. Outside I saw a load of guys with billboards around their necks saying, "Give up gambling. Gambling is a sin." I thought, "What a bunch of wankers." Now I don't buy a paper any more, except for the *Metro*, which doesn't carry the horses. I don't put on *Channel 4 Racing* any more. I don't go near bookies. I've stopped all my betting accounts. Betting on credit is far more dangerous than betting with ready cash – a big bet doesn't feel like a big bet on the phone. I feel ashamed what I've done to my wife, but I'm glad I told her. I can't thank her enough for staying with me. My name's Anthony and I'm a compulsive gambler.'

* * *

Dostoevsky would have empathised with the gambling-induced family problems experienced by Colin, Derek, Steve and Anthony. Dostoevsky wrote about gambling addiction because he himself was an addict for much of his life – something that left him almost permanently impoverished. In fact, *The Gambler* was written in a frenzied twenty-four-day period in order to raise some much-needed cash to finance his gambling debts. Dostoevsky had to face many challenges in his life: the epilepsy that never left him; the early murder of his father, and his time in the gulags of Siberia. Perhaps his addiction to gambling on the roulette tables of Europe's casinos was his greatest challenge.

The Gambler was not the only good thing that came out of his indebtedness: shortly after the novella had been completed, Dostoevsky married Anna Snitkina, the stenographer who had typed up the manuscript. Dostoevsky was a compulsive letter writer to his second wife, and it is in the letters to her, written during a ten-day period in May 1867, that Dostoevsky's addiction to roulette is laid bare. Simultaneously, Anna was keeping her own diary and so we get an insight into the kind of damage – real, financial and psychological – that addicted gamblers inflict upon their loved ones.

On 6 May 1867, Fyodor talks Anna through his day's gambling: 'I couldn't tear myself away; you can imagine how excited I was. I started gambling in the morning and by dinner had lost 16 imperials. I went back after dinner with the intention of being impossibly prudent and, thank God, I won the whole 16 I had lost . . . Here is my ultimate observation: if one is prudent, that is, if one is as though made of marble, cold, and inhumanely cautious, then definitely, without any doubt, one can win as much as one wishes. But you need to play a long time with little if luck is not with you, and not rushing violently at chance.'

Anna writes: 'I received a letter from Fyodor and I opened it in fear and trembling, thinking perhaps it might contain news of losses on his part.'

7 May 1867: 'Yesterday was very bad for me. I lost very substantially. What can I do? With my nerves, my angel, I shouldn't gamble . . . You see, my efforts are successful every time as long as I have the composure and calculation to follow my system, but as soon as a winning streak starts I immediately start to take risks. I can't control myself . . . I'm not writing the details of how much I won and lost; I'll tell you everything when I see you. In a word, as of now, things are very bad.'

On 8 May it is clear that Fyodor's system has gone wonky. 'Would you believe: I lost everything yesterday, down to the last kopec, to the last guilden and in fact I've decided to write to you in a hurry to have you send me some more money so I can leave. But I remembered about the watch and went to a watchmaker to sell it or pawn it. That's all terribly common, that is, in a gambling town.'

Anna's diary entry records that she was expecting her husband home on the day he pawned his watch. She went to the station to meet him, and then returned home via the post office. 'Fyodor,' she writes, 'has lost everything. Full of misery, I went home and cried bitterly.' Anna also wrote to her mother, begging her to secretly pawn a fur coat and to send some money.

The next day, Fyodor went to the post office and his legs 'nearly buckled' when he was told that there was no letter and, therefore, no money from his wife. He pleads with her in his next letter to send the money, so that he can leave town. 'I need to leave,' he wails, 'but I have no money. I've lost even the pawnbroker's money.'

Anna went to the station again, and again she stopped off at the post office on her return. She 'found a letter which upset me dreadfully. More losses! What will be the end of it all?'

On the 10th, his wife's letter and the money arrived. In it, she berates him about his extended stay in Homburg and his losses. Fyodor cannot see beyond his own problems and he scolds her: 'You have been crying, not sleeping and worrying. What was it like for me to read about that?' Once again, he trusts to his system to get him out of trouble: 'I've made an experiment: if you play coolly, calmly and with calculation there is no chance of losing. There's not even a chance.' Blind to his own recklessness, he tells Anna that 'anyone who gambles without calculation, relying on chance, is a madman.' He talks her through his day's gaming. 'I used nearly supernatural powers to be calm and prudent for a whole hour and the result was that I won 300 guildens. I was so happy and so terribly, to the point of madness, wanted to finish it all today, to win at least twice as much and come home, that without allowing myself to rest up and recollect myself I rushed to the roulette wheel, began staking gold, and lost everything, everything, down to the last kopec.' He finishes by imploring Anna to send him twenty more gold imperials.

On the same day, Anna tries a change of tack. 'I made up my mind as to the contents of the letter I should get, namely that everything was lost and that I must send more money, so that when this turned out to be the case I was not particularly overwhelmed.'

On 11 May he implores Anna to send some more money.

On the 12th, Anna 'called in at the post office where I found a letter from him. He has got my letter but not the money and therefore cannot leave. Is it, I wonder, just a pretext for staying on?' Anna was beginning to understand all about an addict's lies and the ensuing loss of trust.

His letter on the 12th begins like this: 'Anna, my dear friend, my wife. Forgive me, don't call me a scoundrel! I have committed a crime, I have lost everything that you have sent, everything. I received it yesterday and I lost it yesterday . . . can you now respect me? What is love without respect?'

On the 13th Anna again goes to the station expecting to meet her husband. She records that, 'From there I went to the post office and thought on the way there would be a letter from Fyodor telling me that he had lost everything and I must send him more money. All of which happened.' Her diary has a resigned tone by this time.

Fyodor finally returned from his gambling expedition on 15 May, having frittered away more than 100,000 francs in all. Anna greeted him lovingly. On the 16th she writes that 'we woke up rather late today', but not for the reasons that you might expect when man and wife have spent ten days apart: 'We have no watch any longer,' she laments. 'It was left behind in Homburg – so we have no idea of the time.'

It doesn't seem, however, as if Dostoevsky's enthusiasm for gambling has been passed down through the genes: in March 2005 his great-grandson, Dmitri, sued Russia's nationwide sports lottery for using Dostoevsky's image on their tickets. What would the great novelist have thought?

In the more liberal atmosphere of the late 20th century, the anti-gambling lobby had to find a new way to express its concerns. It did so by emphasising that gambling was an illness – a sickness to be cured. Although addiction to gambling is as old as mankind, it had not been studied in any detail until the first half of the last century. One of the first to do so was the master of the darkest recesses of the human mind – Sigmund Freud. In a famous article called 'Dostoevsky and Parricide', written in 1928, Freud used Dostoevsky's letters and his writing in *The Gambler* to cast new light on the psychology of addiction.

Freud described Dostoevsky the gambler as in the throes of an 'unmistakable fit of pathological passion'. He explained Dostoevsky's addiction as a substitute for masturbation, using the shaking of the dice box as the analogy. 'The passion for play,' said Freud, 'is an equivalent of the old compulsion to masturbate.' A student of Freud's, Edmund Bergler, took Freud's analysis further. Whereas Freud looked at Dostoevsky in isolation, Bergler expanded the theory to analyse the gambler's condition in general. Addicted gamblers, he argued, often feel guilty about a childhood resentment towards their parents (Dostoevsky had a death wish against his father), and this guilt manifests itself in a peculiar form of self-punishment – an unconscious desire to lose. The addicted gambler, said Bergler, is not happy until he has lost everything and the punishment is complete. The addict, said Bergler, wants to lose.

Where Freud led, a new generation of psychiatrists and psychoanalysts followed. Most agreed that gamblers are irrational neurotics possessed of an unconscious desire to lose. Unconscious because most gamblers have an illogical belief that they were bound or destined to win, that they were somehow in control. This illusion – or 'gambler's fallacy' as it is known – is recognised as a key factor that encourages gamblers to keep on playing even when they are losing. Adrian Scarfe told me of his favourite quote from one of his clients which proves the fallacy: 'I know my system works but I just can't follow it.'

The American Psychiatric Association finally accepted gambling addiction as a mental illness in 1980 and the World Health Organisation recognised gambling as a disease a decade later. The medical research into addiction goes on: doctors in America have recently linked high levels of dopamine in patients to pathological gambling habits. Indeed, dopamine is a drug given to help patients with Parkinson's disease – and a desire to gamble has been an unwelcome side-effect of their treatment. The endgame to this medical approach is the search for a gambling gene, and in the last decade studies have been released indicating that variants of the gene DRD2 are common to many addicts.

In the GA meeting in Hammersmith, there was a latent hostility towards the medical profession throughout the evening. The well-dressed French lady talked of the advantage to be gained by surrounding herself with real people who had real problems. One addict specifically brought up the issue of psychoanalysis: 'Jesus Christ,' he said, 'at one point I was spending more on my psychoanalyst than my gambling! I thought "What's going on here?"'

The clinicians at GamCare take both a practical and psychoanalytical approach. Initially, they look at behavioural change: at family and social factors and at the accessibility of gambling and the games that addicts play, which are often cynically designed to encourage return visits. Since the ability to gamble is a necessary first step to addiction, then the accessibility of gambling is a big factor. If you can gamble online, without having to leave the front door, without having to face another human being, then the opportunity to become an addicted gambler is clearly greater than before. And when the government sponsored gambling, as they did with the introduction of the National Lottery in 1994, allowing advertisements on TV, the phone calls to GA went up by 17 per cent the following year. The UK Gambling Review Report was convinced about the dangers of the increased opportunity to gamble: 'A central question for us has been whether increasing the availability of gambling will lead to an increase in the prevalence of problem gambling. The weight of evidence suggests that it will do so.'

Scarfe is convinced, however, that only a deeper understanding of the issues can lead to a permanent solution and this is where psychoanalysis comes in. 'We believe deeply in psychoanalysis and we all have a background in that. We try to stop the rot first but underneath you have to find out what is driving it. Psychoanalysis is not in the public domain because it is longer term, more difficult and complex to explain and understand, and more expensive. We know cognitive behavioural therapy works in sometimes as short a time as six to eight sessions. But my personal view and my passionate view is that unless you find out what's going on underneath, you can give the patient certain skills to use if they are motivated to stop but they still lack complete understanding. Very early on a patient asked me why, when he walks down the road, his left foot goes one way, into the bookies, and his right foot another. Only a deeper understanding of that person's background can help us solve that puzzle.'

I doubt if the fair-haired young man who had not yet spoken in the GA meeting knew what was driving his addiction. But at least he was attempting to take action early enough to prevent the downward spiral experienced by most of the others in the room. He'd taken his first step to recovery by coming to Hammersmith on a wet spring evening. He was now about to take the next step when Rick invited him up onto the stage for the second time that evening. This time, instead of declining the invitation, he rose slowly from his chair and walked to the front. He was slim, and dressed casually in trainers, faded jeans and a T-shirt. I was surprised, although I don't know why, when he spoke with a clear, posh, Home-Counties accent. It seemed a little out of place in this room of shattered dreams. Addiction cuts across class boundaries.

'My name's Marcus and I'm,' he paused, not for effect, but simply because he was building up courage, 'and I'm a compulsive gambler.'

'Hello, Marcus.'

'I'm 21, so that makes me the youngest member here. I have the feeling that lots of you guys have been where I am now. I started by gambling in the Hard Rock casino in London. To be honest, I didn't really enjoy it at the start. I went more for the drinking and the friends rather than the gambling. Then I began to enjoy it more and more, even though it still wasn't hurting my bank account. Two years ago I got a job on the ships as a cadet. We spend one month on duty and one month off. My last trip was to Singapore and it was with a fantastic crew. We had a great time in Singapore. The Captain mentioned that there was a great casino. I knew there and then I should have said no, but it's hard to say no to the Captain. I lost all my money in that casino. I couldn't stop myself until I had lost it all. When we got back to Southampton I didn't have enough money for a train, so I had to hitch a lift. Eventually, it was the Captain who picked me up on the road. "What the fuck are you doin'?" he said. I told him what had happened. He was so, so sorry for encouraging me. It was him that told me to come to this meeting. That was a week and a half ago, and here I am. I'm glad I came. I was as nervous as hell. Shit-scared, to be honest. My girlfriend and family are very supportive, but I was still shit-scared. But I'm glad I came. I'm Marcus and I'm a compulsive gambler.'

It had taken Marcus an enormous amount of courage to tell his story. He was clearly embarrassed – his whole neck and face was blotchy-red as he returned to his seat, but I had the feeling that his courage in attending his first GA meeting would stand him in good stead in his fight to beat his problem.

Rick was ready to close the meeting. Before he did so, he congratulated Marcus on his good sense in coming. 'It's no disgrace to come here, you know. This is the most expensive club in the world. It's cost most of our members absolutely everything to join. Marcus, this is the best life you are going to get. Don't fuck it up. Keep coming to the fellowship.'

And on cue, after two hours of what seemed to me to be a combination of phoney ritual and storytelling of the most brutal and honest kind, the West London branch of GA chanted in unison: 'God grant me the serenity to accept the things I cannot change, courage to change the things I can and wisdom to know the difference.' It was time for them to leave the comforting cocoon created by fellow addicts. It was time to face reality again – one day at a time.

EPILOGUE

In March 2006 the latest English newspaper to enter an already overcrowded market rolled off the presses. *The Sportsman* is a newspaper dedicated to gambling, and it reflects both the recent expansion of gambling and its rapidly changing scene. Printing presses have encouraged the spread of gambling in the past, notably in the 15th century, when they disseminated playing cards to a wide audience for the first time, and in the late 18th and early 19th centuries, when a glut of sporting newspapers began to print racing cards, form and results, thus contributing to gambling's evolution into a mass leisure activity. Indeed, the title given to this new publication (part funded, incidentally, by the sons of James Goldsmith, the man who formed such an important part of the 'Aspinall set') is a resuscitation of an earlier title which fed the gambling and sporting enthusiasms of 19th-century London.

But whilst earlier printing efforts were instrumental in encouraging the spread of gambling, this latest venture reflects, and is designed to cash in on, the increase in gambling at the dawn of the 21st century. In 2005, gambling in Britain alone was a fifty-billion pound industry. That represents around £800 for every man, woman and child and is a 20 per cent increase on the figures of five years ago. For an accurate assessment of the numbers of regular gamblers, and problem gamblers, we must wait until the newly constituted Gambling Commission has completed its gambling prevalence survey. All the anecdotal evidence suggests that they will find a substantial increase in both since the last survey was completed, seven years ago.

What has struck me in the writing of this book is that the gambling world is both changing rapidly and stuck in the past. Aspinall's and Crockford's unashamedly echo the gaming rooms of Georgian England; betting shops remain well patronised by punters whose methodology hasn't changed in decades; the stock market continues to experience speculative bubbles and financial dislocations; crowds swarm to the races as they always have done; sport continues to be beset by match-fixing problems; and the types of games offered to a punter in casinos are much the same as they were two hundred years ago. The crazy bet struck recently by the comedian Dave Gorman, who bet his mates that he could find fifty-four other Dave Gormans in the world – one for each card in the deck, plus jokers – and spent six months travelling the world to win the wager, recalls many of the absurd wagers struck by aristocrats in the 18th century.

Despite the similarities, the internet has brought changes that even twenty years ago we might have thought unbelievable: the front room is now the ultimate gambling destination and you don't even need a bookmaker any more to strike a bet. Gambling will continue to take advantage of technological advances because it has been embraced by governments and encouraged to become part of a legitimate and mass-market leisure industry, and because that industry is run by conglomerates out to offer entertainment and maximise their profits by exploiting the gambler's eternal fallacy: that he will win despite the overwhelming odds.

The professional gamblers – the winners – that we met throughout the book seemed to have certain things in common: not many of them enjoyed much of a family life; they exhibited a dedication to gambling that limited an awareness of the world around them; making money, rather than the buzz or excitement or enjoyment of gambling, was the prime motivation; and they all had a keen grasp of mathematics and probability theory. They are the gambling minority – as are the addicts we met in the last chapter for whom gambling results in ruination. In between are the vast majority for whom gambling brings various degrees of pleasure and pain – neither in large enough doses to dominate or decimate their lives.

The methods of the majority, however, dictate the fact that the gambling explosion fuelled by new technology will lead to much financial pain.

Despite the fact that probability theory was first mooted by our friend Cardano more than four hundred years ago, and that it has been accepted since as the soundest forecasting method known to man, the majority of gamblers reject probability theory. For them, unseen, mysterious forces such as luck, fate and omens play a more important part in their choices. To watch the craps players in the Bellagio, for example, is to watch superstition at its most powerful. A recent study into the methodology of 412 bingo players showed that most believed in luck in some form or other, whether it be lucky seats, lucky friends, lucky mascots, lucky numbers or lucky pens. A third of them believed in winning streaks and losing streaks. All this despite the complete randomness of the game they play. Unsurprisingly, perhaps, a good number of these bingo players read their horoscopes on a daily basis and believed in astrology and predestination. Today's bingo players and craps players, then, are no different from the gamblers observed at the Groom Porter's by Samuel Pepys over three hundred years ago: 'To see the different humours of the gamesters to change their luck when it is bad – how ceremonious they are as to call for new dice – to shift their places – to alter the manner of their throwing; and that with great industry as if there was anything in it.'

This rejection of science is unsurprising. Probability theory can provide gamblers with an edge, but only in the long term. Thousands of tosses of a coin will result in a fifty-fifty split – or as near as makes no difference. But probability theory won't tell the punter what will turn up on the next toss of the coin. He might back heads, and suffer ten tails before the law of averages – the law of large numbers – equals things out. Whilst professionals have a large enough bank roll, and enough patience and dedication, to defeat such short-term fluctuations, the amateur has not. In that sense, the majority of gamblers today are not much different from the very first gamblers that we met in this book who cast and drew their lots whilst waiting for divine pronouncement. We may not believe in divination any more, but in the absence of the kind of cold, clinical analysis that probability theory demands, gamblers are reduced to believing in nonsensical controlling forces like luck, superstition and omens. Now, as then, gamblers continue to walk in the shadows of Socrates's 'unexamined life'.

POSTSCRIPT

That public and regulatory attitudes towards gambling represent a slow-moving pendulum, which swings constantly between liberty and constraint, has never been better illustrated than by events either side of the Atlantic in the six months since this book was first published. In Britain, the backlash is under way against a Labour government portrayed as the croupier-in-chief because of its support for liberalising and de-regulating legislation that is more than four decades old. In America, meanwhile, the first twitching of opposition to the prohibition of internet gambling has started to take hold within a reinvigorated Democratic Party.

It is easy to wonder whether Tessa Jowell ever regrets posing as a dice-shaking gambler for a PR opportunity to first publicise the overhaul of the gambling laws in this country, such has been its tortuous path. On 28 March 2007, she might have hoped that the end was in sight when the Lords and Commons finally voted on the government's casino policy. Jowell herself was gambling at a high-stakes table, since she asked for an all-or-nothing vote: both houses were asked to accept the government's casino policy in full – that is show their support for both the single so-called 'super-casino' and the 16 smaller regional casinos. Jowell may well have felt the odds were in her favour – gamblers always do – but she lost. While the Commons passed the motion, the Lords rebelled (123 votes to 120) and it left the government's long-touted casino policy in ruins.

Had the super-casino been destined for Blackpool, it is likely that the Lords would have acquiesced. But the Casino Advisory Panel, which had long been debating the relative merits of the municipal councils keen to host the super-casino, had chosen Manchester – a rank outsider – instead. The reasoning given was that they wanted to assess the effects of the super-casino in a relatively 'normal' social environment. Blackpool as a tourist destination in need of regeneration – the perfect venue for such a project many thought – did not fit the bill. According to the CAP, Manchester 'was a good place to test the social impact'.

But for many in the Lords, a deprived part of inner-city Manchester was no place to test gambling theory, and general opposition to the super-casino proposal grew. Baroness Warnock, writing in the *Guardian* shortly after the defeat of the motion, was withering in her condemnation of the government's gambling policy: 'Only Tony Blair,' she wrote, 'is sanctimonious enough to propose casinos as a solution to the problems of the poor.' The Archbishop of Canterbury, Rowan Williams, made a rare intervention in political affairs, echoing his institution's long-held antipathy towards gambling in general, when he said during the debate, 'All addictions are imprisonments for the soul.'

Elsewhere, some urban councils began to see the dangers in the proliferation of casinos on their doorstep. Nottingham, for example, which has already granted eight casino licences, has refused to issue any more this year. One senior councillor said, 'Have we no greater ambition than training our young people to become doormen and croupiers?'

By the time the next round in this contest is fought, Britain will have a new Prime Minister. Gordon Brown is known to be lukewarm towards the government's existing casino policy, an attitude reflected in his last budget as Chancellor of the Exchequer, which announced a hike in taxation paid by casinos. Where does that leave the future of the super-casino? Spin the wheel and place your chips.

While the British government attempts to liberalise, de-regulate and promote gambling, a very different attitude exists in America. The increasingly hostile attitude towards internet gambling had been highlighted with the arrest of David Carruthers, the Chief Executive of online betting firm BetOnSports, in July 2006. Carruthers was arrested as he alighted at Texas en route to his firm's headquarters in Costa Rica. At the time of writing he remains under house arrest in St. Louis, Missouri, subject to electronic tagging and allowed outside just twice a day. For internet gamblers, and internet companies, the warning signs were clear.

With a right-wing, Christian fundamentalist orthodoxy prevailing in Washington it was no surprise that America moved to finally ban internet gambling altogether. In October 2006, the Republican Party attached a clause outlawing internet gambling to an unrelated bill on homeland security. It was passed with little debate just before the mid-term elections. Jim Leach, a Republican from Iowa, encapsulated the feelings of the Republican majority when he highlighted the dangers of internet gambling with the pithy phrase: 'You just click your mouse, and lose your house.'

Although it was a move that had been widely predicted, the effects were immediate for internet companies and their founders worldwide. PartyGaming, for example, dropped out of the FTSE 100 as quickly as it had arrived, and its founders were deleted from the Forbes list of the world's richest people. Within weeks, $3 billion had been wiped off the value of British internet companies.

But it was time for the pendulum to swing again. The draconian nature of the prohibitionist legislation began to disturb some within the Democratic Party, and those, of course, with vested interests. The tiny Caribbean island nation of Antigua and Barbuda, home for many offshore internet companies, complained to the World Trade Organisation. The WTO ruled that, because some American states allowed inter-state electronic betting on horses for

American firms only, prohibition was illegal and discriminatory towards foreign firms. America has yet to respond to the WTO's ruling.

The Democrats have tabled a bill to repeal the ban. This from Barney Frank, a Democrat who chairs the Senate's financial services committee: 'The existing legislation is an inappropriate interference on the financial freedom of Americans and the inter-ference should be undone.'

As ever, the financial argument is compelling. It is estimated that revenues from internet gambling, if legalised, would rake in $20 billion over the next five years. Many states looked on enviously as revenues from gambling on Indian tribal lands topped $22.6 billion in 2006 – more than Las Vegas and Atlantic City combined. Robert Martin, the chairman of the Morongo tribe, whose 775 adult members take home almost $20,000 a month each from the revenues of one casino alone, remarked wryly that, 'it wasn't fashionable to be Indian until recently.' But maybe their privileged position will soon come under threat, despite the $7.6 million spent on lobbying by Native American tribes last year alone. Iowa and Michigan are already in the process of liberalising laws to make it easier for non-Indians to set up casinos.

As governments either side of the Atlantic grapple with gambling regulation in the wake of the dramatic technological changes since the arrival of the internet, they would be wise to take a history lesson first: if history shows anything, it is that people will always gamble. The desire to seek out risk is part of the human psyche. Prohibition, therefore, will never work. Nor is it sensible for responsible governments, given the damage that gambling does to the vulnerable, to encourage people to gamble. An industry that is fairly taxed and carefully regulated, one that is allowed to operate legally but not given the ability to stimulate demand, is the commonsense approach. Such an approach, in fact, was accepted by successive British governments from the 1960s on-wards. Few would argue against the need for an updated set of gambling laws given the changing social environment, and had the government not included its new-fangled casino policy, I can't imagine that its proposals would have caused such an outcry. It is a policy that looks sillier by the day.

As governments dither and debate, fortunes continue to be won and lost. In February 2007, Aspinall's won a court case to recover a further £2 million from a Syrian gambler who had already lost £23 million. 'I know it's wrong to lose money like this, but if you've ever been to a casino then you'll know what it is like,' he told the *Daily Telegraph*. Harry Findlay, a professional gambler, cleaned up on the second day of Cheltenham in 2007, when his own horse Denman won him close to a million pounds. (Findlay actually broke the magic seven figure barrier when he won an exotic bet two months later on 2000 Guineas day in May 2007.) On day one of Cheltenham, the bookmaker Coral had been ecstatic when so many favourites failed to win: 'Three more days like this will make our year,' said spokesman Simon Clare. The battle between the punters and bookmakers goes on.

It is clear that groups previously immune to the dangers of gambling are becoming increasingly drawn to it, because of the ease of access. At King's College Wimbledon, boys were recently reported to be staying up all night playing on gambling sites on the internet. At Harrow School a member of Gamblers' Anonymous has been recruited to address boys on the dangers of gambling, although the headmaster was quick to point out that 'no particular incidents have been brought to my attention'. It is not only the public schools who have concerns over the welfare of their students. The International Gaming Research Unit at Nottingham Trent University estimates that 3.5% of children between the ages of 11 and 15 now have a gambling problem. All the statistical evidence, as well as anecdotal impression, is of an activity on the increase. The helpline GamCare took 30,240 calls in 2006 from concerned gamblers – a 33.9% increase on the year before.

The age-old problem of corruption, which goes hand in hand with gambling, continues to threaten sport's integrity. When the Pakistan coach, Bob Woolmer, was found dead of 'asphyxiation by manual strangulation' (the initial conclusion of the Jamaican police, a conclusion they subsequently changed to death by natural causes) shortly after Pakistan's surprise defeat by Ireland, conspiracy theorists were quick to point the finger at corruption. Since Woolmer had coached Hansie Cronje's South African team during the 1990s, and was also close to a number of Pakistani cricketers who had been investigated by Justice Qayyum, it was felt by many that Woolmer might know a little too much. In any case, with Marlon Samuels, a current West Indian cricketer, presently under investigation by the ICC for his reported links with an Indian bookmaker, it is clear that sport can never be complacent about the threat of corruption.

The International Association of Athletic Federations rightly took action to tighten its own regulations following the news that Robert Wagner, a well-known athletes' agent, had launched AthleticBet. com in January 2007 as 'the world's No. 1 betting site for track & field'. The IAAF responded quickly by voting to 'forbid officials, athletes and representatives, coaches, meeting organisers and trainers from taking part, either directly or indirectly, in betting, gambling and similar transactions connected with athletic competitions under the rules of the IAAF or its members.' Players' Associations for cricket, rugby, football and racing, under the umbrella of the Professional Players' Federation, did themselves little credit by asking for the government to soften measures against their members who are found guilty of providing information to bookmakers.

Sport and betting will always co-exist precisely because of the thrill they generate together. Shortly after this book was published in hardback form, one of the greatest gambles of recent times occurred on the outskirts of Paris one autumn afternoon. Deep Impact, winner of the Japanese Triple Crown, was preparing to take on the best of European horses for the Prix de L'Arc de Triomphe, France's premier horse-racing trophy, and a purse of two million euros. Accompanying Deep Impact were between five and ten thousand Japanese horse-racing enthusiasts, certain to a man and woman that their horse could not be beaten. The Japanese don't pussyfoot around when it comes to betting on horses, wagering as they did last year more than $27 billion on course – more than any other country.

Weeks prior to the off, Deep Impact was chalked up by the bookmakers as the third favourite for a race that no non-European horse has ever won – a realistic assessment of its chances. By the morning of the race, due to a frenzy of activity on internet betting sites, he had been made joint favourite. By the time of the off, such was the scale of betting from the Japanese at the track, Deep Impact went off 1–10 favourite. The size of bets on the horse, to shorten so dramatically, can only be imagined.

The horse lost and was subsequently stripped of his third place for testing positive for a banned substance. A story of gambling and a story of our times.

GLOSSARY

ante-post: a bet made well before the event, when the odds are usually more favourable.

arbitrage: an investment where the profit is made on the margin when the same item is priced differently on two exchanges or in different bookies' odds.

baccarat: a card game in which two or more punters back against the dealer.

backgammon: a board game for two players in which the pieces' moves are determined by throws of the dice.

bankroll: normally used to describe the starting sum of money of players in a poker game.

Betfair: the biggest of the internet betting exchanges. Betfair was formed in 2000 and enables its clients to bet with one another in cyberspace, thus cutting out the need for a bookie.

bingo: a game in which the players buy a numbered card, a caller calls out randomly drawn numbers and the winner is the first to complete the numbers on their card – a Full House. Particularly popular with older working-class women, who enjoy the sociability of the game and take apparent pleasure in the callers' oft-repeated nicknames for the numbers, such as 'Legs Eleven'.

blackjack: a card game in which punters play against the dealer to make a higher hand, to a maximum score of twenty-one – also known as pontoon or vingt-et-un.

bookmaker: (**also bookie**) one who lays odds on the result of any future event, but most commonly in horse racing, where the bookie offers odds against all the runners and maintains a **book** (now, of course, a computer printout) keeping a record of his liabilities in any one race as each individual bet is taken.

bridge: (most often **contract bridge**) a development from **whist,** a card game in which partners contract to make a certain number of tricks by progressive or pre-emptive bids nominating trumps.

casino: a building licensed for gambling and traditionally well-appointed – the predominant games being **roulette, blackjack, craps, punto banco** and **fruit machines** (qv).

chemin: de fer similar to **baccarat.**

craps: a gambling game in which dice are thrown and the punters bet on the numbers resulting from the throw.

croupier: person dealing cards, rolling roulette ball and collecting bets in a casino.

derivative: an investment the underlying value of which depends on that of some other investment.

each way: a bet in which the punter backs a horse to finish in the first three (sometimes four).

football pools: a form of gambling in which the punter fills in a postal coupon forecasting the results of football matches – principally eight draws, although there are other options. See also **pools.**

form: predominantly a horse-racing term meaning the previous performances of a horse.

fruit machine: (also **slot machine** or **one-armed bandit**) a gambling machine in which the player pulls a lever or presses a button to activate spinning discs with symbols (originally, and still often, fruits). Success, or more often failure, is determined by the combination of symbols in a given horizontal line.

futures: making a contract to buy or sell an investment or commodity at a fixed price on or before a specific date in the future. See also **long** and **short.**

Gambling: Commission body appointed by the government in the terms of the new **Gambling Act**, which was passed in April 2005 and will come into full effect in 2007.

hazard: a gambling game similar to **craps** in which two dice are rolled – one of the most popular forms of gambling in the extended Regency period (1780–1830).

hedge: to reduce the risk of a heavy loss in an investment by investing in an equal and opposite risk. Thus a bookie who has taken a large number of bets on a horse, and stands to make a large loss if the horse wins, will himself back the horse to win with another bookie.

index betting: see **spread betting**.

keno: a form of bingo-like lottery, played in casinos or on-line, in which the punter invests in numbers of his choice in the hope that they will be selected and posted to a winners' board.

lay: offer odds.

lay off: the term used when a bookie hedges his bets – see **hedge**.

long: buying long is to buy a futures contract.

lottery: like **pools**, lotteries are the basis for a number of gambles in which tickets are bought and the winning ticket is subsequently drawn.

Margin Call: a call made by a broker to an investor when the investor's margin, or collateral, is below the necessary deposit for a purchase.

National Lottery: re-introduced by the government in 1994 for the first time since 1826. The operating licence remains with Camelot, the original licensee. It is a pool gamble, with the total sum gambled divided between the winners, Camelot and good causes.

odds: the offer made in ratios by the bookie or other person laying the bet, e.g. 2-1, when the punter stakes, say, £10 to win £20; or 5-4, when the gambler stakes, say, £10 to win £12.50. These are **odds against**. When the offer is **odds on**, the ratio is either expressed in reverse, e.g. 4-5, or as '5-4 on' – in this case, a gambler staking £10, if successful, would win £8 plus the stake money back. **long odds** – e.g. 50-1 – are quoted when it is not anticipated that the runner has much chance of winning, and **short odds** – e.g. 2-1 or 5-4 on – are quoted when the runner is one of the favourites.

overlay: where the punter's analysis of a horse's chances of winning are greater than the odds on offer from the bookmaker.

poker: almost two hundred years old, poker is currently the fashion amongst gambling games. The fascination of the game is that the best hand dealt does not necessarily win, because players have to assess whether their opponents may have a better hand and are required to stake money to stay in the game to its conclusion.

pools: (also known as **pari-mutuel**) various forms of gambling in which all the bets made are aggregated and shared between the winners, less a fixed percentage for the organisers. See also **football pools**, **National Lottery** and **Tote**.

Premium Bonds: government bonds which retain their face value – the gamble is risking the potential profit of buying an interest-earning bond against the potential profit of winning one of the monthly prizes.

probability theory: a calculation of the likelihood of an event occurring based on an assessment of available evidence.

punter: in current usage the most common term to describe the bettor or gambler.

Punto banco: a variant of baccarat (qv).

raffle: the most traditional of 'soft' gambles, in which punters, many of whom would be unlikely to recognise themselves as such, pay for a ticket which is then mixed with others, from which winning tickets are later drawn.

Rapido: a version of Keno (q.v.).

roulette: a casino game in which a ball is dropped into a spinning wheel divided into numbers, and players bet on which number the ball will settle on.

scratchcard: a card with the numbers or symbols masked so that the player has the immediate gratification of scratching off the masking to reveal whether it is a winning card – or not.

sharp: a slang word in regular usage in the 17th and 18th centuries to describe a crafty gambler who takes advantage of a flat, or foolish, punter.

short: a term to describe an agreement to a sale of an investment which has not been bought and will have to be bought to complete the transaction. The opposite of long (qv).

spread betting: type of betting offered by index betting firms whereby the punter is offered a spread of possibilities on a future event – e.g. England will score between 375 and 400 in their first innings. The punter can then invest in them scoring fewer or more and, if correct, the winnings will be a multiple of the difference between the actual score and the opening level. Cricket offers many opportunities within the same game – e.g. the performances of individual batsmen, bowlers and fielders.

stake: the amount of money for which a bet is made.

sweepstake: a form of betting where all participants bet the same amount and the winner takes the pot.

Texas hold'em: one of several versions of poker.

Tote: (or **Horserace Totalisator Board**) a form of pool gambling, principally associated with horse racing, in which the total sum bet on a particular race is paid to winners after the fixed overheads and profits of the Tote are deducted. The Tote is a government-controlled body, in that its chairman is appointed and its board members are approved by the Home Secretary.

whist: an early card game in which individuals or partners play to win the most tricks. Less popular today as a gambling game, it was immensely popular in the 18th century, not least amongst the European community in India, where fortunes were won and lost at the whist table.

BIBLIOGRAPHY

Ashton, John: *The History of Gambling in England.* N.Y., Burt Franklin, 1968

Balen, Malcolm: *A Very English Deceit: the secret history of the South Sea Bubble and the first great financial scandal.* Fourth Estate, 2002

Bellin, Andy: *Poker Nation: a high-stakes, low-life adventure into the heart of gambling.* Yellow Jersey, 2002

Bergler, Edmund: *The Psychology of Gambling.* N.Y., International Universities Press, 1985

Bernstein, Peter: *Against the Gods: the remarkable story of risk.* N.Y., John Wiley & Sons, 1998

Birley, Derek: *A Social History of English Cricket.* Aurum Press, 1999

Blyth, Henry: *Hell and Hazard, or, William Crockford versus the Gentlemen of England.* Weidenfeld & Nicolson, 1969

Brenner, Reuven, and Gabrielle Brenner: *Gambling and Speculation: a theory, a history, and a future of some human decisions.* CUP, 1990

Cardano, Girolamo: *Liber de Ludo Aleae.* Translated by Sydney Henry Gould

Cassidy, John: *Dot.Con: the greatest story ever told.* N.Y., HarperCollins, 2002

Cassidy, Rebecca: *The Sport of Kings: kinship, class and thoroughbred breeding in Newmarket.* CUP, 2002

Castleman, Deke: *Whale Hunt in the Desert: the secret Las Vegas of superhost Steve Cyr.* Las Vegas, Huntington Press, 2004

Cellan-Jones, Rory: *Dot.bomb: the strange death of dot.com Britain*. Aurum Press, 2003

Chancellor, Edward: *Devil Take the Hindmost: a history of financial speculation*. Farrar, Straus, Giroux, 1999

Chesney, Kellow: *The Victorian Underworld*. Maurice Temple Smith, 1970

Chinn, Carl: *Better Betting with a Decent Feller: a social history of bookmaking*. Aurum Press, 2004

Clapson, Mark: *A Bit of a Flutter: popular gambling in English Society*, c1823-1961. Manchester University Press, 1992

Cotton, Charles: *The Compleat Gamester, or, Instructions how to play at all manner of usual and most gentile games*. 1674 and several other editions

Craig, Michael: *The Professor, the Banker, and the Suicide King: inside the richest poker game of all time*. Warner Books, 2005

Dale, Richard: *The First Crash: lessons from the South Sea Bubble*. Princeton University Press, 2004

David, F.N.: *Games, Gods and Gambling: a history of probability and statistical ideas*. Griffen, 1962

Davies, Andrew: 'The Police and the People: gambling in Salford 1900-1939' (*The Historical Journal*, 1991)

Davies, Hunter: *Living on the Lottery*. Warner, 1997

Dixon, David: *From Prohibition to Regulation: bookmaking, anti-gambling and the law*. Oxford, Clarendon, 1991

Dixon, Henry: *The Post and the Paddock*, by the Druid. 1857 and various other editions

Dostoevsky, Fyodor: *The Complete Letters of Fyodor Dostoevsky*, edited by David A.Lowe. Ann Arbor, Mich., Ardis, 1988

Dostoevsky, Fyodor: *The Gambler*. Various editions.

Eglin, John: *The Imaginary Autocrat: Beau Nash and the invention of Bath*. Profile Books, 2005

Fay, Stephen: *Beyond Greed*. N.Y., Viking Press, 1982

Fay, Stephen: *The Collapse of Barings*. Richard Cohen Books 1996

Ford, John: *Cricket: a social history 1700-1835*. David & Charles, 1972

Ford, John: *This Sporting Land*. New English Library, 1977

Foreman, Amanda: *Georgiana, the Duchess of Devonshire*. HarperCollins, 1998

Freud, Sigmund: 'Dostoevsky and Parricide' (Complete Standard Works of Sigmund Freud)

Galbraith, J.K.: *A Short History of Financial Euphoria*. N.Y., Whittle Books, 1993

Geertz, Clifford: *The Interpretation of Cultures: selected essays*. N.Y., Basic Books, 2000

Gleeson, Janet: *Millionaire: the philanderer, gambler, and duelist who invented modern finance*. Simon & Schuster, 2000

Gronow, Captain: *The Reminiscences and Recollections of Captain Gronow* 2 vols. John Nimmo, 1900.

Haigh, Gideon: *Game for Anything: writings on cricket*. Aurum Press, 2004

Holden, Anthony: *Big Deal*. Abacus, 2002

Huggins, Mike: *Flat Racing and British Society 1790-1914: a social and economic history*. Frank Cass, 2000

King, Mervyn: *What the Fates Impose*. (8th British annual lecture)

Lejeune, Anthony: *White's: the first three hundred years*. A&C Black, 1993

Mackay, Charles: *Extraordinary Popular Delusions and the Madness of Crowds*. N.Y., John Wiley & Sons, 1996

McKibbin, Ross: 'Working Class Gambling in Britain 1880-1939' (*Past and Present* 1979)

McManus, James: *Positively Fifth Street: murderers, cheetahs, and Binion's World Series of Poker*. Picador, 2004

Malaby, Thomas: *Gambling Life: dealing in contingency in a Greek city*. University of Illinois Press, 2003

Michie, R.C.: *The London Stock Exchange: a history*. OUP, 2001

Munchkin, Richard: *Gambling Wizards: conversations with the world's greatest gamblers*. Huntington Press, 2002

Munting, Roger: *An Economic and Social History of Gambling in Britain and the USA*. Manchester University Press, 1996

Neal, Mark: *You Lucky Punters: a study of gambling in betting shops* (*Sociology* 1998, 32)

Nevill, Ralph: *Light Come, Light Go: gambling – gamesters – wagers – the turf*. Macmillan, 1909

Newman, Otto: *Gambling: hazard and reward*. Athlone Press, 1972

Ore, Oystein: *Cardano, the gambling scholar*. Princeton University Press, 1953

Orford, Jim: *Gambling and Problem Gambling in Britain*. Routledge, 2003

Pearson, John: *The Gamblers*. Century, 2005

Pepys, Samuel: *The Diary of Samuel Pepys*

Pycroft, Rev. James: *The Cricket Field: or, the history and the science of cricket*. Longman & Co., 1854, and several other editions

Rae, Simon: *It's not Cricket: a history of skullduggery, sharp practice and downright cheating in the noble game*. Faber, 2002

Reith, Gerda: *The Age of Chance: gambling in western culture*. Routledge, 1999

Schwartz, David: *Suburban Xanadu: the casino resort on the Las Vegas strip and beyond*. Routledge, 2003

Society for the Study of Gambling: Papers 1–35. University of Salford

Spanier, David: *All Right, OK, You Win: Las Vegas, city without clocks.* Arrow, 1993

Spanier, David: *Easy Money: inside the gambler's mind.* Secker & Warburg, 1987

Thomas, Keith: *Religion and the Decline of Magic: studies in popular beliefs in sixteenth and seventeenth-century England.* Weidenfeld & Nicolson, 1991

Thompson, Laura: *Newmarket: from James I to the present day.* Virgin, 2000

Thompson, Laura: *The Dogs: a personal history of greyhound racing.* Chatto & Windus, 1994

Thormanby: *Kings of the Turf: memoirs and anecdotes of distinguished owners, backers, trainers, and jockeys who have figured in the British turf* . . . Hutchinson, 1898

Thorp, Edward: *Beat the Dealer: a winning strategy for the game of twenty-one.* Transatlantic Book Service, 1967

Underdown, David: *Start of Play: cricket and culture in eighteenth century England.* Allen Lane, 2000

Vamplew, Wray: *The Turf: a social and economic history of horse racing.* Allen Lane, 1976

Vega, Joseph de la: *Confusion de Confusiones, 1688.* Boston, Mass., Harvard Graduate School of Business Administration, 1957

Wheen, Francis: *How Mumbo-Jumbo conquered the World: a short history of modern delusions.* Fourth Estate, 2004

Wilde, Simon: *Caught: the full story of cricket's match-fixing scandal.* Aurum Press, 2001

Wykes, Alan: *Gambling: the complete illustrated guide to gambling.* N.Y., Doubleday, 1969

All the reports on match-fixing can be found on the International Cricket Council's website, www.icc-cricket.com

INDEX

'A Safe Bet for Success' 17, 269–70
Abramoff, Jack, lobbyist 200
addiction to gambling 26, 111–14, 206, 281–302
  Gordon House 284
  psychology of addiction 297–8
Affleck, Ben, poker player 260
Ahmed, Mushtaq, cricketer 186
Aislabie, John, Chancellor 50
Akram, Wasim 186
Alfred Club 81
Allen, 'King', gambler 81
Allied Irish Banks 61
Almack's Club 76–7, 178
Les Ambassadeurs Club 90
American Football, Super Bowl 198–9
American Psychiatric Association 298
Anderson, Brett, casino manager xiii
Anschutz, Philip 268
Anson, George, gambler 81
Anti-Corruption Unit 188
Anwar, Saeed, cricketer 186
Aronstam, Marlon, gambler 182–3
Asian handicap betting 194–5
Aspinall, John 84–7
  Aspinall's Club 87–9, 304, 311
  Clermont Club 86–7
Association of British Bookmakers 114, 160
Ata-ur-Rehman, cricketer 186
AthleticBet.com 312
Auriol, gambler 81
Azharuddin, Mohammad, cricketer 187

baccarat 84, 85, 207

Bacher, Ali, South African Cricket Board 185
Bank of England 54
Barclay, David, casino owner xiv
Barclay, Frederick, casino owner xiv
Barings Bank collapse 58–60
Barings Futures (Singapore) Ltd 58
Barker, Liam, poker player 236, 238, 243
Barnes, Dave 234–5, 237, 239–40, 243
Barnes, Simon 119
Bartlett, Warwick 160
Baruch, Bernard, financier 53
Bath 75
BBC, *Come and Have a Go* 1–6
Beal, Andy, poker player 211–14
Beaufort Club 99
Bedford, Lord, gambler 76, 86
Beldham 'Silver Billy', cricketer 180, 181, 190
Bell, Chris, bookmaker 161
Benaud, Richie, commentator 173, 191
Benter, Bill, probability forecasting 33–4
Bentham, Jeremy 73
Bergler, Edmund 298
Berkshire Hathaway (investment company) 53
Berry, Scyld, journalist 182
Best Mate, racehorse 126, 133
Betdaq 159
Betfair 65–6, 118, 126, 137–9, 154–62, 278, 280
  percent of betting market 157
  sponsored races 19, 154
Betmart 157
BetOnSports 309

betting
  see also gambling
  and sport 313
  horse racing 34, 122
  legislation 95–9, 266–7
Betting and Gaming Act (1960) 16,
  86, 101, 245, 267
Betting Houses Act (1853) 95, 99,
  101, 151, 266
betting houses in London 96–8
betting round 148
betting shops 304
  inner city areas 91–4, 104–10
  opening hours 17
Bianco, Francesco, club owner 72
bingo 17, 305
Binion, Benny, casino owner 207,
  220–1
Birley, Derek, *A Social History of
  English Cricket* 177
Black, Andrew, Betfair 138, 154–8, 161
Black, Sir Cyril, anti-gambling 155
blackjack 84
  card counting 32–4, 246
Blackpool 307–8
Blair, Tony 308
Blakenham, Lord 86
Bland, 'Facetious' Jemmy 149
Bland, Sir John, gambler 73
Bloom, Tony, gambler 192–7
  football betting 194–6
  poker 196
blue chip 63
Blue Square, bookmakers 66
Blunt, John 55
Boeken, Noah 'Exclusive' 233–4,
  236, 240, 243
Bolland, Stuart, punter xvi
Boo.com 52
Boodle's Club 81
bookies' runners 101
bookmakers 101, 122–3, 137–54
  banned from Lord's 181
  and Betfair 137
  match-fixing 173–5, 182–8
  pitches on the racecourse 141–7
  stereotype 139–40
  street bookies 151
  tic-tac men 146

Boone, Mr, gambler 74
Bottomley, Horatio 100
Bowen, Peter, trainer 135
Breen, Father 132
Breitling, Tom, casino owner 208
Bretton Woods agreement 56
Bristol, Earl of, owner/jockey 120
Brodrick, Mr, patron of cricket 179
Brooks, William, club owner 77
Brooks's Club 77–8, 81
Brough, Andy, fund manager 265
Brown, Gordon 308
Brown, Stewart 'Stoogster' 235, 243
Brunson, Doyle 'Texas Dolly',
  poker player 213
Brunson, Todd, poker player 213,
  214–15
Budd, Sir Alan, Gambling Review
  Body 17, 267–9, 272, 299
Buffett, Warren, investor 53
Bull, Phil, racing form 165

Cadogan, Lord, gambler 86
Callaghan, Frank, poker player 229
Camelot 12, 14, 16, 18
  market share 15
  name 3
  randomness of draw 4
  rollover 6
Cantor Index 172
Carberry, Nina, jockey 124
Carberry, Paul, jockey 123–4, 133
card counting 32–4, 246
card games 84
Cardano, Jerome 23–7, 305
  addiction to gambling 26–7, 40
  Liber de Ludo Aleae 25, 26–7, 40–1
Carnarvon, Lord, gambler 86
Carruthers, David 309
Casino Advisory Panel 308
casino resorts 200–19
casino policy 307–11
casinos 86, 269–72, 304
  membership 17, 268
  in Nevada 200, 201, 207
casting lots 6
Cawkwell, Simon, financial bettor
  64–9
CelebPoker.com 60

chance, rules of 29–30
Chancellor, Edward 54
Chandler, Billy, bookmaker 253
Chandler, Victor
  internet poker 194, 253–4
  Victor Chandler Poker 253
Channel 4, *Late Night Poker* 260
Channel 4 Racing 143, 293
Channing, Neil 'Bad Beat', poker
  player 227–9, 243
Chawla, Sanjay, bookmaker 174,
  183
Cheltenham National Hunt Festival
  116–31
  betting 122–3
  Centaur Room 123
  Gold Cup 133–4
chemin de fer *see* baccarat
chess 25
Chesterfield, Earl of 80, 81
Chicago Mercantile Exchange 57
Chicago White Sox and 1919 World
  Series 173, 198
China
  copper trading 61–2
  gambling outlawed xviii
China Aviation Oil 61
Cholmondeley, Lady, greyhound
  racing 102
Church antipathy to gambling 7
Churchill, Alison 'The Lady Killer'
  254
Churchill, Winston, on greyhound
  racing 103
Cibber, Colley 73
City Index 172
Clare, Simon 311
Clary, Julian, lottery draw host 2, 5
Clermont Club 86–7
Clevenger, Rhea, poker player 235,
  238, 240, 243, 254
Clooney, George 204
Cockburn, Alexander, Attorney
  General 99
cockfights 84
Cocoa Tree Club 81
Coke, Lord, gambler 73
Colclough, Dave 'El Blondie', poker
  player 228, 233

commodities market fall 63
computer syndicates 37–8
computer-generated gambling 30–1
  horse racing 35–9, 105
  virtual racing 105–7
Condon, Paul, match-fixing report
  188–90
Cook, Robin, punter 154
copper futures 61–2
Coral 105, 141, 160, 162, 311
corruption 312
Cotton, Charles, *The Compleat
  Gamester* 72
Cotton, Sir St Vincent, gambler 81
coursing 102
Cowell, Joseph 220
craps 26, 206–7
cricket
  1999 South African tour 182–4
  2005 Ashes series 172
  Articles of Agreement 179
  and betting culture 177–80
  and bookmakers 180
  'It's not cricket' 176
  Laws 179
  match-fixing 173–5, 182–8
  one-day cricket 189–90
  and spread betting 172–3
Crockford, William, club owner 79–
  82, 149, 180
Crockford's Club 79–82, 88, 90, 304
Cronje, Hansie, cricketer, match
  fixing 174, 182–7, 190–1
currency markets 56

Daily Mail 74, 271
Daily Telegraph 11
Daly, John, golfer, gambling losses
  xix
Damon, Matt, poker player 260
Dandolos, Nick 'the Greek', poker
  player 220
Davies, William 'Leviathan',
  bookmaker 150
de Buckebergh, Count, wager 75
Dean, Peter 273–4
debts 83, 291–2
Deep Impact 313
Defoe, Daniel 46, 55

DeLeon, Russ, PartyGaming 261–2
de Mere, Chevalier 29
Dennis, Barry, bookmaker 143–8,
    153–4, 158, 162
Dennis, Daniel 160
Dennis, Patrick 160
Derby, Lord, gambler 86
derivatives markets 56, 57–62
Dev, Kapil, cricketer 189
Devonshire, Andrew, Duke of,
    gambler 86
Devonshire, Duke of, owner/jockey
    120
Devonshire, Georgiana, Duchess of,
    gambler 78, 178
dice 25–6, 96
Dikshit, Anurag, PartyGaming 261–2
divination 6–7
dog racing 102
dog throw 25
Donald, Allan 238
d'Orsay, Count, gambler 81
Dorset, Duke of, patron of cricket
    178
Dostoevsky, Fyodor
    gambler xviii 294–7
    The Gambler 288–90, 294
dotcom bubble 43, 52
drawing lots 6–7, 25
Duke, Annie, poker player 239–40,
    254
Duncombe, Tom 81
Durham, Lord 100
Duthie, John, poker player 221–2,
    224
Duvall, Jeff, poker player 245–51
Dwan, Tom, poker player 235, 254
Dwyer's betting shop 150

E&O 121
Eclipse, racehorse 128
Effingham, Lord, gambler 86
Egan, Pierce, chronicler of
    prizefighting 127
Eglinton, Lord, gambler 74
Empire Online 261, 264, 266
England, Dick, bookmaker 149
England and Wales Cricket Board
    188

Enron 63
EuroMillions Lottery 15, 18
Evangelical Alliance, 'Help – there's
    a casino coming' 270
Evelyn, John 71

Farmer Jack, racehorse 126, 134
faro 77
Faversham, Lord 100
Fellows, Harvey, cricketer 176
Fermat, Pierre de, theory of
    probability 29
Fifty St James's Club 88
Financial Services Authority 268
financial speculation 54
Financial Times 61
Findlay, Harry 311
Fixed Odds Betting Terminals 105,
    109, 113–14, 122
Fletcher, Duncan, cricket coach 183
Flood, 'Gentleman' Liam, poker
    player 224, 230, 234, 238
Flutter.com 156
football
    2002 World Cup 195
    2006 World Cup 195–6
Football Association, online betting
    161
football betting 194–6, 276
football pools 103
Forrest, Ted, poker player 213, 214–15
Fowles, John, funeral 19
Fox, Charles James, gambler 76–8, 88
France, gaming 70
Frank, Barney 310
Fraser, Hugh, gambler 89
Freud, Sigmund, psychology of
    addiction 297–8
Fry, Stephen, poker player 260
Furnese, Harry, gambler 73
futures contracts 56, 59

Gage, Sir William, patron of cricket
    179
Galbraith, J.K., economist 51, 60
Gam-Anon 293
Gamblers Anonymous 112, 245, 281,
    284–6, 302, 311
gambler's fallacy 298

gambling
  against the law xviii, 95–6
  definition xviii, 13, 54
  history xvii–xviii
  in schools 311
  legislation 95–104, 151, 266–7, 307
Gambling Act (1774) 55
Gambling Act (1845) 70, 82, 96, 266
Gambling Act (2005) 18, 152, 217, 274
Gambling Act (2007) 270, 272
Gambling Commission 12, 268, 272–4, 303
Gambling Prevalence Survey 13, 273, 282–4, 286
Gambling Review Body 17, 267–8, 299
GamCare 14, 112–14, 282–3, 285, 291, 299
gaming 70–90
Gaming Act (1664) 96
Gaming Act (1710) 96
Gaming Act (1738) 96
Gaming Board see Gambling Commission
gaming houses 72–80
Gavaskar, Sunil, cricketer 189
Geertz, Clifford, anthropologist 84
Geraghty, Barry, jockey 135
Gervais, Ricky, poker player 260
Getmapping.com 49
Gibbs, Herschelle, cricketer 187
Goldsmith, James 303
Goodwood 138–9, 158
Gordon House, home for addicts 284
Gorman, Dave, crazy bet 304
Gosney, Lawrence, poker player 228
Gough, Darren, cricketer 184
Grapes, King Street 79
Green, Philip, gambler 90
Greenspan, Alan, dotcom 51, 52
Greenstein, Barry, poker player 213
greyhound racing 102–3
Gronow, Captain, memoirs 81–3, 90
Groom Porter 43, 44, 71–2, 96, 305
Gryko, Richard, poker player 228
Guardian 11, 264
Guards' Club 80
Gudjohnsen, Eidur, gambler 90

Gully, John, bookmaker 149
Gupta, M.K., bookmaker 187, 191
Guy, Thomas, gambler 283
Haigh, Gideon, cricket historian 191
Halley, Edmund, probability of mortality rates 44
Hamanaka, Yasuo, metals trader 61
Hambledon 180
Harding, David 161
Hardy Eustace, racehorse 123–4, 133–4
Harman, Jennifer, poker player 213, 214
Harrah's, World Series of Poker 221
Harris, Lord 176
Hasselbaink, Jimmy Floyd, gambler 90
Hastings, Marquis of, bettor 129, 130
Hastings, Max, journalist 271
Hawke, John, National Anti-Gambling League 98
hazard 26, 81, 206
hedging risk 59, 148
Hemmings, Trevor, racehorse owner 132
Henderson, Nicky, trainer 131–2
Hill, William, bookmakers, 92–4, 104–5, 108, 112, 115, 141, 160, 162
  football betting 276
  on-course bookmakers 159
  social responsibility 113
  tic-tac 146
Hobbs, Philip, trainer 126
Holden, Anthony, Big Deal 4–5
Holden, Tony, journalist 223
Hong Kong
  gambling syndicates 30
  horse racing 34–5
Hong Kong Jockey Club 35, 38
horse racing 116–36
  betting market 122
  classic races 120–1
  computer-generated gambling 35–9
  Derby winners 128
  history 119–20
  Hong Kong 34–5
  Jockey Club 128

match bets 120
off-course betting 122
and on-course betting 117
owners of great horses 128–9
and Royalty 122, 127
televised races xv
Howard, Lord, gambler 76
Hughes, Ball, gambler 81
Hughes, Dessie, trainer 133
Hughes, Howard 202
Hughes, Merv, cricketer 224
Hussain, Nasser, cricketer 182–4

IG Index 166, 170–1
India
Central Bureau of Investigation 187
illegal betting 189
wins cricket World Cup 189
India and Pakistan cricket matches 189, 190
International Association of Athletic Federations 312
International Cricket Council, Anti-Corruption Unit 188
International Gaming Research Unit 311
internet companies 51–2
Internet Entertainment Group 262
internet gambling xix, 198, 269–70, 284, 304, 309–12
internet poker 224, 250, 252–60
global market 260
stakes 256
internet sales 15
Inzamam-ul-Haq, cricketer 186, 188
Irish punters 132–3
Islam, gambling outlawed xiv
Israel, gambling outlawed xiii
Italy, lottery mania 15–16

Jackson, 'Shoeless' Joe, baseball player 173
James, Stan, bookmaker 66
Japanese stock market 59
Jardine, Douglas, cricketer 176
Jockey Club 128
and online betting 161
Johnson, Ben, bookie 123

Johnson, David, racehorse owner 131, 145
Johnson, Howard, trainer 127
Johnson, Richard, jockey 167
joint-stock companies 55
Jones, Iwan, poker player 228
Jordan, Michael, punter 211
Joseph, Ray, internet gambler 275–81
Jowell, Tessa, Minister 269–71, 307

Kennedy, Colin, poker player 230–1, 238, 242
Kennedy, Josh 'The Tooting Tiger' 254
keno 14
Kerkorian, Kirk, casino owner 211
Kerzner, Sol, casino operator 268
Keynes, John Maynard, economist 18, 63
Kicking King, racehorse, 118–19, 133–5
Kidman, Nicole, poker player 260
Kindleberger, Charles, economist 51
King, Edwin, match-fixing inquiry 186
Kingshott, Simon, bookmaker 141
Kyl, Jon, politician 263

Labour Party, anti-gambling 98–9
Ladbrokes 66, 105, 141, 160, 162, 276
tic-tac 146
Lambert, William, cricketer 181
Langan, John, pugilist 127
Las Vegas
casino resorts 200–19
clients 208–10
Desert Inn 202, 204
slot machines 205–6, 208
Latham, Mark, politician 210
Law, John
gambler and banker 42–6
Mississippi Company 46–7
Lawson, Nigel, Chancellor of the Exchequer 103
Lawson, Nigella, poker player 260
Lederer, Howard, poker player 213, 239

Lee, Graham, jockey 127
Lee, Jack, unlucky punter xv
Leeson, Nicholas, collapse of
    Barings Bank 58–60
Lewis, Chris 188–9
Lichfield, Earl of 80, 81
Lincoln, Lord, gambler 73
Lingfield all-weather track 145
Littlewoods 103
Lockhart, George 43
London International Financial
    Futures Exchange 57
London News 150
Long-Term Capital Management 63
lotteries 6–22, 55
    see also National Lottery
    draws 9–10
    history 7–11
Lottery Commission 268
Lotto 3
Lucan, Lord, gambler 86, 89
luck, belief in 4–5, 19

McCoy, Tony, jockey 126, 167
MacDonald, J. Ramsay, Betting and
    Gambling 98
Mackay, Anthony, poker player 234,
    236–7, 240, 243
McManus, J.P.
    130
    racehorse owner 120, 132
Macmillan, Harold, Premium Bonds
    99
McNamara, Dolores, lottery winner
    18
Maguire, Tom, poker player 260
Maitlis, Emily, quiz master 2
Malik, Salim, cricketer 175, 186
Malmsten, Ernst, Boo.com 52
Manchester 308
Mann, Sir Horace, patron of cricket
    178
March, Lord, gambler 75, 178
Martin, Robert 310
match-fixing 304
    cricket 173–5, 182–8
Maxwell, Robert, fraudster 66
Maxwell-Scott, Ian, gambler 85
May, Theresa, politician 271

Mellor, David, minister responsible
    for the Lottery 12
Mercier, Isabelle, poker player 226,
    239, 254
Metropolitan Street Act (1867) 97
Milbanke, Tony, gambler 74
Milken, Michael, Wall Street junk
    bonds 203
Mississippi Bubble 43, 46–8
Mitchell, Peter, journalist 174
Mitford, Mary Russell, author 180
Mond, Lord, gambler 86
Moneymaker, Chris, poker player
    225, 242, 260
Montford, Lord, gambler 73
Montmort, Pierre de, rules of
    chance 29–30
Moody, Rev Gordon, Gamblers
    Anonymous 284
Moores, John, enterpreneur 103
Morgan, James, journalist 61
Morgan Stanley 58
Morning Chronicle 179
Moss, Johnny, poker player 220–1
Mystic Meg, fortune teller 4

NASDAQ 52
Nash, Richard 'Beau' 73, 76
National Anti-Gambling League 97–8
National Association of Bookmakers
    142
national debt 54
National Joint Pitch Council 143
National Lottery 6–17, 267–8, 274, 299
    see also lotteries
    argument against 14
    draw 2–4
    randomness of draw 4
    started (1994) 11–12
National Lottery Commission 4, 12
Neale, Thomas, gaming house
    owner 43
Negreanu, Daniel, poker player 196
Nevison, Dave, bettor 163–9
Newton, Isaac
    probabilities of dice-throwing 44
    and South Sea Bubble xvii; 49
Nicholls, Paul, trainer 111
Nixon, Richard

Bretton Woods agreement ended
56–7
poker winnings xvii
Nyren, John, cricketer 180
Oasis Casino, Jericho xiii–xiv
odds of winning
Lottery 1
overlays 34
roulette xv
six consecutive sixes 45
Odumbe, Maurice, cricketer 188
O'Dwyer, Conor, jockey 123
Oflot 12
Ogden, William, bookmaker 149
O'Kelly, Dennis, racehorse owner
129, 130, 149
online betting 137, 161, 272, 285
see also Betfair
link to addiction 299
online poker 60
options 56
options trading 247
Orléans, Duc d' 45, 48
Osborne, James, Aspinall's 89
Osborne, Lady 86
overlays 34, 37

Packer, Kerry
cricket promoter 190–1
gambler 89, 210–11
Pakistan, match-fixing 186
Pakistan and India cricket matches
189, 190
Palmer, Alasdair, journalist 11
ParadisePoker.com 260
Parasol, Ruth, PartyGaming 261–2
PartyGaming, internet poker 260–6,
266
PartyPoker, com 252, 255, 260
Pascal, Blaise, theory of probability 29
Pascal's Wager 29
Payne, George, gambler 81
Payton, Simon, copper supply and
demand 62
Pelham, Sir Warner 176
Pepys, Samuel 71, 305
probabilities of dice-throwing 44
Pham, Xuyen 'Bad Girl', poker
player 228

Pimlott, Charlie, bowler 174
Pipe, Martin, trainer 111, 135
pitches on the racecourse 141–7
poker
dead man's hand 223
European Poker Tour 222
game of skill 5, 212–15, 220–22
highest stakes game 212–13
language 222–3
money 241–2
online 60
Texas hold'em 226
World Series of Poker 221, 232
PokerListings.com 252, 253
PokerStars.com 224, 235
pools 17, 102
pools companies, age restriction 17
Poster, Tim, casino owner 208
bets on Guinness consumed 116
football World Cup 196
virtual racing 106
Premierbet 195
Premium Bonds 99
Presley, Elvis 202
Price, Graham, gambler xvi–xvii
primero 26
Private Eye 271
Prix de L'Arc de Triomphe 313
probability theory 27–9, 82, 305–6
card counting 33
dice throwing 44
Professional Players' Federation 312
Purcell, John, bookie 146
Pycroft, Rev James, The Cricket
Field 175–6, 180, 181
Pyrah, Wally, Sporting Index 172, 277

Qayyum, Justice 186, 188
Qibing, Liu, trader 61–2
Quantum Fund 56

Raceform 30
racetracks 35
Grade One 143
Racing Post 30, 118, 147, 159, 161,
165, 167
Ramsay, Sir Andrew 44
randomness of Lottery draw 4
rapido 15

Raymer, Greg 'The Fossilman', poker player 233–4
Reed, Ralph, gambling scandal 200
Reith, Gerda, historian 83
Remote Gambling Forum 273
Reynolds, Dick, bookie 147
Richmond, Duke of, patron of cricket 179
Rickert Ltd 123
Rigby, Mr, gambler 74
Ritz, poker parties 85
Ritz casino xiv
Ritz heist xiv–xv
Roach, Stephen, economist 63
Robinson, 'Crutch' 149
Roman games 7
Rooney, Wayne, gambling losses xviii
Rosebery, Lord, racehorse owner 122
Rothschild Commission 13
Rothstein, Arnold, match-fixer 173
Rous, Admiral 99

Saatchi, Charles, poker player 260
St Leger 120, 128
Salomon Brothers 58
Samuels, Marlon 312
Salvation Army 270–1
Sarakakis, Frank, gambling losses 89
Satellite Information Services 105
Scarfe, Adrian, GamCare 113, 283, 285, 298, 299
Schlaff, Martin, casino owner xiv
Schwartz, David, *Suburban Xanadu* 218
Schwartz, Howard, Gambler's Book Shop 217
Scoop6 xv, 24, 166
scratchcards 14–15
Seagrave, Lord, gambler 81
Sefton, Earl of 80, 81, 102
Segal, Richard, PartyGaming 263
Sharma, Ajay, cricketer 187
short-selling 67
Shrewsbury, Duke of 44
Singapore International Monetary Exchange 58–60
slot machines 205–6
Small, John, cricketer 180
Smartplay machines 3

Smith, Andy, bookie 147–8, 153, 158–9
Snitkina, Anna 294–5
Soros, George, currency speculator 56, 62
South African Cricket Board 185
South Sea Bubble 48–50
speculators 63
Sporting Index 172, 277
Sportingbet 260, 264, 266
The Sportsman 303
spread betting 67, 170–1, 268, 277
and cricket 172–3, 189
Spreadfair 278
Spring, Tom, pugilist 127
St-Simon, Duc de, gambler 44
Stair, Lord, Ambassador 75
Stanley International 88
Stanley, Lord, greyhound racing 102
Stavordale, Lord 76
steeple-chasing 132
Steer, Tim, fund manager 265
Stevens, David, bookmaker 160
Stevens, 'Lumpy', cricketer 178
Stewart, Alec, cricketer 188
Steyn, Rory 186
Stock Exchange 55
deregulation 57
stock markets 51–6, 304
stock-jobber 55
Street Betting Act (1906) 97, 99, 100, 104, 266
Strydom, Pieter, cricketer 184
Suffolk, Lord, gambler 86
Sumitomo Bank 61
Sunday Telegraph 174, 182
Sunday Times 137, 185, 264
Super Bowl 198–9
Sutherland, Duchess of, greyhound racing 102
Sutton, Richard, gambler 74
Svobodney, Mike, backgammon player 247
Swift, Jonathan 49

Taaffe, Pat, jockey 118
Taaffe, Tom, trainer 118–19
Tankerville, Earl of 178
Tann, Willie, poker player 228–9, 231, 232–3, 244, 251

Tattersall, Richard 141
Tattersall's 99, 141
televised horse races xv
Templeton, Sir John 51
Thackeray, William 96
theory of probability 27–9
Thompson, Elaine and Derek,
        lottery winners 18–22
Thormanby 129
Thorp, Edward O.
    Beat the Dealer 32
    car counting 246
Thunderball 3
tic-tac men 146
Timeform 30
The Times 11–12, 119, 120
Tote 122, 124, 152–3, 166
Travellers' Club 81
Trumper, Simon 'Aces' 229
Tun Tavern, Jermyn Street 79
Turpin, Dick, hanged 121
'Two Million Adventure' lottery 55

Ude, Louis Eustache, chef 80
Ulliott, Dave, poker player 251
Underdown, David, *Start of Play* 177
Ungar, Stu 'The Kid', poker player 232
USA
    Atlantic City 219
    casino gambling 199
    gambling legalised in Nevada 200,
        201, 207
    gambling outlawed in certain
        states xviii, 199
    gaming on tribal lands 218
    internet gambling illegal 199
    organised crime and illegal
        gambling rackets 201
    Super Bowl 198–9

Vaswani, Ram 'Crazy Horse', poker
        player 228, 229, 233–4
Venus throw 25
Vernon, Mr, gambler 74
Victoria Club 99, 246
vingt-et-un *see* blackjack
virtual racing 105–7
Vladar, 'Smokin' Steve, poker player
    228

Voltaire, Francois 47, 75
Voyant, Claire, fortune teller 4

wagers 72–5, 83
Wagner, Robert 312
Walpole, Horace 73, 74, 76
Warne, Shane, cricketer 175, 190
Warnock, Baroness 308
Warriston, Earl of 44
Waterloo Cup 102
Waugh, Mark, cricketer 175
Wellington, Duke of 81
Whaley, Buck, gambler 75
Wheeler, Stuart, IG Index 170–1
whist 26
White's Chocolate House 72
White's Club 72–3, 78, 80, 81, 178
    betting book 73–75, 87
Wilde, Simon, journalist 185
Wilkerson, Billy, entrepreneur 202
Wilkinson, Bronwyn, South African
        Cricket Board 185
William, Henry, cricketer 187
William Hill bookmakers *see* Hill,
        William
Williams, A. and P., betting shop 245
Williams, Archbishop Rowan 308
Williams, Freddie, bookie 123
    and J.P. McManus 130, 131
Wilson, Des, poker player 234, 238
Wilson, Edward 43
Wilson, Harold, anti-gambling 99
Winchelsea, Lord, gambler 73, 178
Woods, Alan, gambler 30–9, 165, 275
Woolmer, Bob 312
working-class gambling 91–101
World Health Organisation 298
World Poker Tour 260
World Series of Poker 220–1, 260
Wray, Edward, Betfair 154, 156
Wyatt, Ben and Philip, architects 80
Wylie, Graham, racehorse owner 127
Wynn, Steve, casino owner 203–4,
    208, 209

Younis, Waqar, cricketer 186

Ziemba, *Efficiency of Racetrack
        Betting Markets* 31